RECONSTRUCTING LITERATURE IN AN IDEOLOGICAL AGE

Reconstructing Literature in an Ideological Age

A Biblical Poetics and Literary Studies from Milton to Burke

Daniel E. Ritchie

William B. Eerdmans Publishing Company
Grand Rapids, Michigan / Cambridge, U.K.

255 Jefferson Ave. S.E., Grand Rapids, Michigan 49503 /
P. O. Box 163, Cambridge CB3 9PU U.K.

Printed in the United States of America

01 00 99 98 97 96 7 6 5 4 3 2 1

Library of Congress Cataloging-in-Publication Data

Ritchie, Daniel E.
Reconstructing literature in an ideological age: a biblical poetics and literary studies from Milton to Burke / Daniel E. Ritchie.
p. cm.
ISBN 0-8028-4140-6 (paper: alk. paper)
1. English literature — Early modern, 1500-1700 — History and criticism — Theory, etc. 2. Religion and literature. 3. English literature — 18th century — History and criticism — Theory, etc. 4. Christian literature, English — History and criticism — Theory, etc. 5. Christianity and literature — Great Britain — History — 17th century. 6. Christianity and literature — Great Britain — History — 18th century. 7. Bible — Language, style. I. Title.
PR438.R45R58 1996
820.9′382 — dc20 95-47322
CIP

Our pleasant labors require more hands than ours.

For Abraham, William, and Hilary

Contents

ACKNOWLEDGMENTS ix

INTRODUCTION: Reconstructing Literary Studies 1
A Biblical Poetics as a Response to Ideological Criticism

1 Why Can't Gulliver Learn? 21
Ancients and Moderns in Swift, the Bible, and Our Time

2 Johnson Reading Literature, Johnson Reading the Canon of Scripture 71
The Difference between Literary Pleasure and Religious Happiness

3 Blessing and Naming in Genesis and *Paradise Lost* 119
A Biblical Poetics as an Alternative to Ideological Feminism

4 From Babel to Pentecost 180

George Psalmanazar's "Formosa," Burke's India, and Multiculturalism

5 The End of the Blessing and Its Renewal 232

The Apocalypse, Pope's Dunciad, *and Deconstruction*

Conclusion 289

INDEX 297

Acknowledgments

SINCE THIS BOOK aims to restore our conversations about books and poems, my deepest thanks go to the friends and colleagues whose reading and criticism of my work helped to sharpen my thoughts: Steven Blakemore, Barrett Fisher, Norman Fruman, Paul Fussell, Jeffrey Hart, David Jeffrey, Elizabeth Lambert, Diane McColley, Samuel Overstreet, Mark Reasoner, Leland Ryken, Peter Schakel, and Howard Weinbrot. Their kindness, expressed in disagreement and questions as well as encouragement, but expressed above all in serious communication about literature, was crucial to my understanding of the issues raised by this book.

I would also like to thank the Earhart Foundation, the Lynde and Harry Bradley Foundation, the Marguerite Eyer Wilbur Foundation, and the Bethel Faculty Development Office for financial support during a sabbatical leave.

A shorter version of chapter four appeared in the Spring-Summer 1994 edition of *Christianity and Literature.*

INTRODUCTION

Reconstructing Literary Studies

A Biblical Poetics as a Response to Ideological Criticism

THREE HUNDRED years ago, Jonathan Swift escalated the quarrel between ancient and modern literature into a battle — the Battle of the Books, in his pamphlet of that name. Today Swift's "battle" has escalated again, this time into a "culture war," with the moderns battling against the alleged racism, sexism, and classism of older literature, and its defenders counterattacking with charges of relativism, the loss of standards, and political correctness.

The contest over our view of past literature has become an almost military objective, waged by two fairly well-defined and recognizable sides. On the one side are traditionalists, like William Bennett, Dinesh D'Souza, Allan Bloom, Lynne Cheney, and many who would call themselves "humanists." They believe that we must continue "to learn and propagate the best that is known and thought in the world," in Matthew Arnold's words.[1] Often from positions outside the academy itself, they argue that we should search for standards of excellence that transcend temporary political commitments, and that the great literature of the past raises enduring questions regarding the nature of the

1. For example, Dinesh D'Souza refers to the famous lines from Arnold's essay, "The Function of Criticism at the Present Time," in *Illiberal Education: The Politics of Race and Sex on Campus* (New York: Macmillan–Free Press, 1991), 254.

soul, the problem of evil, the individual and society, the individual and God, and the relations between genders, ages, nations, and races. Moreover, they believe that the past teaching of literature, for all its shortcomings, often succeeded in illuminating these questions.

On the other side are educators who urge the adoption of the more recent approaches to literature, especially deconstruction, multiculturalism, feminism, and Marxism or its descendant, the "new historicism." These people, who occupy far more powerful positions within the academic establishment than their opponents, believe that the literature of the past is largely a manifestation of the oppressive societies where it originated, and that past approaches to older literature merely perpetuated that oppression. Regarding the quotation from Matthew Arnold, Henry Louis Gates Jr. of Harvard steams that these are code words for racism, sexism, and classism — ignoring Arnold's criticism of Anglo-Saxon cultural insularity in the very essay in which these words occur.[2] When the traditionalists quote Arnold, continues Gates, they really mean that we should read "the best" written by, for, and about white males. Gates then vows to "fight against anyone who tries to drag us back" where "God is in *His* heaven and all is white with the world," melodramatically changing Browning's lyric about all being "right" with the world and flouting the biblical mode of referring to God.[3] In the same book, Annette Kolodny, dean of the humanities faculty at the University of Arizona, reminds us that feminist criticism is not only about exposing the biases concerning race, class, and gender in literature. It demands an alliance with the broader forces of liberation, as understood by the political left, to change the oppressive "institutional structures in which truth gets made and codified."[4] Similarly, Terry Eagleton, now the Warton Professor of Poetry at Oxford, classifies Arnold's words with attempts to mystify "such historical trivia as civil wars, the oppression of women, or the dispossession of the English

2. Henry Louis Gates Jr., "On the Rhetoric of Racism in the Profession," in *Literature, Language, and Politics,* ed. Betty Jean Craige (Athens: University of Georgia Press, 1988), 21.

3. Gates, "On the Rhetoric of Racism in the Profession," 24.

4. Annette Kolodny, "Dancing between Left and Right," in *Literature, Language, and Politics,* 36.

peasantry . . . [by placing] in cosmic perspective the petty demands of working people for decent living conditions or greater control over their own lives."[5] Without actually accusing Arnold of any evil, then, Eagleton's contemptuous rhetoric makes clear that Arnold's view of literature leads one to favor the wrong side — and there are only two sides — in women's issues, questions of property rights, and labor. Moreover, one must choose between eternal and temporal realities, in Eagleton's view: if you care about "eternal truths," it must be because you wish to mask your position as a social oppressor.

The message of Gates, Kolodny, Eagleton, and their ideological colleagues is clear: the past is a repository of oppression, and the only morally defensible ways to read and teach literature in the modern world are those they suggest. The traditionalists have struck back forcefully, maintaining that these approaches produce the opposite of what they promise — political correctness instead of liberal learning, ethnic division instead of true multicultural understanding, uniformity instead of diversity.

This book will come at the dispute from another direction, for it seems clear that the two sides understand each other fairly well, but they use such different categories of thought that persuasion is impossible. It will be clear that my sympathies lie with the traditionalists. I believe, however, that traditionalists need to demonstrate more persuasively the value of the literature they love, for the common academic-in-the-ivory-tower is no longer persuaded that literature has something unique to teach us about life. Most teachers are confused and unsure of how to respond to the presupposition that "[l]iterature is an ideology," in Eagleton's words, and that therefore our literary education is spent either in accommodating or in overcoming oppression.[6] If that presupposition is true — and no one can deny that oppression has existed and continues to exist — shouldn't it dominate our approach to literature? Shouldn't we change our approach to literature, the teacher may wonder, either by adding works to make the ideological point, or by teaching the older works in such a way as to make it indirectly?

5. Terry Eagleton, *Literary Theory: An Introduction* (Minneapolis: University of Minnesota Press, 1983), 25.

6. Eagleton, *Literary Theory,* 22.

At present, few teachers, students, and college-educated adults adopt the ideological approach wholeheartedly, but they generally cannot articulate a convincing alternative. Traditional literary study is still practiced, but it often seems otiose in comparison with ideological criticism like that of Gates and Eagleton. The time may soon come when ordinary, college-educated citizens accept the moderns' belief that our institutions are to be understood primarily as embodiments of oppression and that our literature, in turn, is to be read primarily as manifesting the structures of oppression.

Those who dissent from the ideological critique must do more than criticize their modern opponents. They must demonstrate that the literature of the past has values ignored by ideological critics by producing more insightful readings of particular books than their antagonists. If a "humanistic" form of literary study is different from and superior to ideological criticism, the humanist should show how. Some recent critiques of higher education have pointed out the flaws of the ideological approaches and ended there, apparently assuming that the next step is obvious — a backward movement to the "traditional curriculum." But this solution is both unattractive and unexciting. One cannot attract others for very long simply by pointing out the repellant features of the other side. If humanistic literary study cannot be presented as more rewarding than the ideological varieties, it will die. Many people are passionately concerned about the politicized university; few are passionately interested in the traditional curriculum.

My book attempts to avoid a merely nostalgic longing for the traditional curriculum. I do not wish to reconstruct an inert, five-foot shelf of classic books, but rather to revive a conversation about literature. Conversations — even conversations about the same books — change over time. If we attempt to understand books from within the tradition of literary study, we do not simply seek to reproduce the author's original meaning. "Not just occasionally but always, the meaning of a text goes beyond its author," writes Hans-Georg Gadamer. "That is why understanding is not merely a reproductive but always a productive activity as well. . . . It is enough to say that we understand in a *different* way, *if we understand at all*."[7] Tradition always presents us with some-

7. Hans-Georg Gadamer, *Truth and Method*, translation rev. by Joel Wein-

thing other than we had expected. For instance, I have chosen to study some little-read texts by Edmund Burke (an author who has been dropped altogether from the influential *Norton Anthology of English Literature* in recent years) because his India speeches look different in the light of our current disputes over multiculturalism.

In each chapter, I hope to show that traditional literary study is more demanding and insightful than the ideological approaches. I will argue that Edmund Burke has more to teach us about multiculturalism than current multicultural theory, and that we can learn more about gender from Milton than from current feminist critiques of Milton. In short, ideological criticism prevents us from learning what authors such as Burke and Milton have to teach us about culture, human nature, and the very social issues that interest readers like Kolodny and Eagleton.

The Ideological Approach to Literature

My book begins with Swift's *Tale of a Tub* and *Battle of the Books,* which entered into their own "quarrel between ancients and moderns." There are striking parallels between Swift's ancients and today's traditionalists, and between his moderns and today's ideologues. By "ancient" Swift does not mean simply "old." Swift sees himself as an "ancient," and wittily predicts that he will be considered an ancient "200 years hence."[8] Moreover, both ancients and moderns, in Swift's day and ours, read "old" literature. What distinguishes "ancient" literature, in Swift's view, is its enduring quality. Contemporary ancients — that is, readers of any era who share the "spirit" of the ancients — are distinguished by their ability to recognize the enduring qualities of past literature. These qualities, for Swift, are moral, religious, and political as well as aesthetic.

Swift satirizes modern critics for their inability to recognize the good in older literature. He considers their whole approach to the past an abuse of learning. They set themselves above literature and distract

---

sheimer and Donald G. Marshall, 2nd rev. ed. (New York: Continuum, 1994), 296, 297; emphasis in original.

8. Jonathan Swift, *Prose Works of Jonathan Swift,* ed. Herbert Davis et al., 14 vols. (Oxford: Clarendon, 1937-68), 5:201.

attention from the texts of the past to themselves. Their language quickly becomes violent. They avidly seek disciples and quash any dissent from their views. They develop a highly technical vocabulary which seems accessible only to a convert. They fault ancient writers for lacking a modern sensibility. They pretend that the greatest moments in ancient literature are those that run parallel to their own theories.

This sounds so much like recent literary criticism that one could simply note the parallels between Swift's moderns and current ideologues, and turn off the computer. But that too would be an abuse of learning. That would make my own literary study the mirror image of ideological criticism. One reason Swift's satire continues to be pertinent is that he also asks disturbing questions of his own side. He does not stop with attacking his enemies, as Gates and Kolodny do. He sees that there are elements of truth in his opponents' criticism, and he questions himself and the reader.

An "ancient" of today who enters into the spirit of Swift's work should not read him to gather ammunition against his enemies, but rather to enter a conversation about the issues raised by Swift — here the issue of ancients and moderns. Moreover, like great literature in general, Swift's satire can change the reader, not by converting him or her to an ideology, but by forcing him to ask questions that admit no easy, systematic answers. For instance, how is it that Swift, himself an ancient, criticizes the moderns for turning literature into a battleground, when Swift's criticism uses the setting of a battle for its wit? Why is it that the figure who represents the moderate approach to religion and learning in Swift's *Tale of a Tub,* presumably preferred by Swift, is rather boring, while the fanatics are so interesting?

In each of my chapters I hope to demonstrate that literary study of authors like Swift, Johnson, and others is more rewarding than ideological criticism, even on issues parallel to those of ideology. At this point, however, I need to define the term "ideology," which is central to my argument.

* * * * *

"Until well after the Second World War, American institutions of higher education were bastions of a sort of cheery and thoughtlessly jingoistic nativism. . . . [T]he vast majority of the student bodies of America's hundreds of colleges were overwhelmingly U.S.-born, male, Christian, and of Northern European descent, and their faculties were even more so."[9] These lines by Richard Perry and Patricia Williams initiate a typical attack on older curricula, combined in this case with a defense of speech and behavior codes on campus. In their essay, the older or "ancient" side is made to defend a "nativist, racist, anti-Semitic, sexist, homophobic, or . . . monocultural" position — in short, the position of the oppressor. In Gates's essay, as I have already shown, the ancients' position is symbolically made to defend the oppressive institution of slavery: "The return of 'the' canon" urged by Education Secretary William Bennett, says Gates, "represents the return of an order in which my people were the subjugated, the voiceless, the invisible, the unrepresented, and the unrepresentable."[10]

While the current "ancients" and "moderns" agree on little, they both see that the "modern" approach presupposes that the essential significance of literary study is political. But the ancients maintain that politics is just one aspect of Shakespeare's plays, for instance, along with their moral, spiritual, historical, philosophical, and aesthetic significance. While these aspects are connected, it diminishes an understanding of Shakespeare to reduce everything to politics or power relationships. The moderns would respond that these additional ways of explaining Shakespeare are also essentially about the allocation of power, if only the ancients were not blind to their own ideology.[11]

When they address the general public, the moderns usually treat "ideology" as no more than a point of view. On these occasions, it refers to the historical, economic, religious, and social contexts in which literature is written and read. On this rather vague level, of course, all writing, reading, and teaching is "ideological." The ideologue also assumes a misleading public face when he or she becomes embarrassed

9. Richard Perry and Patricia Williams, "Freedom of Hate Speech," in *Debating P. C.: The Controversy over Political Correctness on College Campuses,* ed. Paul Berman (New York: Dell, 1992), 225.

10. Gates, "On the Rhetoric of Racism in the Profession," 24.

11. In addition to Eagleton's book, see (for instance) Michael Berubé's "Public Image Limited: Political Correctness and the Media's Big Lie," in *Debating P. C.,* 147.

about the flaws in his or her argument or is forced to admit to having reduced all significant phenomena to a predetermined system of thought. At this point, the ideologue usually retreats to the position that he or she is merely pointing out, in a commonsense way, that people are influenced by their social surroundings, or that literature must be put into historical perspective. These commonsense notions are true, of course. It is undeniable, moreover, that scholars working from a well-known ideological basis have sometimes advanced our knowledge of the structures of oppression better than traditional scholarship.[12] It would be foolish to deny the elements of truth in many ideological critiques of literature. As my chapter on multiculturalism will show, the structural injustice of British imperial policy in India (for example) was undeniable. In fact, however, Edmund Burke used the literary and historical tradition to reveal its structures, and his work is more rewarding, in many ways, than current ideological theories (such as "Orientalism") about European relations with the East.

The confusion surrounding ideology is similar to the confusion that used to surround the adjective "Christian." It could have the loose sense of general beneficence, as in the phrase "Christian kindness," or the more precise meanings that truly matter to the believer. The confusion may attract some of the unpersuaded for a time, but it is a potentially serious misrepresentation. Likewise, "ideology" refers to a very precise and predictable set of practices among its adherents, far more predictable than studies of the social and historical context of literature. It is this set of practices that guides today's moderns and distinguishes them in a basic sense from other readers.

At its simplest, writes Kenneth Minogue, ideology presupposes that all evil is caused by an oppressive social system.[13] These evils are not basic to the human condition (which would make most of them beyond our power to change), but are rather part of a single system of dehumanization, such as the jingoistic system of education described by Perry and Williams. Nothing short of a complete transformation of the system will satisfactorily end this oppression, and hence ideologues

12. The work of Christopher Hill is one example.

13. Elements of the following description are indebted to Kenneth Minogue's *Alien Powers: The Pure Theory of Ideology* (New York: St. Martin's Press, 1985).

like Annette Kolodny seek "to change . . . the institutional structures in which knowledge gets made and codified."[14] From the institutions of learning, the ideologue moves without difficulty to political and economic institutions, which are also to be understood as manifestations of structural oppression.

For the ideologue, the world is a battlefield between oppressed and oppressor, the powerful and the powerless; therefore "truth" and "knowledge" about the world have no independent existence, and may even serve (as Eagleton believes) to mystify the position of the oppressor. The only knowledge that fully deserves the name, then, is that which succeeds in defining the causes of oppression and in persuading others that one's theory of social change will bring liberation. It is impossible for an ideologue to be wrong about anything, for mistakes are due to some previously unexplained part of the oppressive system. For instance, if an "ancient" points out that women writers were frequently included in older reading lists, or that clever peasants frequently outwit noblemen in earlier literature, the ideologue will have a quick answer: the particular women on those lists merely buttressed the ancient, oppressive order, or the stories of the clever peasant were relegated to folk literature by the elite. In an important sense, then, the "facts" don't really matter to the ideologue; they can always be interpreted in some way to support the ideologue's theory of systemic evil. Even quite significant historical events that would seem to damage the ideological project, such as the fall of communism or the relation between poverty and the collapse of the two-parent family, have caused no widespread soul-searching among literary ideologues at the end of the twentieth century.

The language of ideology is that of denunciation rather than academic argument. Today's moderns denounce their opponents, either for allegedly supporting oppression by their choice of books and mode of teaching, or for "celebrat[ing] literature as pointless but very fine writing."[15] The ideologue sometimes transposes his denunciation into a type of interrogation, calculated to elicit anger. Do you find the analyses of Allan Bloom and William Bennett persuasive? If so, says Gates, you are nostalgic for the days "when women and people of color

14. Kolodny, "Dancing between Left and Right," 36.
15. Berubé, "Public Image Limited," 148.

were voiceless, faceless servants and laborers, pouring tea and filling brandy snifters in the boardrooms of old boys' clubs."[16] This is the language of accusation, not the academic language of explanation and the testing of theories by their coherence and explanatory power. As many a professor in the humanities can attest, the language of interrogation and indictment is now typical fare in the papers and essays thought to represent the cutting edge.

Despite the claim that he or she pays attention to history, the ideologue already "knows" in advance that history will reveal, in each case, a system of domination. This is not really "history," in the usual sense, but a theory of development, since (unlike real literary history, for instance) the ideologue already knows *what* will develop — a power structure that exists through oppression — and needs only to reveal *how* it got there.

A further distinction between ideological criticism and academic inquiry is in the relation between method and outcome. The outcomes of ordinary academic inquiry may be tested with common academic methods by people who disagree with the theorist on any number of fundamental beliefs. Ideology, by contrast, converts itself into a self-fulfilling methodology whose "correct" use guarantees the proper outcome. If essay after essay proposes to show how earlier women writers subverted a surrounding patriarchal order, a common method in earlier feminist criticism, one guarantees agreement on prior but unstated beliefs — that gender relations are to be understood with reference to a patriarchal system of oppression, and that the chief object on the horizon of literary study should be the critique of that system. It follows that previous literary criticism may be largely dismissed as the attempts of oppressive elites to "promulgate the divine mandate for established authorities," as Kolodny says; it should be replaced by a new literary criticism.[17]

Kolodny indicates four other differences between academic inquiry and ideological criticism. She identifies her ideology (feminism) as an essentially activist enterprise that requires solidarity with efforts to form unions, erect anti-apartheid shantytowns, finance local shelters

16. Gates, "On the Rhetoric of Racism in the Profession," 21.
17. Kolodny, "Dancing between Left and Right," 35.

for battered women and children, and so on. "[W]e will proclaim again that theory devoid of activist politics isn't feminism, but, rather, pedantry and moral abdication," she writes.[18] The first difference is that there is one "true" ideology, and it issues in certain political activities: alternative inferences from theory, including "activist" ones that would conflict with Kolodny's, are heresies that must be exposed and quashed. The internecine conflict within Marxism illustrates this insistence upon orthodoxy. Recent conflicts within the discipline of women's studies have now become so intense as to threaten to split apart the National Women's Studies Association into warring caucuses of "Jewish Women, Jewish Lesbians, Asian American Women, African American Women, Old Women, Fat Women, Women Whose Sexuality Is in Transition."[19] The second difference is that one cannot dissent from the furthest reaches of the ideology on any question, or even declare oneself a noncombatant, without risking the charge of "pedantry and moral abdication" or worse.[20] Third, the ideological method claims to overcome the separation between academic life and the rest of life, as seen in the linkage between Kolodny's ideology and current social issues. Fourth, the role of education is not to discover new truth, to evaluate one's own beliefs self-critically, or to engage students in an open-ended conversation about the good life. Rather, its goal is to persuade students that ideological criticism accounts for virtually every significant occurrence, from the law and literature of the eighteenth century to current problems of labor and domestic violence.[21]

18. Kolodny, "Dancing between Left and Right," 35, 36.

19. Christina Hoff Sommers, "Sister Soldiers," *New Republic,* 5 October 1992, 29.

20. Gates demands that literature professors choose a political side — his own side — and use the power of their professional organization, the Modern Language Association, to further the political goals that he enunciates ("On the Rhetoric of Racism in the Profession," 23).

21. One of the winners of the 1992 Teaching Competition of the American Society for Eighteenth-Century Studies combines an understanding of Anita Hill's failed testimony against Clarence Thomas's Supreme Court nomination with the failure of Eliza Haywood and Aphra Behn to attain the stature of Samuel Richardson and Henry Fielding. She suggests an "ideological homology" between the history of the novel and the rules of evidence, both of which reveal the oppression of women. See Susan Sage

Today's moderns are ideologues in these senses, and today's ancients are not. While today's ancients do not doubt that systems of oppression exist and often work for social change — frequently on different sides of the political spectrum — they deny that oppression is the absolute horizon for viewing all culture. They do not doubt that differential power relationships have existed, and that these are reflected in culture. But they deny that culture is simply the manifestation of such power relationships. Unlike the moderns, most ancients place at least as much value on individuals as on structures; they are as interested in the choices made by Antigone as the political structures in which she is caught. The ancient, moreover, believes that no transformation of social structures will solve the most enduring human problems, for most such problems have no rationalistic, structural solution. *Paradise Lost* would not be a better poem if only we could transform the world of Milton and his Adam into the world of, say, the National Women's Studies Association.

There is indeed a separation, for most ancients, between academic life and the rest of life. For all the moral, psychological, and ethical significance of literature, traditional literary study cannot provide an all-encompassing approach to life in the way that ideologies can. Traditional literary study is not complete in itself.[22] Nor does such literary study — again unlike ideological criticism — identify unself-critically with the forces of good against the forces of oppression. In fact, the self-critical gestures of the British literary tradition are among its most obvious, and in my view, its most appealing, characteristics. Finally, there is no single method that guides today's ancients, who produce everything from literary history and textual explication to descriptions of the literature's social and psychological implications. My discussion of Swift, for example, will follow some of the practices of recent "ethical

---

Heinzelman, "Legal Facts and Feminist Fictions: Laws of Evidence and Women's Writing 1688-1760," *Teaching the Eighteenth Century,* American Society for Eighteenth-Century Studies (1993): 21-34.

22. A biblical poetics can ultimately point the interested reader across this separation, to the full message of the Bible, but its purpose is not primarily to gain converts — again, unlike the ideological approaches. I will discuss how a biblical poetics respects the relative autonomy of literary study in chapter 3.

criticism" by considering the significance of his satire for our own relationships to older literature. My discussion of the Tower of Babel story in the chapter on Burke and multiculturalism is compatible with some varieties of reader-response criticism, as I attempt to fill in some of the gaps in the spare Hebrew narrative.

To put the matter slightly differently, today's ancients believe that knowledge is acquired through use and practice according to the customs and traditions of one's field, and that no mere application of technique can do justice to the complexity of the discipline's methods and subject matter. Without by any means extinguishing our background, we nevertheless encounter in the traditional texts of literature something different from ourselves, as Gadamer has written.[23] If we are willing to enter a conversation or dialogue with those texts, we can learn from them. Today's moderns regard these views as naive. They write as if knowledge may be imparted by a technique — the technique of uncovering oppression. This technique is rather easily taught to disciples, who need little previous knowledge of the discipline apart from what the ideology uncovers, but who have little trouble reproducing the technique.

Toward a Biblical Poetics

Some would be content to end with a two-part approach to the current debates in literary criticism: a critique of ideology and a constructive alternative from within the traditional humanities. But I would contend that many defenses of the humanities lack the depth of their ideological opponents because the ideologues, to their credit, explicitly make clear the presuppositions that guide their work. Sensing this deficiency, traditionalists sometimes locate their own deepest foundations in the American political inheritance, Enlightenment skepticism, or Emersonian individualism, as may be seen in David Bromwich's *Politics by Other Means.* While I applaud virtually any good-faith effort to rediscover the grounds for a common American civilization, my own perspectives are rooted in biblical faith. A religious basis for truth-seeking has

23. Gadamer, *Truth and Method,* 269.

historically coexisted, although not without conflict, on the same campuses that have embraced Bromwich's approach. I hope that many secular readers will be able to learn from my readings of Milton, Pope, and the others I have treated. I believe, though, that biblical faith provides the most thorough response to ideological criticism. In particular, it takes seriously the concern for social evil — indeed, its diagnosis of evil is far more profound than that of ideology — without subordinating every aspect of culture to a particular educational and political program.

The third part of my approach, then, is a religious one. Those who are skeptical of ideological criticism commonly believe that the habit of attending to our literary tradition has more to teach than ideology does. I hope to find among such readers, whether they consider the Scriptures "sacred" or not, some who are willing to listen to the central book of that tradition, the Bible. My study proposes a revived religious humanism among the plurality of streams within higher education in general and literary study in particular.

My approach to literature, or "poetics," comes from the Bible as it has been received by the Christian church. It is broader than a "Christian poetics" because it does not formally adopt a particular theology. When appropriate, it takes into account the reception and interpretation of the Bible in church history (especially in the chapters on Johnson and Milton), but it adopts the perspective that all theological doctrines and developments should be evaluated, ultimately, by Scripture.[24] In each chapter, I will look at how the Hebrew and Christian Scriptures shed light on certain issues in literary history to see how they can illuminate our current disputes.[25]

24. I realize that my emphasis on Scripture and the very choice of a "biblical" (rather than, say, "sacramental") poetics reflects a Protestant tilt. The reader familiar with the theology of "common grace" will also discern that Calvinistic doctrine at various points, especially in the chapter on Milton. Moreover, my second chapter, on the recognition of the New Testament canon, goes outside the Bible to examine why the early church received certain writings as its New Testament. No use of the Bible is innocent of theology or church history. Since all Christians acknowledge the Bible, however, I believe that a biblical poetics, rather than a theologically or historically particular one, offers the greatest possibilities for agreement.

25. By the Hebrew Scriptures, I mean what the Christian church has called the

Many critics have treated literature from a religious perspective or have looked at the theological significance of literature. Relatively few, however, have asked the basic questions of a biblical poetics: what is the Bible's sense of itself as "the Word"? How might the Bible's own negotiations with language affect our view of literature? Among current critics, Michael Edwards has provided one thoughtful example of how such a poetics might proceed. In *Towards a Christian Poetics,* he considers the Bible in very broad terms, locating a three-part "ternary dialectic" in its cosmology, history, anthropology, and theology, corresponding to paradise, fall, and redemption. He finds a similar "ternary" structure in the possibilities of language itself. Before the fall, for instance, there is no problematic link between word and referent, as in Adam's naming of the animals. With the serpent's speech to Eve, however, concealment, obscurity, and deception enter into language. Human language after the fall — which is, of course, all the language we know — preserves elements of both the "grandeur" of paradise and the "misery" of the fall. In such stories as the Pentecost account, the Bible records a third element as well, the possibility of the redemption of language, implied at Pentecost but never to be realized fully on earth. Edwards argues that literature often reenacts this three-part structure. In a tragedy like *Romeo and Juliet,* for instance, the "grandeur and misery" of the plot is completed by the final possibility of renewal — the establishment of peace between Capulet and Montague. "If the biblical reading of life is in any way true," writes Edwards, "literature will be drawn strongly towards it."[26] Comedy, tragedy, and narrative, without offering salvation, nevertheless "contest the fall" by offering possibilities of renewal that are analogous to the renewal found in the Bible.

In a somewhat different way, Thomas Jemielity has pointed out how Hebrew prophecy and the satire of Juvenal, Pope, Waugh, and others is mutually illuminating. Both forms of writing employ ridicule

---

"Old Testament." I realize that this already narrows my scope by excluding the oral Hebrew law, ultimately recorded in the Mishnah and Talmuds. For a criticism of this procedure, see Jacob Neusner, *The Oral Torah* (San Francisco: Harper & Row, 1986).

26. Michael Edwards, *Towards a Christian Poetics* (Grand Rapids, Mich.: Wm. B. Eerdmans, 1984), 12.

to exploit shame in their objects; both assume a quasi-judicial authority; both give moral reasons for their vindictiveness and hatreds; both forms attack language itself in order to shatter the complacency of their audience.[27]

For the purposes of this book, I have adopted Edwards's premise that the Bible's "teaching about language is rigorously exact."[28] Although few readers will be able to accept the truth of that assumption, my hope is that many will agree to its usefulness. Perhaps some will find my interpretations of Swift, Johnson, Milton, Burke, and Pope sound enough to grant the value of my theoretical basis; others may consider that biblical language is worth our attention simply because of the Bible's centrality in the literary tradition. I have asked the following basic questions in each chapter (with some variation in chapter 2): What can we learn from biblical ways with language with respect to its treatment of older texts (chapter 1), gender issues (chapter 3), ethnic diversity (chapter 4), and the apparent arbitrariness of language itself (chapter 5)? How does this language provide a basis for literary study in the texts of Swift, Johnson, Milton, Burke, and Pope? How does biblical language and the study of these writers differ from that of recent ideological approaches?

A biblical poetics, then, begins by inquiring how the Bible itself uses language, then asks about the significance of that inquiry for literature. Since so few critics in recent years have asked these questions, my scope will be relatively narrow and practical. I will focus on discrete issues currently under debate in higher education to show the present value of a biblical poetics. For instance, the chapter on Pope will propose that biblical apocalyptic sheds light both on *The Dunciad* (through Pope's allusions) and on deconstruction; the chapter on Johnson will show how Johnson's criticism and the actual process of New Testament canon formation make one question recent attacks on "the literary canon." My conclusion will draw out some of the implications of a biblical poetics.

I believe that something like a "bright line" test can be used to

27. Thomas Jemielity, *Satire and the Hebrew Prophets* (Louisville: Westminster/John Knox, 1992), 11-61.

28. Edwards, *Towards a Christian Poetics*, 2.

distinguish an "ideological" reading: if the reading *depends upon* a prior acceptance of the perspective (its power to analyze social reality, its particular program of liberation, etc.), then one is dealing with "ideological criticism." If the conclusions may be shared by many who are skeptical of the reader's underlying perspective, the conclusions have a much broader appeal. This test, one should notice, could also distinguish valid insights of feminist and deconstructive critics from those that follow circularly from the assumptions of those schools.

I have discovered that a biblical poetics does not govern my reading of Milton, Swift, or the other writers in the way that ideological theory governs its criticism. Of course, the Bible may be, and has been, turned into an ideology. Indeed, Swift's *Tale of a Tub*, the subject of my first chapter, warns against just such a Calvinist misuse of the Bible.[29] But a more deeply biblical poetics, unlike the current ideologies, accommodates a great deal of autonomy for the academic disciplines. In fact, by accommodating so much autonomy, the Bible may seem almost irrelevant to literary study.

I have several responses to this potential problem. The autonomy for literary study in my approach is a strength, not a weakness. It means, for instance, that someone like David Bromwich may agree with my reading of Burke without having to accept my poetics as a whole. It means likewise that I can agree with Bromwich's excellent readings of Hazlitt and Wordsworth without fully accepting the secular foundations of his approach. This autonomy allows for truly pluralistic readings, where people of diverse ultimate commitments can join together to advance knowledge. This autonomy makes conversation possible. The ideological theories of literature disallow such autonomy, I will argue, and at their extreme they merely produce permutations on themselves. It is a strength, in short, that a biblical poetics does not govern the methods and conclusions of literary analysis in the manner of ideological criticism.

The biblical basis for the relative autonomy of literature will be fully explained in the chapter on Milton, under the subject of "bless-

29. There is at present a small sect of Christian "Reconstructionists" who seem to misuse the Bible in this manner as well. The title of my book in no way suggests agreement with their approach.

ing." In brief, the opening chapters of Genesis locate human culture, from agriculture to music, under God's blessing. Blessing is the means by which God establishes his attachment to creation, but blessing also situates the man and woman in a place of relative autonomy, where they are to cultivate the garden. After the fall, this blessing is badly damaged. To reestablish a faithful knowledge of God, God must initiate a covenant relationship with his people. God's blessings, however, including viticulture, technology, family, and other basic components of human culture, abide for all mankind, regardless of their covenantal status. Paul's sermons and letters assume that the pagan world has continually enjoyed God's blessing through the agriculture, poetry, and wisdom of their civilizations.

A biblical poetics, then, should not expect that literary beauty or even the social and religious implications of literature will lead to a full knowledge of God. It does not "save" anyone; poetry is not a means of grace. It cannot promise the degree of liberation that ideological criticism does. Where an ideologue demands that criticism lead to liberation, a biblical poetics explores the dimensions of cultural "blessing." Consequently, the stakes of literary interpretation are, in a way, far lower and far different for a Christian, whose sensibility is shaped by the Bible, than for an ideologue. C. S. Lewis perfectly illustrated this difference in his criticism of T. S. Eliot's notion that *Paradise Lost* was best judged by "the best contemporary practicing poets":

> If I make Mr. Eliot's word the peg on which to hang a discussion of this notion, it must not, therefore, be assumed that . . . I wish to attack him *quâ* Mr. Eliot. Why should I? I agree with him about matters of such moment that all literary questions are, in comparison, trivial.[30]

Because ideology regards each word as either advancing or retarding the liberation from oppression, nothing is comparatively trivial. Liberation is the ideological parallel to salvation. But for an ideologue, there is no parallel to "blessing." As long as oppressive structures remain,

30. C. S. Lewis, *A Preface to "Paradise Lost"* (New York: Oxford University Press, 1942), 9.

there can be no realm of relative autonomy. This lack of autonomy is especially evident when ideologues have to deal with conflicts among people who "should" agree with them. One prominent multiculturalist, for instance, writes that Booker T. Washington should be seen as one "who helped Whites to conquer or oppress powerless people rather than [one] who challenged the existing social, economic, and political order."[31] In this scheme, there is a single, ideologically correct understanding of every significant aspect of our culture, including the way one should regard the debate between these two historical figures: W. E. B. Dubois's confrontational approach is correct, and Washington's approach of education and self-development is wrong. Washington is to be numbered among the oppressors. There is no possibility for disagreement, no middle ground, no real diversity. For the ancient, by contrast, "knowledge" and "truth" are not primarily weapons to be wielded, but goals to be sought in patient conversation with many people, both those who share our convictions and those who deny them. Moreover, new knowledge and new truths can indeed penetrate our previous commitments in religion, politics, economics, and aesthetics, making us perhaps doubt some views, confirm others, and introduce us to new ones.

Denunciation may occur in the rhetoric of today's ancients as the Battle of the Books erupts again, but its purpose is not to destroy all structures other than those of the ancients' own making, nor is it the form of speech most favored by the ancients. Literary history is not, for the ancient, a confirmation by examples positive and negative of his or her beliefs regarding society. "[W]riters [like Wordsworth, Dickens, and George Eliot] don't necessarily endorse our current opinions and pieties," writes the socialist Irving Howe. "Why should they?"[32] Nor are all academic disputes treated as either irrelevant, at one extreme,

31. James A. Banks, "A Curriculum for Empowerment, Action, and Change," in *Empowerment through Multicultural Education,* ed. Christine E. Sleeter (Albany: State University of New York Press, 1991), 131.

32. Irving Howe, "The Value of the Canon," *New Republic,* 18 February 1991, 43. It is noteworthy that in their obituary to Irving Howe, the editors of the *New Republic* write, "It was one of Howe's lessons, and we took this lesson very seriously, that the synchronization of culture with politics was the slippery slope to a fake culture and a mean politics" (31 May 1993, 10).

or heretical, at the other. I shall argue that Gulliver's misanthropy at the end of *Gulliver's Travels* is essentially different from Swift's own position, but I may be wrong, and no "ancient" who disagrees with me will think it necessary to denounce my views. Today's ancients welcome a true diversity within their ranks, which include a socialist like Howe, a skeptical analytic philosopher like John Searle, a Marxist like Eugene Genovese, a Platonist like Allan Bloom, and still others whose approach is rooted in biblical faith.

This book will have done its work if it leads some to question the popular ideologies of the day and provides others with a path out of the modern wilderness. I hope that it will help to show why locating authors with respect to current ideological fashions is fundamentally different from true education. But above all, I hope to help reconstruct an atmosphere where teachers, students, and educated citizens will wish to enter a conversation with Swift and Johnson, Milton, Burke, and Pope for their enjoyment and intellectual growth.

CHAPTER 1

Why Can't Gulliver Learn?

Ancients and Moderns in Swift, the Bible, and Our Time

In the course of teaching *Gulliver's Travels* many times, I have often been struck by a question that the vast amount of scholarship on Swift has not answered. Why is it that Gulliver, a traveler characterized by his appetite for knowledge and placed in the most suitable of all eighteenth-century careers for gaining knowledge, never seems to learn anything? At its most obvious, why does he almost never reflect on earlier voyages later in the book? More importantly, why do we not see the experience of a lifetime reflected in this man? Why is Gulliver's final enlightenment, in a utopia of horses, really his first enlightenment, and why does it cause him to go mad?

Some would say that these questions treat Gulliver as novelistic character, and since Swift's book is a satire they cannot be answered. But even allowing for the differences between Gulliver and a satirical character of Austen or Trollope, Gulliver remains the focus of the book. Everyone finds his final madness interesting; many find it disturbing. Some suggest that he cannot return to the real world after seeing the horse utopia, any more than the enlightened man can willingly return to the cave in Plato's allegory. But I don't believe we need to go outside of Swift at all to find at least one major contributor to Gulliver's madness. Over two decades before he began writing *Gulliver's Travels*, Swift had entered the "quarrel between ancients and moderns" with two satires, *A Tale of a Tub* and *The Battle of the Books.* Between them, the two pamphlets portray madness as a malady of the modern mind, whether that mind is captivated by new religions, new empires, new critical theories, or new scientific systems. According to Swift's satires, the moderns have relinquished the ancient habits of mind that produce moral and psychological health, and have successively adopted habits that are trivial, pedantic, and even insane.

My argument is that Gulliver's insanity has a similar root. His is a modern, "scientific" mind and its modernity (as Swift uses the term "modern") prevents him from learning the most important lessons on his travels. It precludes the most important kind of knowledge — moral, self-knowledge — and leaves him helpless when he is confronted by his own shortcomings. Moreover, Swift's satire of the quarrel between ancients and moderns has strong parallels to the current battles between modern, ideological interpretations of ancient literature and more traditional ones. Certain biblical negotiations between ancient and modern texts, I will argue, provide a better model for understanding older literature than those practiced in ideological literary criticism. Such a model could help to end the current "battle of the books."

As a young man serving as secretary to Sir William Temple, Jonathan Swift was a firsthand observer of the *querelle,* as the quarrel between ancients and moderns was already known in France. Sir William wrote the first major English essay in the quarrel during the very year in which Swift joined his household, 1689. As the next decade progressed, the issues separating the two sides became clearer and the disagreements sharper.[1] The partisans for the ancients believed that the achievements of Greek and Latin culture in literature, history, and science deserved our admiration and imitation. The moderns believed that they had surpassed the ancients in their own day, certainly in the sciences and possibly in literature and history. By the time the quarrel died down in the 1730s, it seemed that moderns could rightly claim to have surpassed the ancients in the cumulative disciplines, like the sciences and philosophy, while the ancients could confidently assert

1. The discussion below is indebted to Joseph Levine's definitive account in *The Battle of the Books: History and Literature in the Augustan Age* (Ithaca: Cornell University Press, 1991).

that the classical masters had never been excelled in the imitative arts, such as literature.

Ironically, the very tools developed in the Renaissance to recover the classical world, especially philology, ultimately undermined the ideal of "the classic." For as Renaissance scholars learned more about the classical world, they came to realize the profound separation between their world and that of antiquity. They began to see Greek and Latin culture as a product of a particular era and, naturally, came to doubt whether its ideals were "timeless." It was but a short step to consider whether the culture of the Renaissance might equal — and even surpass — that of antiquity.

For most European educators of the sixteenth, seventeenth, and eighteenth centuries, however, a complete education for the future man of affairs could be provided by the classical authors of Greece and Rome.

> The student must model himself on his ancient predecessors for style and substance, in his speech and his behavior, and he is not likely to surpass them. Perfection can only be imitated. The goal is eloquence joined to moral and political wisdom. It is a renewal of the Ciceronian ideal of *humanitas* and the means are the classical humanities: grammar and rhetoric, poetry, history, and moral philosophy. . . . When the eighteenth-century English gentleman read the letters of (say) Cicero or Pliny the Younger, he discovered in them a mirror image of himself and he naturally identified with his ancient Roman forebears. . . . But it was a style of life and an outlook on culture, not a specific political posture, that gave the Greeks and Romans their general modern appeal.[2]

Swift's "Letter to a Young Gentleman, Lately entered into Holy Orders" (1720) commends the ancients for similar reasons. A clergyman and by this time dean of St. Patrick's Cathedral in Dublin, Swift adopts the voice of a layman to give his advice. He laments the tendency of preachers to disparage the ancient philosophers as heathens, for while they cannot "make us wise unto salvation," they can assist in enforcing

2. Levine, *The Battle of the Books,* 5, 6. By "modern appeal," Levine here means the contemporary appeal that the eighteenth-century gentleman, an "ancient" in sentiment, felt for antiquity.

"the moral part of the gospel."[3] Swift recommends the "principal [ancient] orators and historians, and perhaps a few of the poets" for the young clergyman's study, and proceeds to describe the benefits and purposes of reading:

> [Y]ou will soon discover your mind and thoughts to be enlarged, your imagination extended and refined, your judgment directed, your admiration lessened, and your fortitude increased. . . . If a rational man reads an excellent author with just application, he shall find himself extremely improved, and perhaps insensibly led to imitate that author's perfections; although in a little time he should not remember one word in the book, nor even the subject it handled: For, books give the same turn to our thoughts and way of reasoning, that good and ill company do to our behaviour and conversation; without either loading our memories, or making us even sensible of the change.[4]

Swift values ancient orators, historians, and poets for reasons similar to those given above: their moral wisdom and the judgment that acquaintance with the ancients can give. But most significant is the attitude toward life and culture that Swift indicates in the final phrases. Even if we forget the actual texts, we acquire a certain "turn to our thoughts and way of reasoning" from the literature that has endured. Such an education teaches a habit of thought that prepares one for a public life, a life of "affairs," or as Swift and his friends would say, the life of a "gentleman."

The "Letter" also shows that Swift's interest in the ancients was of long standing. It was first published in 1720, over twenty years after Swift had entered the lists by writing *A Tale of a Tub* and *The Battle of the Books.* Moreover, the "Letter" shows that he was thinking of these

3. Jonathan Swift, *The Prose Works of Jonathan Swift,* ed. Herbert Davis et al. (Oxford: Blackwell, 1939-68), 9:73. In this and other citations from Swift, I have kept the older punctuation but modernized the italics and capital letters of Swift and other writers for clarity's sake.

4. Swift, *Prose Works,* 9:74, 76. After the ellipses, Swift does not limit his reference to authors of Greece and Rome. He refers to "excellent" authors, who may be of any era. Swift's concern throughout *The Battle of the Books* is with the *qualities* of writing that produce excellent, lasting, and therefore "ancient" literature.

issues near the period in which he began work on *Gulliver's Travels,* which supports the possibility that Gulliver's moral and intellectual problems derive in part from his "modernism."[5]

The English phase of the quarrel between ancients and moderns had begun in 1690 when Temple, a distinguished, retired diplomat and man of letters, responded to works by Thomas Burnet and Pierre Fontenelle.[6] Temple tried to refute two assertions that he attributed to Burnet and Fontenelle: first, that we have more knowledge than the ancients because we know both their work and our own; and second, that human nature had grown progressively better. In truth, most of the moderns of Temple's day did not accept the second assertion, at least in that form. With regard to the first assertion, Temple went so far as to deny that the new sciences of astronomy, physics, and medicine could rival the achievements of Greek science. Significantly, Swift did not follow his mentor's critique of modern science, focusing his satire of science on the absurdity and viciousness of a modern science that loses sight of its human purposes. The more lasting aspect of Temple's "Essay Upon Ancient and Modern Learning," however, concerns his belief that the moderns have nothing to compare with ancient achievements in the subjects that are (for Temple) most fundamental to civilization: poetry, history, philosophy, and eloquence. When William Wotton responded to Temple with his *Reflections Upon Ancient and Modern Learning* (1694), Wotton agreed that the ancients had "set the standards" of moral and political knowledge, but argued that it was still possible for moderns to "rival their achievement."[7] He also agreed that the ancients were better poets and orators, but his survey grants superiority to the moderns in chemistry, anatomy, physics, astronomy, mathematics, and medicine. Wotton had urged "'joining ancient and modern Learning together . . . in those things wherein they severally

5. We know that Swift was at work on *Gulliver's Travels* by April 15, 1721, when he writes his friend Charles Ford that he is "writing a History of my Travells. . . ." *The Correspondence of Jonathan Swift,* ed. Harold Williams (Oxford: Clarendon, 1963-65), 2:381.

6. My treatment here is indebted to Levine's first, second, and fourth chapters in *The Battle of the Books:* "Wotton vs. Temple," "Bentley vs. Christ Church," and "The *Querelle.*"

7. Levine, *The Battle of the Books,* 35.

do excel,'" but his irenic counsel went unheeded. Already the French were deep in controversy over the value of Homer's *Iliad*—whether its heroes were capricious brutes who would have been better bred had they lived in the seventeenth century, or whether the *Iliad* as a whole was second only to the Bible in its wisdom, nobility, and morality.

When Wotton entered this controversy on the side of the moderns, he was not yet thirty years old. His critics viewed him as a mere scholar, while Temple had served in the diplomatic core, helping to construct the Triple Alliance in 1668 and to arrange the marriage of the monarchs who had saved England from tyranny, William and Mary. If the purpose of education was to produce a gentleman like Sir William Temple, shouldn't there be some sense in which he was correct?

Fortunately for the partisans of "ancientness," or *ancienneté,* and especially for Jonathan Swift, the next phase of the quarrel expanded the issue and sharpened the matter of "character." One passage in Temple's 1690 "Essay" had bluntly proclaimed that the oldest books were the best, and that the most ancient prose works were Aesop's *Fables* and the *Epistles of Phalaris.* This passage had deeply offended the most learned philologist of the age, Richard Bentley, the royal librarian, who knew he could show, on the basis of modern scholarship, that Aesop was written relatively late and that the *Epistles* were not only late but forgeries to boot. When an Oxford student, Charles Boyle, published the *Epistles* (in 1695) and insulted Bentley in the preface for refusing to lend a manuscript, Bentley was more than eager to respond. Two years later, Bentley's "Dissertation upon the Epistles of Phalaris" appeared as an appendix to a new edition of Wotton's *Reflections.* He proved his point (although some continued to doubt him), but compromised the superiority of his modern scholarship by its seeming alliance with his arrogance, contentiousness, tactlessness, and studied lack of style. The ancients' most effective response to Bentley, both for Boyle's allies at Christ Church College and for Jonathan Swift, was satire. Modern scholars like Wotton and Bentley may be correct on this or that point, they realized, but the ultimate question concerned the purpose of education: was a true knowledge of the classics accessible only to professionals in modern philology, who turned out to be pedants like Wotton and Bentley, or to amateurs as well, who were better fit for public life? Levine writes:

> The Christ Church men — it is Macaulay again who describes them — were "dominant at Oxford, powerful in the Inns of Court and the College of Physicians, conspicuous in Parliament and in the literary and fashionable circles of London." These were no mere scholars but in every sense men of the world; and like gentlemen and men of taste in their time, they were accomplished Latinists and convinced disciples of antiquity. In this respect they much resembled Temple . . . in contrast to Wotton and Bentley, who knew little of life outside the academic cloister.[8]

Swift composed *A Tale of a Tub* and *The Battle of the Books* in 1696-98, during the heat of the pamphlet war that followed Bentley's "Dissertation," and published them in 1704, when they occasioned another outbreak of hostilities. Temple and Boyle, Bentley and Wotton, Aesop and Phalaris all appear in these works. Readers have generally agreed that the *Battle* is less a separate work than an expansion of the *Tale*'s ideas regarding literary criticism, and indeed the two works have generally been printed together since their first appearance.[9] Swift translates the "quarrel," as the controversy was known in France, into a "battle" and changes its front from footnotes about Aesop to the larger significance of education. In both of these respects, Swift's strategy runs parallel to today's controversialists, who have produced books and essays with titles like *The Book Wars, Culture Wars,* and *Beyond the Culture Wars.*[10] We have seen in the introduction how Gates and D'Souza use the metaphors of "allies," "reinforcements," and the language of combat. But today's war does not primarily concern the addition of some excellent works of art by women or minorities any more than Swift's battle concerned the antiquity of Aesop. The contest today is over whether older literature has something worthwhile to teach us — something that should command our attention and shape

8. Levine, *The Battle of the Books,* 54.

9. A third work, *The Mechanical Operation of the Spirit,* is also printed with the other two. All subsequent quotations from the *Tale* and the *Battle* are taken from the standard, fifth edition of 1710, *A Tale of a Tub, to which is added "The Battle of the Books" and "The Mechanical Operation of the Spirit,"* ed. A. C. Guthkelch and D. Nichol Smith, 2nd ed. (Oxford: Clarendon, 1958).

10. By James Atlas, James Davison Hunter, and Gerald Graff, respectively.

our minds, or whether it represents "the educational kingdom built to accompany the era of white supremacy," in the words of Molefi Kete Asante.[11]

Swift's Satirical Pamphlets and Current Controversies over the Curriculum

The first part of Swift's *Battle of the Books* is a note from the "Bookseller to the Reader," which maintains that the pamphlet treats books only, not persons. Swift counts on us to recognize the ethical problem of separating the self from the word, a problem he examines in *Gulliver's Travels* as well. "I must warn the reader," writes Swift's "bookseller,"

> to beware of applying to persons what is here meant, only of books in the most literal sense. So, when Virgil is mentioned, we are not to understand the person of a famous poet, call'd by that name, but only certain sheets of paper, bound up in leather, containing in print, the works of the said poet, and so of the rest.[12]

One of the strengths of current ideological criticism is its apparent linkage between literature and historical context. But that linkage is often bought at the price of eliminating the individual author and considering his or her work as emanations of the oppressive systems it allegedly serves. For instance, when multiculturalist Asante responds to an article by Diane Ravitch, he associates her work with the " 'the neo-Aryan' model of history" and the system of the "South African Boers," with its odor of Naziism and apartheid.[13] Asante doesn't really need to respond to Ravitch's particular words or the cultural traditions she describes. His ideological presuppositions enable him to consider everything she writes against the backdrop of various systems of oppression. Like Swift's bookseller, Asante makes the person disappear.

The *Battle* begins with the ancients and moderns peacefully oc-

11. Molefi Kete Asante, "Multiculturalism: An Exchange," *American Scholar* 60 (1991): 267-72.

12. Swift, *A Tale of a Tub,* 214.

13. Asante, "Multiculturalism," 267, 268.

cupying two different peaks on Mount Parnassus, the Greek mountain sacred to the muses and symbolic of the achievements of classical culture. The moderns complain that their view is spoiled by the ancients' peak, the higher and larger of the two, and they propose to trade places or reduce the ancients' peak to the level of their own — or to begin a war. Swift's ancients cannot understand the very language of the moderns' demand. They accuse the moderns of "either folly or ignorance" in proposing to equalize the two peaks by "pulling down that of the ancients" and suggest instead that the moderns raise their peak, offering to help them in the effort. The moderns reject this proposal "with much indignation." War then breaks out between the two sides, which foreshadows the later conflict between the books in which the authors' spirits have been preserved.

Like the controversies of today, the "battle" in Swift's satire is fought not over different ways of valuing the past, but rather over the very notion that past authors are valuable. Although he lived before the development of ideology in its modern form, Swift's "pulling down" anticipates the tendency in ideological criticism (like that of Eagleton, for instance) to portray the traditions of the past in an extremely negative light.[14] Swift's ancients can no more understand the moderns' language, to the satisfaction of the moderns, than Diane Ravitch can "understand" Molefi Kete Asante: in its pure form, ideology regards true understanding as entailing a kind of conversion or transformation, as we shall see in the chapter on multiculturalism. Swift's contemporary ancients could not comprehend how philology could seriously challenge the entire classical tradition of education. Today's ancients are similarly handicapped by their skepticism of the vocabulary of modern theory — "hegemony," "privileging," "implicating," "valorizing," and so on — and the translation of such terms into a technique of analysis. Like

14. Michael Oakeshott describes the ideological tendency of "the Rationalist" thus: "There is, of course, no question either of retaining or improving such a tradition [of ideas], for both these involve an attitude of submission. It must be destroyed. And to fill its place the Rationalist puts something of his own making — an ideology, the formalized abridgement of the supposed substratum of rational truth contained in the tradition" (*Rationalism in Politics and Other Essays,* new ed., ed. Timothy Fuller [Indianapolis: Liberty Press, 1991], 8-9).

Swift's moderns, today's variety indignantly reject as "vague," "muddled," and "patently absurd" suggestions such as those of E. D. Hirsch that certain kinds of knowledge can initiate the ignorant into the habits of our culture.[15]

Swift's *Battle* continues by reporting that both sides claimed victory in the first phase of the war between ancients and moderns. The setting then changes to the present — "last Friday," in fact. The site moves from Parnassus to St. James's Library, which has recently acquired the latest controversial books on the battle, books described as "instinct with a most malignant spirit." In his capacity as royal librarian, Richard Bentley has been rearranging the books, giving the best spots to the moderns and displacing the ancients to obscure corners. The discord then begins among the books themselves. The ancients demand to have their priority restored, but negotiations between the two sides fail.

At this point the narrative is interrupted by an accident in the highest corner of the library. A bee has flown through a broken window pane and crashed into a spider's web. The bee extricates himself and is cleaning off the remnants of the ruined web when the angry spider confronts him. Their interchange is later interpreted by Aesop, a chief of the ancients, as an allegory for the entire battle, with the bee representing the ancients and the spider representing the moderns. The spider speaks first, angrily swearing at the bee for having destroyed his web. This first speech reflects Swift's belief that responsibility for the outbreak of hostilities lay with the moderns, and that Bentley's violent language was itself a moral indicator of the moderns' position. The spider boasts of having constructed his web entirely by himself, with no need to rely on the materials of others or to set foot outside the "four inches round" of his corner in the library. The bee freely acknowledges that he visits "indeed, all the flowers and blossoms of the field. . . . [B]ut whatever I collect from thence, enriches my self, without the least injury to their beauty, their smell, or their taste."[16] In the interpretation

15. Barbara Herrnstein Smith, "Cult-Lit: Hirsch, Literacy, and the 'National Culture,'" in *The Politics of Liberal Education,* ed. Darryl J. Gless and Barbara Herrnstein Smith (Durham, N.C.: Duke University Press, 1992), 90.

16. Swift, *A Tale of a Tub,* 231.

of Aesop, the spider's claim of self-sufficiency parallels the moderns' scornful disavowal of any obligation to past traditions. By contrast, says Aesop, the procedure of the bee reflects the ancients' willingness to "[range] thro' every corner of nature," which presumably requires them to leave the library and enter the public worlds of law, medicine, politics, and the church, where the Christ Church wits had distinguished themselves. Aesop concludes by contrasting the inner qualities of the ancients and moderns: "instead of dirt and poison [which make up the spider's entrails], we have rather chose to fill our hives with honey and wax, thus furnishing mankind with the two noblest of things, which are sweetness and light" (234-35).

This portion of the *Battle* does not parallel our situation in one important respect: unlike Bentley and Wotton, who believed that the only person fit to comment on literature was one who had spent an entire lifetime in the academy, both today's ancients and today's moderns want educated men and women to bring their learning into their public and professional lives. In other respects, however, the allegory of the spider and the bee is disconcertingly apropos. Teaching the technique of ideological criticism requires but a narrow range, for once learned, the lesson of systemic oppression may be found everywhere. Spenserian romance will yield the very same lesson as Harlequin Romance. Further, ideology lays claim to a complete understanding of cultural dynamics, parallel to the spider's belief in its self-sufficiency, and must therefore regard contributions and opinions from outside itself negatively. This is why older writers must be spoken of derisively (as "dead white males," for instance) or shown to be part of a hegemony that excluded others.

The bee, by contrast, treasures the floral objects of his attention and does little or no harm to them in his effort to produce honey and wax. Similarly, today's ancients see part of their role in preserving cultural artifacts, for the "sweetness and light" needed to sustain our own culture cannot come from any merely contemporary system of thought and practice, whether liberal or conservative, religious or secular, parochial or cosmopolitan.

Aesop's words, hardly calculated to bring peace, heighten the tensions, and the two sides prepare for battle. Several things happen in the course of the battle to raise Swift's satire above a narrowly partisan pamphlet, although his sympathies for the ancients are never in doubt.

First, Sir Francis Bacon, associated then as now with the modern, scientific method, is not even touched when Aristotle shoots an arrow at him. The fate of other modern scientists, especially medical scientists, is left purposely blank in Swift's text, with two sets of ellipses that ironically indicate a faulty text. The point is that Swift is unwilling to grant superiority to ancient science over modern, although his later works contain plenty of sharp satire for a science that has lost its moorings in ethics, human purpose, and common sense. Second, and perhaps even more surprising, in the final episode Bentley succeeds in carrying off the armor of Aesop and Phalaris, which suggests that Swift is willing to grant Bentley's narrow point that the two authors are not, chronologically, ancients. Although the battle is not ultimately about the narrow questions of scholarship in Swift's day or ours, Swift suggests that a true ancient is willing to admit mistakes.

Most readers have seen Swift's *Battle of the Books* as an expansion of one of the two themes of *A Tale of a Tub.* An extraordinarily complex work, the *Tale* satirizes contemporary abuses in learning (which Swift attributes to the moderns) and in religion (which Swift attributes primarily to the "enthusiasts"). The *Battle,* of course, picks up on the first of these themes, the satire on modern learning, but the *Tale*'s satire of religious enthusiasm is significant for my purpose as well.

By religious "enthusiasm" Swift meant a form of private revelation, accessible only to initiated members of one's particular group. The enthusiast in the *Tale* is Jack, representing John Calvin and his English descendants, the Puritans, who had gained control of Parliament and waged a victorious civil war against king and church a couple of generations earlier. The plot of the *Tale* concerns Jack and his brothers, Peter (the Catholic Church) and Martin (the Church of England), who quarrel over the coats left them by their father in his will, symbolizing the later quarrels over Christian doctrine as given by Christ in the New Testament. Jack abandons normal, "unrefined" reason and uses the "will" to answer absolutely every question in life, as the Puritan extremists had used the Bible for guidance in every question of politics, cultural life, and church government.

> He had a way of working it into any shape he pleased; so that it served him for a night-cap when he went to bed, and for an umbrello

> in rainy weather. . . . His common talk and conversation ran wholly in the phrase of his will, and he circumscribed the utmost of his eloquence within that compass, not daring to let slip a syllable without authority from thence.[17]

Jack is not a hypocrite in the *Tale,* which distinguishes the *Tale* from other satirical portraits of the Puritans: he is mad. It is insane, Swift suggests, to take one element of life for the whole, then force all phenomena to conform to a previously arranged system. It is mad to fence one's language, down to the smallest syllable, by a system. In its treatment of madness, the *Tale* brings together Swift's two themes, the abuses of religion and of learning, and raises some relevant questions for our present quarrels.

Section 9 of *A Tale of a Tub* is Swift's "digression" on madness. The typical actions of madmen like Jack are "the establishment of new empires by conquest[,] the advance and progress of new schemes in philosophy[,] and the contriving, as well as the propagating of new religions." Swift was a severe critic of England's imperial ambitions, particularly as they affected his native Ireland, but my concern is primarily with the second activity, the advancing of new schemes in "philosophy," which here includes "natural philosophy" or what we call "science." The narrator begins by wondering how anyone could "advance new systems with such an eager zeal, in things agreed on all hands impossible to be known. . . . For what man in the natural state, or course of thinking," Swift continues, "did ever conceive it in his power, to reduce the notions of all mankind, exactly to the same length, and breadth, and height of his own? Yet this is the first humble and civil design of all innovators in the empire of reason."

How can Jack possibly reduce the complexity of life to the simplicity of his system? Or how, one might ask in parallel fashion, can the most complex questions of literature be reduced to the simple analyses given by the ideologies of race, class, and gender? The "problem" in every text for the modern is discovering the correct critique of oppression. If you disagree with the critique or place a greater emphasis on other issues, you are "naive and irresponsible," according to Henry

17. Swift, *A Tale of a Tub,* 190-91.

Louis Gates Jr.[18] His ally Gerald Graff wonders "what is to be done with those constituencies which do not happen to agree . . . that social transformation is the primary goal of education."[19] Like Jack, these modern critics believe that their opponents just don't get it. They believe that "the notions of all mankind" must conform to their own if "the primary goal of education" is ever to be achieved.

Swift's narrator next asks about the madman's tendency to proselytize: "Let us therefore now conjecture how it comes to pass, that none of these great prescribers, do ever fail providing themselves and their notions, with a number of implicite disciples." The narrator suggests a "secret necessary sympathy" or a "string of harmony" which has "the same tuning" among various individuals. Later he implies that the "thought of subduing multitudes to his own power" motivates the systematizer to seek disciples. In their purest forms, modern ideologies, like the systems of Swift's characters, have always been accompanied by a large will-to-power. This gives them tremendous force, untapped by their opponents. Any doubts about the exercise of power have previously been quieted by the self-justifying moral aspects of ideology. "We, as a body, possess an enormous amount of collective authority and power," Gates tells the Modern Language Association, "power which as yet remains unharnessed and untapped, inert and merely potential."[20] But why would a prospective disciple prefer to enlist under a new system rather than acquire knowledge in the old ways? An earlier digression in Swift's *Tale* supplies the answer: "to enter the palace of learning at the great gate, requires an expence of time and forms; therefore men of much haste and little ceremony are content to get in by the back-door" (sec. 7). In the systems provided by modern critics, according to Swift's narrator, actual "authors need be little consulted, yet criticks, and commentators, and lexicons carefully must." In short, learning a system is easier than entering the spirit of older literature. By mastering a system, the disciple can hope

18. Henry Louis Gates Jr., "On the Rhetoric of Racism in the Profession," in *Literature, Language, and Politics,* ed. Betty Jean Craige (Athens: University of Georgia Press, 1988), 23.

19. Gerald Graff, "Teach the Conflicts," in *The Politics of Liberal Education,* 70.

20. Gates, "On the Rhetoric of Racism in the Profession," 23.

that one day he or she will occupy the position of subduing other multitudes.

"But to return to madness," as Swift's narrator says. The digression on madness explicitly contrasts the modern student of philosophy, politics, and religion with one who accepts the older, ancient approach to learning:

> [T]he more he shapes his understanding by the pattern of human learning, the less he is inclined to form parties after his particular notions; because that instructs him in his private infirmities, as well as in the stubborn ignorance of the people. (171)

The "pattern of human learning" teaches us our "infirmities" and discourages us from forming parties. This passage, where the voice sounds straightforward and void of irony in light of Swift's other writings, could hardly be further from Gates's call for the modern professor to exercise power in pursuit of what Graff calls social transformation. It is the voice of self-criticism, willing to express doubts about one's own righteousness.

The quarrel between ancients and moderns appears more explicitly in section 3 of the *Tale,* "A Digression concerning Criticks." Here Swift adopts the voice of one who sympathizes with the moderns' treatment of ancient texts in order to explore the nature of the "true [that is, modern] critick." Just as the *Battle* had extended ancient qualities to persons like Temple and Boyle who lived in the present, this digression finds "modern" qualities in certain critics of the ancient world. The true, modern critic is in fact descended from the stock of Momus, Zoilus, and other men of antiquity whose criticism was a byword in the eighteenth century for partial, trivial, or carping analysis. The critic is "a discoverer and collector of writers faults." Now in Swift's day a "fault" was something like the apparently incredible description of the shield of Achilles in the eighteenth book of the *Iliad.* Today the modern detects the faulty "gender, race, and class assumptions in literature and criticism," in Annette Kolodny's words, as the first step in her project of ideological criticism.[21] The type of fault has changed,

21. Annette Kolodny, "Dancing between Left and Right," in *Literature, Language, and Politics,* 36.

but the impulse is the same: the "noble moderns . . . have with unwearied pains made many useful searches into the weak sides of the antients, and given us a comprehensive list of them," says Swift.

A more curious characteristic of modern scholarship in Swift's satire is that "the noblest discoveries those antients ever made, of art or of nature, have all been produced by the transcending genius of the present age." Swift satirizes the modern scholars of his day for their tendency to recognize value in the ancient world only in those aspects that run parallel to their own modern notions. He then illustrates the arrogance of modern critics by his narrator's claim to have "[taken] in the whole compass of human nature" and "easily concluded" that the ancients are really imitators "of their masters the moderns." In our own day, we see a similar gesture when women's writing is valued primarily because it anticipates modern feminism, or Shakespeare because his plays are implicated in oppressive structures that only a new historicist critique adequately reveals.

In Swift's "Digression," the modern critic grossly overestimates his own importance by persuading himself that "the perfection of writing correct was entirely owing to the institution of criticks." In other words, the critic really considers himself more vital to the art of literature than literary artists themselves. His pronouncements are as dreadful as the "braying of an ass" that put to flight "a vast army of Scythians." His vocation turns into a form of hunting in which the critics, "like young wolves, [grow] up in time, to be nimble and strong enough for hunting down large game." In our own time, perhaps Milton's *Paradise Lost* is the largest trophy to have been mounted on the ideologues' wall, brought down for its alleged misogyny: an essay in the influential pedagogical journal *College English* takes it for granted that teachers are morally bound to show how that poem is "implicated in the ongoing oppression of women in our society."[22]

Donald Greene has noticed the parallel between this part of Swift's *Tale* and current criticism as well: "The implied injunction to 'revaluate' literary texts using the 'critical methods or ideologies of the present day' is ominously reminiscent of the Hack's program of critical modernism

22. Ronald Strickland, "Confrontational Pedagogy and Traditional Literary Studies," *College English* 52 (March 1990): 297.

in *A Tale of a Tub*."[23] Yet an ancient too can read back his or her own preoccupations in older literature, like Swift's, essentially duplicating the strategy of the moderns: he or she too can turn Swift into a partisan for his current battles. If an ancient values Swift *only* because he anticipates the present quarrels with the moderns, the ancient is mimicking the gestures of the moderns in *A Tale of a Tub*. No one should think himself safe from Swift's satire.

A more careful reading of Swift will prevent this misuse. Swift's preface to the *Battle* is especially important at this point: satire is a sort of mirror, says Swift, "wherein beholders do generally discover every body's face but their own" (215). This suggests that we should indeed see our own face in his satire, whether we sympathize more with the ancients or with the moderns. Without denying the importance of the cultural battle, Swift locates the problem in a more profound confrontation within the individual and in the infirmities of human nature. Swift argues that the purpose of satire is to "mend the world," but by satirizing Jack as mad rather than hypocritical, he has chosen a character who is unmendable.[24] Jack's madness comes from natural causes, not from moral choices, and he therefore cannot, ultimately, be considered culpable for his words and actions. Jack's disciples believe that their inspiration comes from "wind," which they consider "the original cause of all things" and have even compiled a systematic treatment of winds called "Æolism" (142, 150, 162). But the narrator does not accept this as a full explanation of Jack's madness. When he promises to "unravel this knotty point" in the "Digression on Madness," the text is interrupted by five lines of ellipses:

23. Donald Greene, "Literature or Metaliterature? Thoughts on Traditional Literary Study," *Theory and Tradition in Eighteenth-Century Studies*, ed. Richard B. Schwartz (Carbondale: Southern Illinois University Press, 1990), 26. "The Hack" is the name given by many scholars to the narrator of the digressions and the prefatory matter of the *Tale*. See Ronald Paulson's *Theme and Structure in Swift's "Tale of a Tub"* (New Haven: Yale University Press, 1960), 45-52. I believe, however, that Gardner D. Stout Jr.'s thesis is more persuasive — that the narrator is Swift, often parodying several different narrative voices in single sections of the *Tale* yet sometimes commenting on the *Tale* in his own voice. See Stout, "Speaker and Satiric Vision in Swift's *Tale of a Tub*," *Eighteenth-Century Studies* 3 (1969): 175-99.

24. See Stout, "Speaker and Satiric Vision in Swift's *Tale of a Tub*," 187.

> There is in mankind a certain * * *
> * * * * * * * *
>
> *Hic multa desiderantur* * * . . . . . . *
> * * * And this I take to be a clear solution of the matter.
>
> (170)

Today's ideologues combine Jack's enthusiastic systematizing with the "modern criticks' " attitudes toward the past. But Swift does not pretend to comprehend Jack. Perhaps Swift is suggesting a useful warning: believing one can even comprehend, let alone mend the disputes of the day is something beyond us. One may have a duty — satirical, prophetic, or scholarly — to try, but the ultimate result will be failure.

Like the moderns he satirizes in the *Battle,* Swift reduces persons to combatants, to books, and even more tellingly to "sheets of paper" and "print" (214). In other words, the most effective response to the modern challenge — a satirical battle rather than a disinterested and possibly even charitable essay — adopts the methods of his enemy. After all, it is the enemy, philologist Bentley, whom Swift accuses of having more interest in the black marks comprised in texts than in the meanings of texts. But if one must adopt the methods of one's opponents to win the battle, is it worth the fight? Swift doesn't say.

Swift implies that the battle cannot really be won after all. No modern will be persuaded by the *Battle,* no enthusiast by the *Tale,* and no ideologue by my analysis. Nor did Swift really expect any of his opponents to be persuaded by his satire, as the epigraph to the *Battle* suggests: no one will see himself mirrored in these pages. The ironic "Letter from Captain Gulliver" which precedes the *Travels* speaks of the same issue, satire's ultimate failure, in a different context. Purportedly written after his cousin has persuaded him to print the *Travels,* Gulliver complains that none of the "reformations" promised by the cousin have actually occurred. "[F]or instead of seeing a full stop put to all abuses and corruptions . . . behold, after above six months warning, I cannot learn that my book hath produced one single effect according to mine intentions."[25] In this way, the satirical intent of

25. Jonathan Swift, *Gulliver's Travels,* in *Prose Works,* 11:6. All citations from *Gulliver's Travels* are from this edition.

Gulliver's Travels is itself satirized, a crucial point of continuity between the later *Travels* and the earlier *Tale.* As Stout says, "recent criticism of the *Travels* has increasingly recognized that in Gulliver's final posture Swift presents an ironic self-parody of the satirist's motives — his anger, pharisaical pride, and desire to convert others — and a mocking, sympathetic exposure of satire's impotence to 'wonderfully mend the world.'"[26]

Swift's satire in the *Tale of a Tub* and *Battle of the Books* questions himself in a way that one cannot imagine a modern ideologue doing. Swift's gesture of self-questioning rests upon the assumption of a flawed human nature, which modern ideology regards as naive. The ideologue thereby loses the capacity for moral progress that Swift's satire offers, proposing instead a transformed cultural order that is just over the horizon of the newest scholarly advances. But Swift knew about new orders whose basis was an enthusiasm for the latest learning. *Gulliver's Travels* is the story of a modern man with a similar vision, who denounces his past and goes on to lose his humanity altogether. This loss, which reaches its climax in the last of Gulliver's voyages, is one of the richest themes of the book.

Gulliver's "Modernity": Learning All the Wrong Lessons

Gulliver's fourth and final voyage, to the land of the Houyhnhnms, unsettles his mind and turns him into a misanthrope. Typically discussions of Gulliver's madness and misanthropy begin with the final voyage rather than the beginning of the book. His insane antipathy to mankind, however, is apparent from the prefatory material, especially in the letter to his cousin Sympson. Here he refers to Englishmen as "Yahoos," the vicious, human-like brutes of Houyhnhnm-land who are ruled by passion in contrast to the horses, the Houyhnhnms, who rule their land rationally. In this letter, Gulliver's mind is deeply divided over whether he has maintained the Houyhnhnms' level of rational virtue or slipped back to the filthy depravity of the Yahoos. The final paragraph of the letter to his cousin, the final words written by "Gul-

26. Stout, "Speaker and Satiric Vision in Swift's *Tale of a Tub*," 197.

liver" in the fictional world of the book, captures his tortured ambivalence:

> I have other complaints to make upon this vexatious occasion; but I forbear troubling myself or you any further. I must freely confess, that since my last return, some corruptions of my Yahoo nature have revived in me by conversing with a few of your species, and particularly those of mine own family, by an unavoidable necessity; else I should never have attempted so absurd a project as that of reforming the Yahoo race in this kingdom; but, I have now done with all such visionary schemes for ever. (8)

Gulliver accepts "Yahoo nature" as his own, but considers Yahoos "your" species, not his. He recognizes his corruptions, but maintains that they are not really his fault. Rather, they are due to his regrettable need for close association (the older meaning of "conversing") with human beings. Like the narrator in the *Tale,* he cannot conceive of any third possibility — the possibility that he is neither Houyhnhnm nor Yahoo, but a human being, a mixture of reason and passion, virtue and vice.

In the nineteenth century, several influential commentators laid Gulliver's obvious misanthropy at the feet of Swift himself — Thackeray going so far as to discourage the reading of the final voyage. "It is Yahoo language; a monster gibbering shrieks and gnashing imprecations against mankind," he wrote.[27] Since the 1940s, however, many readers have argued for a "soft" reading of *Gulliver's Travels:* Since Gulliver is not Swift, perhaps Gulliver (rather than mankind) is the butt of Swift's satire. After all, Gulliver's words are rarely those of Swift speaking in his own voice. Moreover, the humor of the book, from first to last, depends on our rapid recognition of meanings that escape Gulliver, whether it is his inordinate pride in achieving the distinction of "Nardac" (the Lilliputian equivalent of duke) or his proficiency in speaking the Houyhnhnm tongue to his English horses. The purely rational Houyhnhnms are not the ideal for humanity, say the advocates for the "soft school," any more than the Yahoos are an accurate depiction of real human beings. Gulliver reports that the Houyhnhnms

27. Milton Foster, ed., *A Casebook on Gulliver among the Houyhynhmns* (New York: Crowell, 1961), 86.

> are endowed by nature with a general disposition to all virtues, and have no conceptions or ideas of what is evil in a rational creature; so their grand maxim is, to cultivate reason, and to be wholly governed by it. Neither is reason among them a point problematical as with us, where men can argue with plausibility on both sides of a question. . . . (267)

Gulliver goes mad and loses his humanity because he adopts this ideal as his own. He is blind to his own nature, which is not naturally disposed to all virtues, and deceived as to the sufficiency of human reason. Moreover, he does not see the weak sides of the horse utopia. The Houyhnhnms lack nearly all significant emotion, for instance. They are willing to exchange children to achieve a balance of genders and do not grieve for the death of their mate (270, 275). None of the Houyhnhnms even has a name, the most basic of all human identifiers. By adopting an ideal that is both unreachable and ultimately contrary to human nature, Gulliver sets himself up for catastrophic disappointment and misanthropy. But Swift sees what Gulliver does not, and while his satire is sharp, its point is aimed primarily at Gulliver and people like him, who harbor deep illusions about the sufficiency of reason in overcoming human vice.

Against this interpretation, other scholars have proposed a "hard" reading. The soft reading allows the reader to escape the troubling consequences of the final voyage by suggesting that Swift himself was merely recommending, say, Christian humanism or criticizing the Houyhnhnms as excessively rational, like the deists of his day. These readers point out that even if Gulliver does not speak in Swift's voice in the Voyage to the Houyhnhnms, his moral conclusions are often similar. For instance, Gulliver provides his Houyhnhnm master with this description of "the art of war":

> a description of cannons, culverins, muskets, carabines, pistols . . . ; ships sunk with a thousand men; twenty thousand killed on each side; dying groans, limbs flying in the air: smoak, noise, confusion, trampling to death under horses feet. . . .
>
> I was going on to more particulars, when my master commanded me to silence. He said, whoever understood the nature of Yahoos might easily believe it possible for so vile an animal, to be capable

> of every action I had named. . . . But when a creature pretending to reason, could be capable of such enormities, he dreaded lest the corruption of that faculty might be worse than brutality itself. (247-48)

There is no question but that Swift would agree with the Houyhnhnm master's comments and with Gulliver's later "detestation" of war and many similar corruptions described in the middle chapters of the fourth voyage. Although most readers now seem to agree that Gulliver's fatal conclusion that human beings are Yahoos is not to be taken as Swift's, the advocates of the "hard" reading believe the Houyhnhnms do represent an ideal for humanity. Claude Rawson puts the case for this interpretation of *Gulliver's Travels* convincingly. Admitting that we cannot "identify [Gulliver's] voice with Swift's" and that we rarely "accord Gulliver our whole-hearted respect," Rawson nevertheless writes:

> The volume as a whole has been establishing, bleakly and massively, the grounds for an attack on man; and we as readers are left alone with Gulliver's voice at the end, for Swift has taken care to provide no competing point of view to help us towards a more comforting perspective. Swift is readily dissociated from Gulliver's rant, but hardly from the indictment it embodies.[28]

Rawson is surely correct to warn us of an easy retreat that keeps us from seeing ourselves in Swift's satirical mirror: we are not Yahoos, but we have all made Yahoo-like compromises with evil. To turn away from the mirror is to accept the moral complacency in which we usually live.

One of the questions that has been too little discussed is why Gulliver is particularly susceptible to the misanthropic madness that overtakes him. For some this question is inappropriate, for it may suggest that Gulliver is like a character in a novel, when it is clear that Swift treats him externally and inconsistently, unlike a true novel character.[29] Nevertheless, Gulliver remains the focus of the book, from

28. Claude Rawson, *The Character of Swift's Satire: A Revised Focus* (Newark: University of Delaware Press, 1983), 78.

29. Claude Rawson, *Gulliver and the Gentle Reader* (London: Routledge & Kegan Paul, 1973), 27.

beginning to end, and his end is morally fascinating: Gulliver cannot recognize the humanity of the man who rescues him, Pedro de Mendez. When his wife takes him in her arms and kisses him, "the touch of that odious animal," says Gulliver, causes him to fall "in a swoon for almost an hour" (289). The prefatory letter to his cousin is, if possible, even more misanthropic, for Gulliver quarrels over meaningless dates and spellings, prefers the neighing of his English horses (whom he identifies with the Houyhnhnms) to praise from "the Yahoo race," and complains of the failure of his "project" "to correct every vice and folly to which Yahoos are subject" (6-8). Swift wants the satire to sting every reader of Gulliver's final words. But Gulliver is mad. His education at the hands, or rather hoofs, of the Houyhnhnms, has not made him more virtuous and rational than other humans, but more vicious and irrational. Why, of all people, should a traveler, someone defined by his appetite for knowledge in Swift's day, end up like Gulliver?

"Modern Science," Gulliver's Sensibility, and Madness

One reason Gulliver learns his lessons wrongly, in Houyhnhnm-land and throughout his travels, is that he is a "modern" in spirit. Gulliver is not primarily a modern critic, like the ones described in the *Tale of a Tub* (although he has some of their faults as well), but rather a modern scientist. Swift was ambivalent, as we have seen, about the achievements of modern science. But he was downright skeptical of the newly developing scientific method insofar as it reduced the acquisition of knowledge to a technique that required no familiarity with any tradition of knowledge, human or divine, outside itself. Divorced from older wisdom about the purpose of knowledge, yet imperial in his claims to answer all significant questions of human life, the modern scientist was just beginning to feel his strength in Swift's day. In our own, he has skeptics as well — but certainly none of the caliber of Swift, whose satire suggests the absurdities and ultimate inhumanity of a purely self-contained science.

Modern science in Swift's Britain was associated most conspicuously with the Royal Society of London for Improving Natural Knowledge, which met at Gresham College, Bishopsgate Street, in London.

Just west lay Bethlehem Hospital, or "Bedlam," where the insane were housed. Bedlam was thus strategically placed between Gresham and, further west, Grub Street, where many of Swift's modern, hack writers lived. Swift picks up this coincidence in the *Tale of a Tub*'s "Digression on Madness," linking critic, scientist, and lunatic together by neighborhood association.[30] It is not particularly surprising, then, that a madman, in Swift's fictional world, should be associated with modernity either in its literary or scientific forms. Gulliver too is associated with the Royal Society, for after he returns from the gigantic land of Brobdingnag, he sends three wasp stings "to Gresham College" (110).

Gulliver's modern sensibility is apparent even before his very first voyage, to Lilliput. While Gulliver's professional education as a surgeon consisted of an apprenticeship, his three years of university took place at Emmanuel College, Cambridge. Some have suggested that Swift chose Emmanuel to pay tribute to his patron, Sir William Temple, a graduate of the college, but a comparison to Gulliver is a very ironic compliment indeed. Since Emmanuel was known for its strong Calvinist leanings, a student who claims (like Gulliver) to have "applied my self close to my studies" would have imbibed the Puritan spirit of the place. Puritans were enthusiasts for the new science — the Americans Cotton Mather and John Winthrop, for example, were members of the Royal Society. More specifically, in *A Tale of a Tub* Swift associates the Calvinist Jack with the modern approach to learning by linking his madness for "new religions" with that of advancing "new schemes in philosophy," which includes both what we would call "philosophy" and "science."

Gulliver's enthusiasm for scientific, technological advance is apparent in the first voyage, when he brings home Lilliputian beef cattle and sheep for the improvement of British agriculture and woolen manufacturing. These animals are less than three inches high, a fact

30. In the "Digression Concerning Madness," the narrator suggests that Parliament appoint commissioners to "inspect into Bedlam, and the parts adjacent," which would include Grub Street and Gresham College. In section 10, the linkage between critics and scientists is more explicit ("my worthy . . . friends at Will's coffee-house and Gresham-College, and Warwick-Lane, and Moor-Fields"). Will's was a gathering place for literary critics; Bedlam was in Moorfields.

that escapes Gulliver's notice in the enthusiasm of his project. As is typical in the book as a whole, Gulliver literally loses perspective in his new land, then multiplies that loss in matters scientific, political, and moral. His is a one-track mind, generally captive to his current environment. The excellence of the Lilliputians' beef and fineness of their fleeces blind him to all the practical difficulties of his project (64, 80). The result of his loss of perspective is merely absurd in this voyage, nothing more serious. Later, however, Gulliver's loss of perspective, his systematizing mind, and his Jack-like tendency "to reduce the notions of all mankind, exactly to . . . his own" drive him mad.

In his second voyage, to Brobdingnag, Gulliver's more obviously modern sensibility comes into conflict with that of an "ancient," the king of Brobdingnag. From the outset of the voyage, Gulliver adopts the technical language of the specialist. The account of his outward journey sounds like that of other modern travel writers, notably the popular William Dampier. The jargon-filled paragraph on his shipwreck is drawn almost word for word from a contemporary magazine: "We reeft the foresail and set him, we hawled aft the fore-sheet; the helm was hard a weather. The ship wore bravely. We belay'd the foredown-hall. . . ." The technical jargon is meaningful only to the specialist, comical in its pretentious inaccessibility to everyone else. One of the main charges against the moderns in the *querelle* was their presupposition that the only person qualified to comment on learned subjects was the specialist, one whose entire life was devoted to learning the specialized language of modern scholarship. The ancients' response, as reflected in Swift's satirical paragraph, is that such scholarship results in pedantry and narrows the scope of learning from the large, public world of "gentlemen" to the narrow, cloistered society of scholars.

Like the modern scientist with his recently developed microscope, Gulliver's relatively small stature in this land of giants gives him far greater powers of observation, yet even so he longs for a microscope. But what more would he really "see"? What does he truly hope to contribute to the world of learning? He describes the cancerous breast of a Brobdingnagian woman, the wen in the neck of a man, and wishes for a microscope to dissect a louse. Swift's "satire on microscopic vision," Robert P. Fitzgerald has noted,

> reflects the assumption of the Ancients and the humanists that we have in our own nature the powers to deal with questions really fundamental. One may use a scientific instrument to discover facts of evidence, but he who looks to an instrument for wisdom will begin to see the world in a distorted, non-human way. The Modern who becomes obsessed with what is to be seen through the microscope will be reduced, like Gulliver, to the level of the lice and the wasps.[31]

Gulliver's size associates him with the moderns as well in book 2, for both sides in the *querelle* spoke of the moderns as "dwarfs" standing on the shoulders of ancient "giants." The moderns asserted that this perspective enabled them to see further than the ancients, while the ancients pointed out their inferiority and indebtedness to their predecessors. Gulliver's sense of superiority to older traditions of learning is perhaps clearer here than in any other book. He delivers an attack on Aristotelian science in the context of reporting (favorably) on the inquiry of the Brobdingnagian scholars into his own nature:

> After much debate, they concluded unanimously that I was only relplum scalcath, which is interpreted literally lusus naturæ ["a freak of nature"]; a determination exactly agreeable to the modern philosophy of Europe: whose professors, disdaining the old evasion of occult causes, whereby the followers of Aristotle endeavour in vain to disguise their ignorance; have invented this wonderful solution of all difficulties, to the unspeakable advancement of human knowledge. (104)

Swift is not endorsing ancient science, unlike his patron Sir William Temple, but his skepticism of the "unspeakable advancements" of modern science is clear.

31. Robert P. Fitzgerald, "Ancients and Moderns in Swift's Brobdingnag," *Literature in Wissenschaft und Unterricht* (Kiel, Germany) 18 (1985): 91. Allan Bloom reads the entire book through the prism of the quarrel between ancients and moderns in "An Outline of *Gulliver's Travels,*" in *Ancients and Moderns,* ed. Joseph Cropsey (New York: Basic Books, 1964), 238-57. I consider Bloom's reading too programmatic — it forces the Houyhnhnms to be "ancients," for instance — but I agree that the issue is more important to the book than we have realized up to now.

Of all his voyages, Gulliver feels most negative towards the one to Brobdingnag. "The learning of this people is very defective," he complains, "consisting only in morality, history, poetry and [practical] mathematicks" — in short, the subjects of greatest interest to the ancients. He is unable to "drive the least conception" of more up-to-date concerns with "ideas, entities, abstractions, and transcendentals" into their heads (136).

On perusing a book of "morality and devotion" that belonged to "a grave elderly gentlewoman," Gulliver is disappointed to find "all the usual topicks of European moralists; shewing how diminuitive, contemptible, and helpless an animal was man in his own nature . . ." (137). These topics, of course, are the very ones that Gulliver could have learned, had he been disposed, from ancient books. Gulliver has read ancient literature; so had the "modern criticks" in *The Battle of the Books.* The point is that he had learned nothing from the ancients because he felt there was nothing to be learned. He condemns the gentlewoman's book, along with those of the entire tradition of European moralists, as among "the quarrels we raise with nature. And, I believe upon a strict enquiry, those quarrels might be shewn to be as ill-grounded among us, as they are among those people" (137-38). True. But then again they might be shown to be as *well* grounded. A "strict enquiry" might end by recommending a book of morality for combatting the same problems in Gulliver that concerned the grave gentlewoman of Brobdingnag.

The king of Brobdingnag is "as learned a person as any in his dominions," especially in philosophy and mathematics, but presumably educated as well in the three subjects already mentioned — morality, history, and poetry. When Gulliver graphically describes the uses of gunpowder, associated with "modern" technological advance at least since Bacon's *New Atlantis,* the king is horrified: "He was amazed how so impotent and groveling an insect as I . . . could entertain such inhuman ideas, and . . . commanded me, as I valued my life, never to mention any more" (134-35). Now Sir William had expressed reservations about this "modern" invention of gunpowder as well, and many have recognized touches of Swift's patron in the king's character. But Gulliver simply cannot understand his reaction: "A strange effect of narrow principles and short views!" He has already accused the king of "prejudices," a typical complaint made by the moderns against the ancients from Swift's day to our own. Perhaps the king's prejudices are due to his relatively small library, for a small collection of books is typical of an ancient, not a modern.[32] Gulliver ultimately attributes the king's scruples to the general "ignorance" of the Brobdingnagians, who have not yet "reduced politics into a science, as the more acute wits of Europe have done." The notion that politics can be so reduced is a peculiarly modern one, as Fitzgerald points out, beginning with Machiavelli.[33] It is typical of Gulliver, in Swift's satire, to speak as a modern without even an awareness of the provenance of his ideas.

While the king of Brobdingnag has many of the characteristics of an ancient, he is not the embodiment of all moral goodness. Swift is not writing an allegory of the quarrel, nor does he have an idolatrous view of the tradition he embraces. The king's lowest point comes in chapter 8, when we find that he has no intention of helping Gulliver return home. Rather, he has "given strict orders" to capture any ship with normal-size human beings aboard so that Gulliver "might propagate the breed." If we are surprised by the king's callousness, however, the king himself is aware of the failings of his own race. After hearing Gulliver talk of domestic politics, the king takes him up in his right hand, and

> after a hearty fit of laughter, asked me whether I were a Whig or a Tory. Then turning to his first minister . . . he observed, how contemptible a thing was human grandeur, which could be mimicked by such diminuitive insects as I: And yet, said he, I dare engage, those creatures have their titles and distinctions of honour. (107)

Unlike Gulliver, the king actually learns from his experience, in this case, his experience with Gulliver. He learns, or rather re-learns, the lessons of human fallibility that Gulliver rejects when he finds them in the gentlewoman's book of morality and devotion. The king does not require a microscope for this kind of learning. Nor does this learning

32. In *The Battle of the Books,* the ancients are "much fewer in number" than the moderns. Swift refers to only about fourteen ancients, as opposed to a much larger number of moderns (*Battle,* 238).

33. Fitzgerald, "Ancients and Moderns in Swift's Brobdingnag," 92-93.

give him the power that modern systems promise. Rather, it leads him to question his own "titles and distinctions of honour," which is to say his own previously held values, as any lively acquaintance with a tradition of learning will.

On his return, Gulliver retains the physical perspective of the Brobdingnagians, worrying about trampling English travelers when he meets them on the road, but he learns nothing from their moral perspective. His modern contempt for the kind of wisdom represented by the king of Brobdingnag insulates him from understanding his experiences there. To the captain who rescues him, for instance, Gulliver says that he does not plan to write about his travels, for they "could contain little besides . . . the barbarous customs and idolatry of savage people" — as if the Brobdingnagians were savages (147)! Gulliver, in short, has learned nothing. He has become familiar with no tradition (in his reading or his experiences) for comprehending human nature and human weakness. And when he is confronted with his weaknesses again, in the fourth voyage, he will be driven insane.

The third voyage, to the floating island of Laputa, has usually been thought to be the weakest artistically. Since the inhabitants of Laputa and its earthbound dominions are normal size and human, Swift cannot exploit the comedies of distorted perspective and bodily functions, which contribute so much to the rest of the book. Another reason for the weakness of book 3, however, is that it lacks a level of irony present in the rest of the book. With one exception, the inhabitants of Laputa and the professors in the capital city of Lagado are "moderns," especially in their approach to science. They perform the very experiments in their "Grand Academy" that Gulliver's friends were undertaking at the Royal Society. Because both Gulliver and his hosts are modern, the third book shrinks the ironic gap, so evident elsewhere, between Gulliver's experiences and his perception of those experiences.

The Laputans value the very kind of knowledge Gulliver had tried to force on the Brobdingnagians: ideas, entities, abstractions, and transcendentals. They despise practical geometry but love abstract forms; they have no "imagination, fancy, and invention," by which literature and history (in Swift's understanding) produce knowledge of human nature, but they have superior instruments (like the telescope) for acquiring knowledge of the heavens. Gulliver's initial accounts of

Laputa are themselves modern and scientific, now giving an absurd philological account of the etymology of "Laputa," now describing the physics of the floating island. Gulliver soon complains of the Laputans, but his principal objection is that he is "very little regarded" (173). He still overestimates his own importance, like the moderns in Swift's *Tale,* and disapproves of their abstract speculations primarily because they detract from proper treatment of himself.

After leaving the floating island of Laputa for the earthbound metropolis of Lagado, Gulliver meets the second embodiment of *ancienneté* (after the king of Brobdingnag), "Lord Munodi," a former governor of Lagado who now lives in disgrace. He is an exception to everything Gulliver has experienced in the third voyage to this point. It is significant that of the three positive characters in the book, two of them are decidedly "ancients."[34] Before reaching Lord Munodi's estate, Gulliver "could not discover one ear of corn, or blade of grass." But on the border of his estate, "the scene was wholly altered":

> we came into a most beautiful country; farmers houses at small distances, neatly built, the fields enclosed, containing vineyards, corngrounds and meadows. Neither do I remember to have seen a more delightful prospect. . . .
>
> We came at length to the house, which was indeed a noble structure, built according to the best rules of ancient architecture. The fountains, gardens, walks, avenues, and groves were all disposed with exact judgment and taste. (175-76)

Lord Munodi then reports that soon he will have to raze his houses and build them "as modern usage requires." Gulliver is amazed at this, but Lord Munodi assures him that his "admiration . . . would cease" when he learns the background to the Laputans' new methods. He tells Gulliver that

> about forty years ago, certain persons went up to Laputa . . . and after five months continuance came back with a very little smattering in mathematicks, but full of volatile spirits acquired in that airy

34. The third positively drawn character, Pedro de Mendez, is the Portuguese captain who rescues Gulliver in the fourth voyage.

> region. That these persons upon their return, began to dislike the management of every thing below; and fell into schemes of putting all arts, sciences, languages, and mechanicks upon a new foot. To this end they procured a royal patent for erecting an Academy of Projectors in Lagado. (176)

As Marjorie Nicolson and Nora Mohler point out, "about forty years ago" would place the new-modeling of the arts at about the same time as the opening of the quarrel between ancients and moderns in France.[35] Since that time, to return to the world of Gulliver, similar, provincial academies had been established as well, with their own projects for technological and scientific advancement:

> a palace may be built in a week, of materials so durable as to last for ever without repairing. All the fruits of the earth shall come to maturity at whatever season we think fit to chuse. . . . (177)

The only problem, Gulliver reports, is "that none of these projects are yet brought to perfection; and in the mean time, the whole country lies miserably waste, the houses in ruins, and the people without food or cloaths." In Swift's fiction, even Lord Munodi accepts the censure of his countrymen, who denounce his lack of enterprise and innovation and rebuke his preference of personal ease to the nation's improvement. Similarly, Gulliver can physically see the benefits of Lord Munodi's manner of life, and even praise it, but he fails to comprehend its source. He simply reports on it. Lord Munodi encourages Gulliver to visit the projectors' "Grand Academy," describing Gulliver as "a great admirer of projects," and Gulliver accepts the description "for I had my self been a sort of projector in my younger days" (178).

The word "projector" is an important one here. In *A Tale of a Tub*, the projector is associated with madness and with modern "revo-

35. Marjorie Nicolson and Nora Mohler, *Science and Imagination* (Ithaca: Cornell University Press, 1956), 134. We know from the *Correspondence* that Swift had nearly finished *Gulliver's Travels* by April 1724, and that he wrote the *Voyage to Laputa* last (*Correspondence,* 3:5, 11, 87). Thirty-seven years earlier, in 1687, Charles Perrault opened the *querelle* by reading a poem to the French Academy, *Le Siècle de Louis le Grand*, which maintains that contemporary French culture had surpassed that of Rome under Augustus.

lutions . . . in philosophy, and in religion."[36] The "volatile spirits" that inspire the projectors in *Gulliver's Travels* sound very similar to the "winds" that inspire the mad "Æolist" in the *Tale.* The projectors in both works are systematizers; in both, they are characterized by an earnest search for disciples; in both, they are "moderns."

Gulliver is not telling the full truth when he limits his projecting days to his youth. The introduction of Lilliputian sheep and cattle into Britain is a "project" as ridiculous as the Grand Academy's project of propagating a "breed of naked sheep" (182). Far more important, however, is Gulliver's final project. Gulliver's last words, in the prefatory letter to his cousin, regret his attempting "so absurd a project as that of reforming the Yahoo race in this kingdom" (8). Gulliver is a projector from first to last in the book. And when he finally sees the absurdity of the projecting mind, which is his own mind, he is driven mad.

I have said that the third book shrinks the ironic gap between the reader's perception and Gulliver's perception of his experiences. By merely reporting what he sees, Gulliver's voice lacks the ironic richness it has in the other voyages. But it is not at all true that Gulliver's reactions to the Grand Academy of Lagado are the same as Swift's. For instance, Gulliver is shown a machine "for improving speculative knowledge by practical and mechanical operations." By operating this machine, any ignoramus may "write books in philosophy, poetry, politicks, law, mathematicks, and theology, without the least assistance from genius and study" (182, 184). The machine is a checkerboard affair, with the words of the Laputan tongue written on every square. The professor's pupils turn the squares by means of iron handles, wait for the squares to change, then record the nonsensical results. Gulliver's reaction? He promises to proclaim this professor as "the sole inventer of this wonderful machine" and even inserts a picture into the *Travels,* presumably for the sake of science (183, 185). Gulliver is similarly sympathetic to a later project to abolish words, reporting with a straight face on the advantages of carrying around all of the objects about which one wishes to communicate. In fact, the only project of which Gulliver disapproves is one to persuade monarchs to choose their advisors according to their wisdom, abilities, and virtue. More to his liking are the mechanical political projectors, who have

36. Swift, *A Tale of a Tub,* 171, 174.

reduced all the flaws of politicians to medical causes, and who recommend administering the appropriate remedies of "lenitives, aperitives, abstersives, corrosives, restringents . . ." as each politician requires. "This project could not be of any great expence," he reports, "and might, in my poor opinion be of much use" (187-88).

Many of the scientific "projects" in the Grand Academy (and other important aspects of the third voyage) are drawn from experiments actually recorded in the *Transactions* of the Royal Society or in the works of its members.[37] The Laputans' fear of the earth falling into the sun, their wildly inaccurate use of such instruments as the quadrant, their virtual equation of music with mathematics — all of these have historical sources. So do most of the works of the experimental scientists of the Grand Academy, from setting a spider to spin silk stockings, to employing a blind man to mix colors for paint, to extracting sunbeams from cucumbers. Gulliver reports all of these in an objective, scientific tone, similar to the tone of their original description by Gulliver's modern friends in the Royal Society. A neutral, "scientific" tone is also exploited, at key points, in *A Tale of a Tub*.[38]

Shortly after leaving the Grand Academy, Gulliver comes directly into contact with the ancients, summoned from the dead on the island of Glubbdubdrib. His interviews with the ancients occur in chapter 8, entitled "A further Account of Glubbdubdrib. Antient and Modern History corrected." The title itself indicates a modern mind, for instead of finding in history the models of behavior to shape a "gentleman," Gulliver is interested primarily in discovering the taste of Spartan broth and the endless instances of previously undiscovered corruption. On summoning Homer and Aristotle, Gulliver must be told what a contemporary ancient would already have known: that their commentators

37. This paragraph is indebted to Nicolson and Mohler, "The Scientific Background of Swift's *Voyage to Laputa,*" in *Science and Imagination,* 110-54.

38. In several of the *Tale*'s digressions, Swift adopts the neutral tone of contemporary scientific writing, in part to show that an objective appearance can cover an inhumane obtuseness: "Last week I saw a woman flay'd, and you will hardly believe, how much it altered her person for the worse. Yesterday I ordered the carcass of a beau to be stript in my presence. . . . Then I laid open his brain, his heart, and his spleen . . ." (*Tale,* 9:173). Ronald Paulson discusses the *Tale*'s satire of scientific language in *Theme and Structure in Swift's "Tale of a Tub,"* 52-65.

are strangers to them because they lack "a genius to enter into the spirit of a poet" (197). Aristotle freely admits his mistakes in science, but predicts that even the contemporary theory of gravity, so unqualifiedly endorsed by the scientists of the time, would ultimately give way to a new theory. The true ancient, the interview suggests, realizes that his word is not the last word, which is something Gulliver never learns.

I have been arguing that Gulliver learns very little in the course of his travels, and often what he learns is somehow wrong. For Swift and the other ancients, the most enduring part of learning was its moral significance. The "pattern of human learning" instructs a person in his infirmities, said the *Tale.* Nevertheless, despite all his reading of the ancients and all his travels, Gulliver admits in the final book that he had learned nothing until he came to the land of the Houyhnhnms. In fact, he is confronted with no more "data" regarding human depravity in the horse utopia than he had heard from the lips of the king of Brobdingnag and seen in Lilliput. But when Gulliver sees horses behaving reasonably and compares their lives with actual, depraved human behavior, he cannot bear the experience. Not only does he again accept the perspective of his hosts, he identifies the human race with the savage Yahoos. Unlike Swift's Aristotle, who is capable of admitting his mistakes without losing his mind, Gulliver has no capacity for incorporating new knowledge of the most important sort. In this respect he is like Jack in *A Tale of a Tub.*

For many years we have known that Swift is satirizing a particular kind of rationality in the fourth voyage.[39] Swift had disliked the approach to logic that he had been taught at Trinity College Dublin, which stressed rationality as pertaining to humans and irrationality as foreign to humans. It was even typical to use horses as examples of the irrational animal. A textbook widely used at Trinity put the matter thus:

> Man feels, a plant not: but a horse also feels, and likewise other beasts. Divide we therefore animal corporeal feeling substance into

39. The historical scholarship for this view was initially done by R. S. Crane in "Houyhnhnms, Yahoos, and the History of Ideas," in *Reason and the Imagination,* ed. Joseph A. Mazzeo (New York: Columbia University Press, 1962), 231-53. The quotation from Burgersdicius is found on pp. 247-48.

> rational and irrational. Here therefore are we to stand, since it appears that every, and only man is rational.

This passage appears in a 1697 commentary by Burgersdicius on the third-century logician Porphyry, who is himself a commentator on Aristotle. In other words, the writer is at two removes from his source, and likely as much a stranger to Aristotle as "the great Philosopher's" commentators in Laputa. The modern commentator has taken a single aspect of the ancient understanding of rationality for the whole. By reversing the dichotomy of human-rational/brute-irrational, Swift satirizes this partial, modern understanding of rationality. He sharpens his satire by making the Houyhnhnms act in an invariably rational manner and the Yahoos in an invariably brutal manner.[40]

In two famous letters to Alexander Pope, Swift identifies his book as a rejection of the unqualified definition of man as a rational animal, saying that it is precisely this view that leads to misanthropy:

> I hate and detest that animal called man, although I hartily love John, Peter, Thomas, and so forth. . . . I have got materials towards a treatis proving the falsity of that definition *animal rationale;* and to show it should be only *rationis capax* ["capable" of reasoning]. Upon this great foundation of misanthropy (though not Timons manner) the whole building of my travells is erected: And I will never have peace of mind till all honest men are of my opinion. . . .
>
> I tell you after all that I do not hate mankind, it is vous autres [you others] who hate them because you would have them reasonable animals, and are angry for being disappointed. I have always rejected that definition and made another of my own.[41]

In the first letter Swift has in mind his masters at Trinity College Dublin, particularly Narcissus Marsh, whose logic book was written for student use. Marsh's book adopts the human-rational/brute-irrational dichotomy, illustrating the specimen "human" by the Latin names for "John,

40. See Irvin Ehrenpreis, "The Meaning of Gulliver's Last Voyage," in *Swift: A Collection of Critical Essays,* ed. Ernest Tuveson (Englewood Cliffs, N.J.: 1964), 138.

41. *Correspondence,* 3:103, 118 (29 September 1725; 26 November 1725).

Peter, Thomas, and others," later remembered by Swift.[42] Swift's letter warns Pope against the misanthropy that follows from having too high of expectations regarding human rationality, and too little acquaintance with actual people named John, Peter, Thomas, and so forth.

Narcissus Marsh was conspicuously associated with modern science, having helped to found the Dublin Philosophical Society during Swift's student days. Similar in spirit to the Royal Society of London, the Dublin society was "centred in the dons of Trinity College," and its members too conducted experiments like the ones remembered in the Grand Academy of Lagado.[43]

The point is that the satire in the fourth book is of a piece with the satire earlier. The frame of mind represented by the Grand Academy is kindred to a mind like Gulliver's that expects pure rationality from the human mind. Because Gulliver's understanding is shaped by his hosts rather than by the ancient "pattern of human learning," he cannot discriminate the utopian rationality of the Houyhnhnms from the modicum of reason that real humans possess. Because he lacks the true self-knowledge of the "private infirmities" known to the ancients, he is utterly overwhelmed when the Houyhnhnms' manner of life shows up the depravity of human existence. Gulliver finally comes to realize that human life is not the purely rational life. But then he unfairly concludes that human life must be that of the Yahoo.

Twice in book 4 Gulliver indicates that he has completely adopted the intellectual assumptions of his current hosts. "[T]he many virtues of those excellent quadrupeds placed in opposite view to human corruptions, had so far opened mine eyes, and enlarged my understanding, that I began to view the actions and passions of man in a very different light" (258). A bit later he says: "I freely confess, that all the little knowledge I have of any value, was acquired by the lectures I received from my master, and from hearing the discourses of him and his friends" (278). Gulliver's eyes could not have been closed to human corruption had he been capable of learning anything from an ancient like the king

42. Crane, "Houyhnhnms, Yahoos, and the History of Ideas," 251-52.

43. Irvin Ehrenpreis, *Swift: The Man, His Works, and the Age* (Cambridge: Harvard University Press, 1962-83), 1:80. Ehrenpreis describes the significance of the Dublin Philosophical Society and Swift's intimate knowledge of its members at 1:47-56, 78-88.

of Brobdingnag, or from the ancient and modern writers he claims to have read on shipboard. Yet he maintains that "all" his knowledge of value comes from the Houyhnhnm master. The effect of this learning turns Gulliver, modern that he is, into a worse person. Like the modern critics of *A Tale of a Tub*, Gulliver's knowledge turns to arrogance and querulousness. When combined with the modern attraction to "projects," especially "that of reforming the Yahoo race," Gulliver's knowledge becomes misanthropic. Pure abstractions such as "rationality" may be found in the anonymous Houyhnhnms, but when pure rationality is demanded by persons with real names like Gulliver — and "John, Peter, and Thomas" — human nature breaks out in war on itself.

The projecting mind possesses great and attractive powers: its promise of material and scientific advance; its claim to give mastery over human weakness and moral imperfection; its refusal to be bound by mystery; its unquenchable hope of future improvement. If "projects" were entirely unattractive, *Gulliver's Travels* would be an entertaining farce but not a satire that challenges every reader. Swift seems to assume that his readers will live in an age — like his and ours — where the attraction of the projecting mind is taken for granted, and yet felt to be questionable by some. Swift does not leave us with a comfortable "counter system" to that of the projector. He leaves us with Gulliver. But the ancients, like Lord Munodi and the king of Brodingnag, while not representing a "system," do represent a manner of life that is distinct from Gulliver's. It involves acquaintance with a traditional "pattern of learning." Participating in this pattern is different from exercising a technique of ideological criticism. Rather, it involves a self-critical and tactful evaluation of the present as a moment whose future is morally dependent upon an imaginative encounter with the past.

The satirist, like the Hebrew prophet, speaks to some who will hear and some who will not. But he also assumes a third audience, as Thomas Jemielity has written, namely those who already accept the moral or religious ideals against which his description of the present comes into its satirical or prophetic force, with all its attendant ridicule, derision, and horror.[44] The "pattern of learning" represented by the ancients is one

44. Thomas Jemielity, *Satire and the Hebrew Prophets* (Louisville: Westminster/John Knox, 1992), 81.

source of the moral and rational ideals crucial to Swift's satire. Still more important for Swift are certain forms of communication like Scripture, the sermon, and the sacrament, all of which called forth Swift's faithful service. Is it not worth our consideration to ask whether those forms provide an alternative to the modern, ideological approach to the past? Can the scriptural negotiation between modern and ancient texts provide part of an alternative poetics to the ideological variety?

A Biblical Poetics and Ideology

One weakness of today's "ancients" is their inability to suggest a compelling alternative to the ideological understanding of earlier authors. Many of those authors, including Swift, believed that the basis for most human understanding was to be found in religion. Without denying the validity of discipline-specific approaches to history and literature, they saw the arts and sciences in the context of one's relation to God. Milton said the end of education was to "repair the ruins of our first parents," and there is no doubt that Swift and Milton considered Christ's incarnation and crucifixion the final "repair." If we wish to reconstruct a conversation about these authors for our own day, perhaps we should look again at their most important source, the Christian Bible.

The question I have addressed throughout this chapter is the relation of ancient and modern learning. Now unless one writes on a very high level of abstraction, I doubt one can find much in the Bible on this subject. Indeed, the attempt to make the Bible speak, directly and specifically, on every issue of aesthetic, social, economic, and political life is to make Christianity into the kind of system that Swift satirizes in the character of Jack. The possibility of turning Christianity into an ideology should be acknowledged, for there are similarities between the two kinds of faith, as Kenneth Minogue explains.[45] For both, faith is inseparable from understanding the world: "I believe in order to understand," as Augustine said. Both depend upon a "revelation" of some

45. See chapter 6, "The Ideological Revelation," in Kenneth Minogue, *Alien Powers: The Pure Theory of Ideology* (New York: St. Martin's Press, 1985), 118-46.

kind: God's biblical self-revelation for the Jew or Christian; the enlightenment regarding systemic oppression for the ideologue.

While Christianity may be (and has been) turned into an ideology, however, Swift considers the project of transforming the faith into an all-embracing system to be mad, as mad as all other "projects." I will explore the ultimate distinctions between Christianity and ideology in chapter 3, but at this point I wish to indicate some differences between my approach and ideological criticism. A biblical poetics regards Christian revelation as a foundation for education, but it is nevertheless compatible with many discipline-specific methodologies. For instance, the tools that I have used — the history of ideas, biography, and the ethical interpretation of literature — have an integrity of their own, which is validated by their usefulness in advancing knowledge. Ideologies, by contrast, provide their own methodology and see discipline-specific methods as "implicated" in the "system of knowledge production," as Kolodny says, which is but an aspect of larger oppression. Indeed, one question that current ideologues ask is whether they should even use "'the master's tools'" to destroy the slavemaster's house.[46]

Unlike the ideologue, the Christian can share the wider cultural tradition with those who do not share his or her faith, for since culture is the result of human interaction with the created world, it shares in the original blessing of God on creation and human beings. There is no more profound demonstration of this than Swift's own acceptance of the value of ancient, pagan authors. On the other hand, a biblical poetics recognizes human culture as sinful, and therefore its products stand in a subordinate relation to biblical accounts of deliverance. As a consequence, no part of human culture — ancient or modern, "Christian" or secular, British or Native American — can be absolutized. Nor can the work of culture be equated with the work of Christ. Perhaps this is why a Christian like Swift felt he should satirize a Calvinist figure who (in his view) had tried to do just that.

In failing to distinguish between the work of "deliverance" (or

46. Carey Kaplan and Ellen Cronan Rose ask this in *The Canon and the Common Reader* (Knoxville: University of Tennessee Press, 1990), 164. They are quoting from Audre Lorde, "The Master's Tools Will Never Dismantle the Master's House," in *Sister Outsider: Essays and Speeches* (Freedom, Calif.: Crossing, 1984), 112.

transformation) and the works of cultural life, the ideologue is partly right: human beings and the world stand in need of transformation. But by failing to delight in or even acknowledge any good — any "blessing," to use biblical terms — outside of his own system of deliverance, the ideologue falls into the same trap as Swift's Jack: all of life is seen through a monistic system.

I have stated that a biblical faith may serve as the foundation for education without becoming an ideological methodology. In the remainder of this chapter, I will show what that might mean for the relation of "ancient" and "modern" texts in the Gospel according to Matthew, Swift's favorite account of the life of Christ.[47]

Ancient Texts and the Gospel of Matthew

Biblical scholars have long recognized the distinctly Hebrew nature of Matthew's Gospel. Henry Hammond, the most important theological influence on Swift's patron (Sir William Temple), believed that Matthew was originally written in Hebrew. This view is not generally accepted at the present, but its germ of truth is that Matthew clearly knew Hebrew and Aramaic as well as Greek.[48] The book's Hebrew character is visible in the rabbinic tracing of the genealogy of Christ, the affirmation that not one "jot or tittle" of the Jewish law will become invalid, and the mention

47. The relation of the New Testament to the Old Testament is, to put it mildly, an extremely complex issue. Even my general conclusions below would be different if I had chosen to work with the book of Hebrews or the Gospel of John rather than Matthew. The great New Testament textual critic Matthew Black suggests that the principles by which New Testament writers interpreted the Hebrew Scriptures are mostly taken from the Jewish hermeneutics of their day ("The Theological Appropriation of the Old Testament by the New Testament," *Scottish Journal of Theology* 39, no. 1 [1986]: 1-17). Yet it must be confessed that we do not fully understand those interpretive procedures very well, and that even distinguished Christian scholars have made many mistakes in trying to find rabbinic sources for the methods of New Testament interpretation. See Samuel Lachs, "Rabbinic Sources for New Testament Studies: Use and Abuse," *Jewish Quarterly Review* 74 (October 1983): 159-73.

48. See C. P. Daw, "Swift's Favorite Books of the Bible," *Huntington Library Quarterly* 43 (1980), 209, and Ehrenpreis, *Swift,* 1:93. Hammond's views were published as *Paraphrases on the New Testament.*

of Jewish customs and phrases without explanation. More relevant to my purpose is the fact that Matthew is packed with quotations from and allusions to the Old Testament, approximately a dozen of which are said to be "fulfilled" by some event in the life of Christ. The Gospel of Matthew commends itself, both by Swift's preference and its own emphasis on "fulfillment," as a model for dealing with the Hebrew Scriptures. How does Matthew, as a "modern" writer, look back to these ancient texts?

There is no doubt that Matthew, and the New Testament writers generally, considered the recent words and deeds of Christ to be superior to those of the Hebrew Scriptures. But they are not superior in the sense of overthrowing or casting down the older tradition. Christ is seen as the "fulfillment" of the very Hebrew Scriptures which contemporary Christians shared with Jews, and the New Testament writers frequently make their appeal "according to the Scriptures." In Thessalonica, for instance, the apostle Paul, "according to [his] custom . . . reasoned with [the Jews] from the Scriptures" (Acts 17:2). Moreover, the portions of the Hebrew Scriptures generally used by the Christian apologists were not proof-texts, quotations taken out of context and used to justify a belief. Rather, says C. H. Dodd, they rest on the "*total context* that is in view" in the Old Testament passage. Having embraced the basic Christian proclamation, or "kerygma," about the life, death, and resurrection of Jesus, the New Testament authors interpret the Old "upon a genuinely historical understanding of the process of the religious . . . history of Israel as a whole."[49] Now one may conclude that

49. The quotations are from C. H. Dodd, *According to the Scriptures* (London: Nisbet, 1952), 126, 133, italics in original. Dodd's thesis has held up remarkably well over the decades, winning respect from all sides of the theological community. See, for instance, Black, "The Theological Appropriation of the Old Testament by the New Testament," 6: "Most scholars since Dodd accept his basic premise on the primacy of the Kerygma: the Kerygma came first, the proclamation of the 'facts' or 'events' of the life, death, resurrection of Jesus of Nazareth, the latter attested by many eye-witnesses (1 Cor. 15,4f) — 'facts' or 'events' to which the Apostles bore witness and saw as fulfilled in ancient prophecy." Significantly, Dodd's theory that the New Testament writers have full Old Testament "text-plots" in mind (rather than mere proof-texts) is accepted by the two standard works on Matthew's use of the Old Testament: Krister Stendahl, *The School of St. Matthew* (Philadelphia: Fortress, 1968); and Robert Gundry, *The Use of the Old Testament in St. Matthew's Gospel* (Leiden: Brill, 1967).

their historical understanding was ultimately flawed, and that the new "revelation" they received from Jesus was no revelation at all. But one may not argue that they, like modern ideologues, held that the older writings reflected and often caused oppression, which only the new revelation could explain and alleviate.[50]

In Matthew, Jesus is seen as a "greater Moses," greater, that is to say, than the central human figure and author (it was believed) of the Hebrew Scriptures. Like Moses, he escapes a "slaughter of the innocents" as an infant and later returns to his own people (Matt. 2:13, 20).[51] Like Moses, Christ shines with glory on a mountain and institutes a covenant in blood (Matt. 17:2; 26:28). But the likeness ultimately points to Christ's superiority to Moses, particularly in the Sermon on the Mount, where Christ reinterprets the law of Moses on his own authority (Matt. 5–7). It is significant that these were Swift's favorite chapters of Matthew, and that they are singled out for praise in the anonymous, seventeenth-century book of devotion so important to Swift's spiritual formation, *The Whole Duty of Man.*[52]

Matthew prepares the reader for viewing Jesus as the culmination of the Old Testament by concentrating many of his "fulfillment" texts

50. The closest the New Testament comes to this negative view of the Old Testament is in Paul's criticism that the "letter" of the law kills, while the Spirit gives life (2 Cor. 3:6). The early Christian Marcion went so far as to deny the validity of the Old Testament for Christians altogether, and to exalt only certain portions of the New Testament writings (Paul and the Gospel of Luke). His views were declared heretical, and as we shall see in chapter 3, a similar misuse of 2 Cor. 3:6 gave rise to an unrestrained allegorical interpretation of the Old Testament. A consideration of Paul's relation to the Old Testament, and particularly the law, would have to consider this matter in great detail, but one point is clear: Paul sees an ultimate continuity in the purpose of the Hebrew Scriptures and the gospel, for they both bear witness to the saving activities of the same "author."

51. See Gundry, *The Use of the Old Testament in St. Matthew's Gospel*, 209, for the allusions to these verses and to 17:2 and 26:28. In recent years the importance of the "greater Moses" reading of Matthew has been disputed. Without attempting to take sides in the dispute, I believe Matthew's treatment of the relation of Jesus to Moses is indicative of how he relates new to old revelation.

52. Henry Hammond wrote the prefatory letter to the first edition of *The Whole Duty of Man* in 1658. Its significance to Swift is discussed in Ehrenpreis, *Swift*, 1:39-40. See also Daw, 209-10n.30.

in the first chapters of the Gospel. Five times before the beginning of the Sermon on the Mount, certain events are described as "fulfilling" the Old Testament; others are described as the referent for other Old Testament texts. For instance, John the Baptist is said to be "the one referred to by Isaiah the prophet, saying 'The voice of one crying in the wilderness . . .' " and the birthplace of Christ said to be anticipated by "the prophet" (Matt. 3:3; 2:6; cf. Isa. 40:3; Mic. 5:2). By the time we reach the Sermon on the Mount, Christ's first "discourse" in the Gospel, the reader knows he has met a character whose life is being presented as the consummation of "the word of God" up to this point.

Matthew 5:17-18 and 7:12 are beginning and ending points for the Sermon's treatment of Jesus as a greater Moses. In 5:17-18 Jesus says, "Do not think that I came to abolish the Law or the Prophets; I did not come to abolish, but to fulfill. For truly I say to you, until heaven and earth pass away, not the smallest letter or stroke shall pass away from the Law, until all is accomplished." In this passage, Jesus accepts the most exalted possible view of the Hebrew Scriptures, affirming its validity until its overarching prophetic purposes are accomplished.[53] In 7:12, Matthew concludes this portion of the sermon with the "Golden Rule": "Therefore whatever you want others to do for you, do so for them; for this is the Law and the Prophets." The interpretation of this latter passage is not unique to Jesus: Rabbi Hillel had summarized the law in a similar (though negatively framed) fashion a few years earlier. But in between 5:18 and 7:12, Jesus speaks on his own authority, claiming far more for himself than a contemporary rabbi would.[54] Six times in 5:21-48 Jesus contrasts the popular

53. See D. A. Carson, *The Expositor's Bible Commentary,* gen. ed. Frank E. Gaebelein (Grand Rapids: Zondervan, 1984), 8:144-46. Some argue that the "all" to be accomplished is limited to the cross, but my statement reflects Carson's wider view. I am indebted as well to Carson's locating the major theme of the Sermon on the Mount in the manner of life appropriate to the kingdom of heaven (122-28).

54. The thesis that Jesus is merely a rabbi, or more precisely a "proto-rabbi," is advanced by many, perhaps most cogently by Phillip Sigal, *The Halakah of Jesus of Nazareth according to the Gospel of Matthew* (Lanham, Md.: University Press, 1986). The thesis notes similarities between Jesus' teachings and contemporary rabbinic derivation of practical rules of conduct from the law (halakah). However, the thesis must downplay or reinterpret the verses in which Jesus claims his own authority for fulfilling the law in

understanding of the law with his own pronouncement on the direction of the law. For example: "You have heard that the ancients were told, 'You shall not commit murder,' . . . but I say to you that every one who is angry with his brother shall be guilty before the court . . ." (5:21, 22). Similar guidance on adultery, divorce, oaths, revenge, and love for enemies is given in succeeding verses. In no case, here or elsewhere in the New Testament, is Moses an object of criticism.[55] But neither are these the words of a mere teacher or commentator on the law of Moses. Rather, they are the words of one who claims an authority far beyond that of Moses, to admit persons into the kingdom of heaven (7:21-22). This authority, if legitimate, validates in turn the sermon as a whole, which concerns the manner of life appropriate to the kingdom of heaven.

As one moves through the Gospel of Matthew, the allusions to the Old Testament take on greater urgency. In Matthew 11:29, for instance, Jesus himself (rather than the narrator) alludes to the Hebrew Scriptures: "Take My yoke upon you, and learn from Me, for I am gentle and humble in heart; and you shall find rest for your souls." The last phrase is a quotation from Jeremiah 6:16, where the prophet says:

> "Thus says the Lord, 'Stand by the ways and see and ask for the ancient paths.
> Where the good way is, and walk in it;
> And you shall find rest for your souls.'"

Jesus compares his "yoke" with God's "ancient paths," putting himself in God's place with his promise of "rest" for the faithful follower. His use of ancient texts himself makes his identity — is he the Messiah or not? — a more urgent issue.

In the "third discourse" of the Gospel (Matt. 13:1-52), Jesus maintains that by explaining the parables of the kingdom of heaven to his disciples and not to outsiders, he is fulfilling Isaiah 6:9-10:

---

word and deed, as well as the messianic and eschatological implications of Christ's teaching. See Carson, *Expositor's Bible Commentary,* 8:142, 195.

55. See David Hay, "Moses through New Testament Spectacles," *Interpretation* 44 (July 1990): 240-52.

> "And in their [the outsiders'] case the prophecy of Isaiah is being fulfilled, which says,
>
> 'You will keep on hearing, but will not understand;
> And you will keep on seeing, but will not perceive;
> For the heart of this people has become dull. . . .'
>
> But blessed are your [the disciples'] eyes, because they see; and your ears, because they hear. For truly I say to you, that many prophets and righteous men desired to see what you see, and did not see it. . . ."
>
> (Matt. 13:14-17)

Jesus is laying claim to having fulfilled the prophecies of Isaiah. Such a man may be a fraud. But if he is not, Matthew wants us to ask, who is he? Simon Peter gives his answer a bit further on in his confession: "Thou art the Christ, the Son of the living God" (Matt. 16:16).

Beginning in the Sermon on the Mount, Matthew contrasts "abolishing" old texts with "fulfilling" them. The older texts direct themselves toward Christ, Matthew maintains, first by his words, later by his deeds.[56] With the triumphal entry into Jerusalem (Matt. 21ff.), allusions to the Old Testament increase again. This time the focus is on Jesus as the royal Messiah and as the greater son of David. The animal ridden by Christ refers back to Zechariah, the hosannas and ultimate rejection of Christ to a "royal Psalm," and his treatment of blind and lame (in 21:14) to David's life.[57] Twice during his betrayal and capture, Jesus refers to the events as fulfilling Scripture. He refuses to call down legions of angels by asking, "How then shall the Scriptures be fulfilled, that it must happen this way?"

56. Despite Matthew's efforts to interpret Christ's words as fulfillments of the law, the eminent Jewish scholar Jacob Neusner recognizes that their ultimate sanction is in the divine privilege to adapt or modify Torah. Imagining a conversation with a disciple of Jesus, Neusner asks, "Is your master God?" Neusner's rejection of Matthew's presentation of Jesus is especially interesting for my purposes because he agrees that Matthew *attempted* to show Jesus in the manner I have described, as fulfilling Torah, even though Neusner ultimately rejects Matthew's presentation. See *A Rabbi Talks with Jesus* (New York: Doubleday, 1993), 74.

57. See Gundry, *The Use of the Old Testament in St. Matthew's Gospel*, 140, 208-10.

and shortly afterward tells his captors that "all this has taken place that the Scriptures of the prophets may be fulfilled" (Matt. 26:54, 56). In the Sermon on the Mount, the older texts are said to be fulfilled by Christ's words. In these later chapters, they are fulfilled by his deeds. The ultimate deed, of course, is Christ's resurrection from the dead: "He is not here," says the angel to the women at the tomb on Easter, "for He has risen, just as He said" (Matt. 28:6).

* * * * *

Matthew's procedure has two striking parallels for our current quarrels. First, before he begins a reinterpretation of the older texts, he embraces the tradition they represent. It is true that he rejects certain current traditions of interpreting the law, such as the casuistry surrounding oath-taking (Matt. 5:33-37). It is also true that he thinks that many traditions of the Pharisees deaden the true religious life (e.g., Matt. 15:1-9). But in such cases Matthew goes back to the law to search for a more central direction. This gesture could not be more at odds with the typical ideological approaches. Instead of searching for a more central thread within the literary tradition, their reinterpretations usually begin by denouncing the tradition or by assuming that the work participates in the traditional structures of oppression. They go on to propose a reading that "problematizes" the past in a way that really solves the past: by situating a text within an ideological critique, all of its problems are clarified, for one can then see how Swift or Milton or Chaucer are placed with respect to the ideological revelation.

Instead of embracing older texts and searching for their ultimate direction, as the New Testament writers believed they were doing, the modern ideologue is often content with analogies that provide fortuitous resemblances between text and ideology. For example, a recent feminist has written that Gulliver's Laputa "is a representation of a female body which is entered by, and controlled by, men," primarily because the author sees a physical resemblance between the island and a uterus, with a vagina-like hole in the center through which men descend.[58] Since the

58. Susan Bruce, "The Flying Island and Female Anatomy," *Genders* 2 (Summer 1988): 60-76.

ultimate direction of Swift's text must move toward her previously believed ideology — the alleged male effort to "wrest away from women their control over their own bodies" — she needn't seek any confirmation of the uterus/island parallel in the general design of Swift's text.[59] Analogies or "homologies," as the current school of new historicism calls them, will do. In this case, a series of eighteenth-century writings on midwifery are enough to suggest an "indirect connect[ion]" between the failed attempts to control women's bodies in Swift's day and the representations of science and language in *Gulliver's Travels*.[60]

In the terms of current literary discussion, the ideologues are "reader-centered." On the basis of their authority as readers possessed of a supposedly accurate social analysis, they exert an interpretive freedom to reshape texts bounded only by their ideology. Their ideological revelation is the bridge between apparently unconnected historical events; it provides the connection, of which eighteenth-century figures were unconscious, between widely disparate ideas.[61]

The New Testament writers, by contrast, are "author-centered." Their interpretive freedom is usually expressed by going back to what they consider a deeper, more central tradition of the Hebrew Scriptures to explain the "new" testament of Christ. Sometimes they appear to go beyond this tradition, for instance in identifying some rather far-fetched "types of Christ" in the Old Testament. But still, their freedom is limited in ways that the ideologues' is not. They engage in this kind of freedom much less frequently, for one thing, which suggests that such fortuitous resemblances are not essential to their interpretive strategy.[62] Moreover, the typological interpretations by New Testament writers do not negate other, more straightforward readings of the Old Testament. When such a negation has taken place in the history of Christian interpretation,

59. Bruce, "The Flying Island and Female Anatomy," 68.

60. Bruce, "The Flying Island and Female Anatomy," 72.

61. See Bruce, "The Flying Island and Female Anatomy," 72-73.

62. The New Testament writers even avoid exploiting some obvious possibilities for typological "proofs" of Christ — the figure of Joseph, for instance — which suggests a rather large measure of interpretive restraint (see C. H. Dodd, *History and the Gospel* [1938], 61-63). More akin to current ideological freedom with the text are the allegorizing techniques found in certain Christian interpretations, beginning with the apostolic fathers.

the Christian reader has converted the Bible into an ideological instrument. He or she has used it as a total explanation of culture, refusing to grant true integrity to any other interpretive method.

To conclude, even the interpretive freedoms exercised by New Testament writers are used within the context of accepting the earlier writings, not abolishing them. The express ideological project, by contrast, is to subvert, problematize, and decenter older literature, or at least the interpretation of older literature.

A second parallel between ideological interpretation and Matthew's view of "fulfillment" is the common belief that an authoritative revelation should, in some way, be fundamental to one's reading of older texts. For the ideologue, these are revelations about race, gender, or class that are validated by the ideology's unqualified aim to account for human culture from within a single system of thought. The ideologue sees (correctly) that the individual disciplines in the liberal arts provide only partial explanations of culture; ideology completes them. The ideologue rightly observes that reforms made through the existing political process are only partial; his ideological program promises to complete them. Even if one disagrees with the ideological use of literature, one must admit that it offers to a secular world the satisfactions that religion can no longer provide for many. Again, the problem with ideological criticism is not that it is entirely wrong, but that it is half right.

For the writers of the New Testament, Christ's revelation is validated by his death and resurrection, both of which happened "according to the [Hebrew] Scriptures" (1 Cor. 15:3-4). A new revelation would presuppose the advent of a new messianic age — and a great deal of the rhetoric of current ideological approaches has a messianic or apocalyptic tone to it. But it seems to me that the authority of one risen from the dead will admit no competition: one revelation on that order is sufficient. Even if one agrees with parts — even large parts — of the ideological critique, then, a biblical poetics would have to regard with skepticism the project as a whole, with its large claims to account for evil and to show the way to social transformation.

Rather than providing the means for social liberation, a biblical poetics could learn from the example of the Gospel of Matthew, and view interpretation as a way of "fulfilling" the meaning of older texts.

Unlike ideological criticism, this need not mean reconciling older texts with a certain dogma. My readings of Johnson, Milton, and others attempt to "fulfill" certain questions raised in their texts. But I think it would be a mistake to try to bring the thematic concerns of those authors into conformity with revealed truth, or to impose biblical dogmas on their texts. The thematic approach is typical of the ideological mode, not of a biblical poetics as I will develop it.

I am using "fulfillment" as an analogy for my own strategy, but I do not claim (as a new historicist might) that this strategy may be found in Swift by virtue of the fact that he was a Christian, a clergyman, and a devoted reader of the Gospel of Matthew. Rather, "fulfillment" commends itself because it is consistent with biblical ways with older texts, it suggests a way to end the current battle of the books, and it grants the integrity of older literature. As a strategy for interpreting literature, it embraces older texts and attempts to discern a more central or neglected tradition behind a contemporary reinterpretation. As a strategy for concluding the current battle of the books, it grants that older literature should have a contemporary significance without abolishing the past tradition of which we are heirs.

A parallel to "fulfillment" may be found in T. S. Eliot's description of how the individual literary talent enters the tradition. Before my reading of Swift, there was a tradition of Swift interpretation which had its own shape. This tradition did not exist in an ideal realm nor in an inert set of books, but in a cooperative, imaginative relationship — what Michael Oakeshott would call a "conversation" — between Swift's readers of the past and present, and myself. In proposing that we see Gulliver as a modern, I hope to have altered the relations between those earlier readings. It is a slight alteration and merely attempts to "fill up" something I found lacking, not an attempt to domesticate Swift to biblical revelation. Accepting my reading of Swift demands neither a conversion to my view of the world nor an adoption of a certain poetics, as ideological criticism, in its purer forms, often seems to do.

The joy of discovering new knowledge can be genuine, unaffected, and full in a biblical poetics, without any irritable reaching out for converts. Cultural achievement is related to God through the language of blessing, which places in a properly human sphere the advancement of human welfare and the pleasures of a responsible use of creation. Some of the most intriguing explanations of literature's role in both of these areas, through its moral instruction and its powerful pleasures, may be found in Samuel Johnson. Johnson's writings are also helpful in distinguishing these roles from those of Scripture, a distinction that has been almost entirely obscured by ideological treatments of the literary canon. To those issues I now turn.

CHAPTER 2

Johnson Reading Literature, Johnson Reading the Canon of Scripture

The Difference between Literary Pleasure and Religious Happiness

ONE OF THE most frequently discussed questions in literary study today concerns the "canon" of literature. Which books will be taught? Who decides? On what basis will the decision be made? Who made these decisions in the past? What were their criteria? What outside forces influenced their decision?

Although current accounts often suggest that these are new and challenging questions, educators have always asked them in various ways, and it's a mistake to consider them particularly unusual. Plato himself enters the debate over Homer's reputation as the "educator of Hellas." Today's moderns generally pose their questions less with respect to individual books than to the supposed collection of books as a whole. This supposed collection, or canon, provides them with an object for questions similar to those I treated in the first chapter, but directed instead against the system that this collection is said to serve. In this chapter I will call them "the new canon-makers" (instead of "moderns") in recognition of their purposes and characteristic ways of answering these questions.[1] Their

1. The phrase "new canon-makers" is used sympathetically by Carey Kaplan

critique of this supposed canon of literature is but one front among many in the larger conflicts over higher education.

Among the older critics examined by the new canon-makers is Samuel Johnson, whose periodical essays on literature, Shakespearean criticism, and *Lives of the English Poets* helped establish many of the biographical and critical tools used in modern literary studies. It is particularly Johnson's last major work, the *Lives of the English Poets* (1779-81), that attracts the attention of the new canon-makers, for that work began as a series of prefaces to a collection of certain poets who wrote from about 1660 to 1771, which suggests to the new canon-makers a "canon" of English literature. Moreover, Johnson has the reputation of being a magisterial authority, which makes him especially useful in what they consider a discussion of cultural power.

The term "canon" comes from a Greek cognate word *(kanon)* for "rule" or "measure," but it is most commonly applied to the books of the Bible. It is crucial for the new canon-makers to parallel the canonization of the sixty-six biblical books with the process of literary evaluation. It turns out, however, that whether they are writing about Johnson or the Bible, their categories are ideological rather than historical or textual, and they often obscure the issues more than clarify them. By using "the canon" to suit their own purposes, the new canon-makers produce a parody of Scripture and literature, for they miss the reasons why billions of people have been drawn to the sacred texts and to secular, imaginative writings. Instead, they offer such unattractive explanations for the existence of the canon that one ought to wonder why any gospels are meditated or any books are read.

Like all ideological explanations, the one for the canon is quite simple: biblical and literary canons are a function of power. "Cultural power," "institutional control," "category of power," "power and authority," "ownership," and "the power to control the meaning of a work" — all of these phrases are from recent work, much of it influential, on the biblical canon, the "canon of literature," or Johnson's criticism.[2] The

---

and Ellen Cronan Rose in *The Canon and the Common Reader* (Knoxville: University of Tennessee Press, 1990), 23.

2. They are from, respectively, Barbara Herrnstein Smith, "Contingencies of Value," in *Canons,* ed. Robert von Hallberg (Chicago: University of Chicago Press, 1984),

power in question is not supernatural in the case of the Bible, nor imaginative in the case of literature. Rather, the canon's power is understood socially by these critics as the tool of a cultural elite to maintain its dominance (economic, religious, academic) by an appearance of legitimacy, which disguises the elite's essentially arbitrary position.

The new canon-makers sometimes maintain that their questions put issues of literary value in historical context, but in fact precisely the opposite occurs. By relying on the "category of power" to explain how we came to value certain literary or biblical books, they need to ignore literary history and the history of the biblical canon. They overlook, disguise, or distort the very history they are pretending to reveal. For instance, they have overlooked the use Johnson actually made of the canon of the Bible. They have missed the historically significant controversy over the canon of the New Testament in the eighteenth century, and the contribution of one of Johnson's direct religious influences, Samuel Clarke, to that controversy. To make their point about power, they employ the distorting figure of a dictatorial "Doctor" Johnson, largely created by Boswell and Macaulay rather than derived from Johnson's own critical writings. Perhaps most important for literature, their presuppositions have the devastating effect of removing what Johnson considered the key ingredient to good books, namely, their capacity for giving pleasure. In place of the pleasures that readers have actually found in literature, the new canon-makers look for power.

Johnson is therefore very much worth considering in this matter of "the canon" of literature. His writings can help remove some of the confusion surrounding the issue, for he believed strongly in the biblical canon, but his manner of using the Bible shows how differently he read sacred and secular literature. He shows how the two types contribute to human life, but he displays humility, not dictatorial power, in his approach. His realistic, self-critical, and skeptical manner is the opposite

---

33; Frank Kermode, "Institutional Control of Interpretation," *Salmagundi* 43 (1979): 72; Gerald L. Bruns, "Canon and Power in the Hebrew Scriptures," in *Canons,* 81; Frederic Bogel, "Johnson and the Role of Authority," in *The New Eighteenth Century,* ed. Felicity Nussbaum and Laura Brown (New York: Methuen, 1987), 208; Kaplan and Rose, *The Canon and the Common Reader,* 25; and Alvin Kernan, *Printing, Technology, Letters, and Samuel Johnson* (Princeton: Princeton University Press, 1987), 233.

of the ideological manner that the new canon-makers bring to these questions.

Moreover, by considering Johnson in the context of one of the major influences on his view of Scripture, Samuel Clarke, one begins to question the very terms of the current discussion. Like Clarke, Johnson ultimately denied the conflict (in Hume, for instance) between "reason and revelation."[3] Like the eighteenth-century rationalists, and unlike Johnson, the new canon-makers write as if their new historical revelation — namely, viewing literature as part of a more general history of power — provides them with the key for reinterpreting older texts. From the dual nature of Christ and his resurrection to Johnson's view of the common reader and "the category of 'literature'" itself — all of these have been reinterpreted by the new canon-makers as efforts by some class of persons to gain or to maintain power.[4]

Reading through Johnson after spending time in the "canon wars" is a refreshing experience, for it reminds one of the prodigious pleasures that Johnson found in secular literature and the eternal happiness he found in religion. It may also remind one — it has certainly reminded me — why one reads books in the first place. Johnson did not treat literature as "the canon." Such parallels that exist between Johnson's treatment of sacred and secular literature often show the profound differences between the two. But both the parallels and the differences may help us recover Johnson's emphasis on pleasures of reading, which would be no small benefit for our day.

3. Robert Scholes offers an example of this assumed conflict when he writes, "The trouble with establishing a canon — the great, insuperable problem — is that it removes the chosen texts from history and from human actualities, placing them forever behind a veil of pieties" ("Aiming a Canon at the Curriculum," *Salmagundi* 72 [Fall 1986]: 114). The practice of the early Christians who canonized the New Testament is almost the opposite of what Scholes suggests. They recognized the New Testament writings as canonical precisely because of the historical attestation of particular books and their relevance to the "human actualities" that confronted the early church.

4. The quoted phrase is from Bogel, "Johnson and the Role of Authority," 207.

The Canonization of the New Testament

The process by which the Bible came to its present form is extremely complicated. An adequate treatment of this process, even as it affects the New Testament alone, is impossible in a short space. If one wishes to understand the making of the canon, therefore, one must choose to undertake the hard work of historical inquiry, and not rest content with the authority of inspiration, on the one hand, or of ideology on the other.

With regard to the Hebrew Scriptures, an earlier consensus that it was canonized in three stages corresponding to the three divisions of the Hebrew Bible (Law, Prophets, Writings), has now broken down.[5] Given our limited knowledge of the canonization process, one would think that literary scholars would refrain from drawing conclusions about the criteria involved in the selection of the Hebrew texts. And yet one of the essays most widely quoted among literary critics does precisely that. Drawing on the hypothesis of the radical historian Ellis Rivkin (not himself a biblical scholar) that the production of the Hebrew Scriptures was the work of "'a class struggling to gain power,'" Gerald Bruns concludes that "canon is not a literary category but a category of power."[6] Whether this is correct or not is hardly an answerable question in light of our present knowledge. It is an assumption that the new canon-makers present as a conclusion without much historical analysis. Bruns, for instance, makes much of the presence of "Hilkiah" both at the rediscovery of the Torah under Josiah (2 Kings 22–23, where he is high priest) and at Ezra's reading of the Torah to the returned exiles (Neh. 8:1-9): "Hilkiah! The name is an allegory of priestly power. . . . The lesson of Hilkiah is that canon is not a literary category but a category of power."[7] The historical problem is that these

5. Two important books on the canon of the Old Testament are Roger Beckwith, *The Old Testament Canon of the New Testament Church* (Grand Rapids, Mich.: Wm. B. Eerdmans, 1985), and John Barton, *Oracles of God* (New York: Oxford University Press, 1986). James Barr goes so far as to question whether the term "canon" may be meaningfully applied to the Hebrew Scriptures. See *Holy Scripture, Canon, Authority, Criticism* (Oxford: Clarendon, 1983).

6. Bruns, "Canon and Power in the Hebrew Scriptures," 78-79, 81.

7. Bruns, "Canon and Power in the Hebrew Scriptures," 81; cf. 68-69.

two events and characters were separated by nearly two centuries. The relation that these two Hilkiahs bear to each other, then, is an "allegory," as Bruns says, and not a historical relation at all. It is a relation, in short, that comes from Bruns's presuppositions.

In order to challenge the value of older writings — of Scripture or literature — the new canon-makers assume that ideological categories (such as "power") explain the shape of the canon, and they then read history and literature allegorically to bear out their assumptions. They assume that the primary significance of the canonical texts (biblical and literary) is their canonicity itself. They then attribute characteristics to these texts that flow from the new canon-makers' own assumptions about power, but which are hard to discern in the texts themselves. Their argument, then, is circular: given their assumptions, it is no wonder they find that the primary function of the collected texts is to legitimate a social class desperately trying to gain or retain power. Such theories tell us little about scriptural or literary texts, but rather create a fiction that ironically tells us a great deal about the new canon-makers, as we shall see with their treatment of Johnson.

Our knowledge of the canonization of the New Testament is in a better state than that of the Old Testament, and its story is arguably more appropriate as an analogy to literature. It will be my final position, however, that this analogy applies only within very narrow limits — far narrower than is typical, for instance, in the literary criticism of new historicists — and that Johnson himself is a good indicator of those limits. No one denies that Johnson is deeply committed to both the New Testament and the criticism of secular literature. He is therefore a good practical example of how both secular and sacred writings have been valued. Terms like "power" and "control" are singularly inapt for describing his view of Scripture. One must rather look to terms like "happiness" if one is to understand how he read Scripture, and to his concept of "pleasure" if one is to understand his reading of literature.

The standard English work on the canonization of the New Testament is Bruce Metzger's *The Canon of the New Testament: Its Origin, Development, and Significance.* The book is a monument of historical scholarship by a man who is among the most knowledgeable scholars on this subject in history. It is depressing, then, to see how rarely literary critics refer to his work, or to the work of the many other biblical scholars who have worked in this field.[8] Instead, literary scholars often follow the theory of Bruns, or the reasoning popularized by feminists (especially Elaine Pagels) that the New Testament canon was established in order to exclude "all forms of revelation that did not support a patriarchal and hierarchical view of society and the church."[9]

Metzger makes a crucial distinction between understanding the canon as (1) an authoritative collection of books versus (2) a collection of authoritative books. He plainly favors the second conception as truer to the history of the canon itself.[10] It is a distinction that will seem obvious to all practicing Christians — who, after all, are the only people who acknowledge the authority of the New Testament canon in the first place. If the *books* are authoritative, as Christians believe, one will be concerned with their content, their authors, and with what others have said about their content and authors. Christians see the primary theme of the books in their witness to Jesus — his life, death, and message. They naturally give the greatest weight to any writings of the

8. Gerald Bruns and Frank Kermode are honorable exceptions to this generalization. See Bruce Metzger's bibliographical chapters in *The Canon of the New Testament* (Oxford: Clarendon, 1987) for a description of other treatments of the canonization process.

9. Lynne Courter Boughton, "From Pious Legend to Feminist Fantasy," *Journal of Religion* 71 (July 1991): 368. Though less often cited by literary critics, the other feminist biblical scholars who adopt this view, as Boughton notes, are Rosemary Radford Reuther and Elisabeth Schüssler Fiorenza. Boughton's essay is an excellent analysis, from a Catholic perspective, of one of the apocryphal "Acts" of the apostles, *Acts of Paul/Acts of Thecla*. This apocryphal work has become popular among feminists who wish to find priestly functions for women in the early church, for it recounts the story of a woman, Thecla, who baptized herself. (The New Testament does portray women as catechists and missionaries, argues Boughton, but not as exercising priestly powers.) The primary reasons for its rejection were the evidence that it was a fictitious rather than authentic account, its portrayal of God taking possession of human personalities, and its spiritualized concept of the resurrection of Jesus (377, 379, 383). Boughton's essay takes issue with the feminist position that the work was rejected because of its allegedly favorable portrayal of a woman.

10. Metzger, *The Canon of the New Testament*, 282-88. The distinction may have a Protestant flavor to it, since it seems to demote the authority of the church in declaring the authority of Scripture. However, even at the Council of Trent, which reasserted its magisterial authority against the institutional threats of a Scripture-based Lutheranism, the Roman Catholic Church reaffirmed the authority of Scripture.

disciples of Jesus and of those who heard the disciples. Testimony regarding the authenticity of those writings, especially from the churches actually founded by those disciples, will carry considerable weight.

A great deal of historical evidence surrounds these issues. Establishing the evidence requires patience, and drawing valid conclusions from it requires careful reasoning. Metzger ultimately suggests that the early church used three criteria for canonicity.[11] The first is theological: "conformity to what was called the 'rule of faith.'" The second and third criteria are historical. One was "apostolic origin" — that is, evidence that the book was written by an apostle, like Paul, or by someone closely associated with the apostles, like Luke or Mark. The third and final test for authority was whether the "Church at large" accepted it. Thus, Jerome (in A.D. 414) urged all Christians to accept both Hebrews and Revelation, despite doubts of their apostolic authorship, on the grounds that the Western churches accepted Revelation and the Eastern churches Hebrews. Significantly, these criteria had developed by the second century, two hundred years before the canon was closed.[12]

If the *collection* of the New Testament is authoritative, by contrast, then one's focus will be on the collectors (rather than the authors), their alleged authority, and the somewhat mystical concept of "a canon" as an unalterable, inspired, and perfect entity. This is the view of canon that the new canon-makers accept — and criticize — as their typical line of questioning makes plain. "[S]trictly speaking," says Bruns, the content of the Torah delivered by the high priest Hilkiah "does not matter."[13] The content of the New Testament does not matter either. The dual nature of Christ, the physical resurrection, the monotheistic nature of God, the believer's fate of martyrdom — all of these issues may be re-read as "serv[ing] the needs of the emerging institution" of the church.[14] Its "needs," in Pagels' analysis, cannot be understood in

11. Metzger, *The Canon of the New Testament,* 251-54.

12. For a somewhat broader classification of these same criteria and an excellent description of how they worked together, see F. F. Bruce, *The Canon of Scripture* (Downers Grove: InterVarsity Press, 1988), 255-69.

13. Bruns, "Canon and Power in the Hebrew Scriptures," 69.

14. Elaine Pagels, *The Gnostic Gospels* (New York: Random House, 1979), 120.

the words of the New Testament itself, namely, bearing witness to the gospel of Jesus. Rather, the needs of the church were for self-preservation, which it achieved by "accept[ing] the status quo," maintaining a pattern of denigrating women and feminine spirituality, and above all by upholding the hierarchical rule of bishops.[15] For instance, the collected texts that testified to the physical resurrection of Christ, in Pagels' analysis, had an essential political function of legitimizing "the authority of certain men who claim to exercise exclusive leadership over the churches."[16]

The emphasis on an authoritative *collection* rather than authoritative *books* carries over into the literary debates as well. To return to the introduction and previous chapter, the "ancient" emphasizes the content of the books he or she values, even when (as I quoted Irving Howe as saying) the books do not endorse his or her own opinions. The "modern" emphasizes the collection itself as a "'system of power' that controls which texts are taught," and directs his or her questions to the allegedly oppressive structure which the collection supposedly legitimates.[17] The modern (unlike the ancient) is then in the position to perform ideological analysis, which can explain every item in the canon, and every historical record that attests to the canon, with reference to the maintenance of structural power and the history of oppression.

Now there are many problems, both theoretical and historical, with looking at literature or social institutions in this way. For instance, by attempting to explain the church in terms of self-preservation, the new canon makers adopt an approach that is insufficient to account for any organism, natural or social. In an essay entitled "Teleology, Darwinism, and the Place of Man," Leon Kass puts it this way: "A mature organism shows itself as a whole, maintains itself as a whole, and functions as a whole in characteristic ways *above and beyond merely maintaining itself.*"[18] Kass is speaking primarily of purposive behavior

15. Pagels, *The Gnostic Gospels*, 107, 66, 118.

16. Pagels, *The Gnostic Gospels*, 6.

17. Kaplan and Rose, *The Canon and the Common Reader*, 8.

18. Leon Kass, *Toward a More Natural Science* (New York: Free Press, 1985), 255, emphasis in original.

in the animal kingdom by way of noting that Darwinism by no means excludes questions of purpose. The point is that one must ask what the church thought the New Testament writings were *for,* and not rest content with a preconceived notion about the way those writings (and doctrines and rituals) maintained an existing organization. By way of analogy, one must ask what Johnson thought literature was for, especially in view of his lengthy testimony on this subject.

Next, the emphasis on an "authoritative collection" rather than authoritative books is untrue to the historical record. As Metzger points out, "During the second and succeeding centuries, this authoritative word [of God] was found, not in the utterances of contemporary leaders and teachers, but in the apostolic testimony contained within certain early Christian writings."[19] It was not the collectors who bestowed authority on the writings. Nor is it precisely true to say that the writings, in some mystical way, bestowed authority on the collectors or the collection. If the writings had authority, it was because they were believed, by their readers, to bear witness to the gospel that Jesus actually preached, and because they met the historical criteria of apostolicity and general use in the church.

None of the books of what came to be known as the New Testament was written with an eye to its future inclusion in that collection. When the earliest Christians referred to "the Scriptures," they meant the Hebrew Scriptures. Only one New Testament book lays claim to being "inspired": the book of Revelation, and that claim was thought to tell *against* including it alongside other, better attested writings. That is, "inspiration" was not a criterion of canonicity, and was only applied retroactively to the New Testament books.

The canonization of the New Testament was long and continuous, extending over three centuries. It began with the writing of the documents in the one hundred years after Christ's death. It may usefully (if not entirely accurately) be said to end in 367, when St. Athanasius, bishop of Alexandria, wrote a festal letter listing precisely the twenty-seven books of the New Testament as the only canonical ones. The recognition of most of the books of the present New Testament by widely scattered churches, however, came much earlier — by the end

19. Metzger, *The Canon of the New Testament,* 287.

of the second century.[20] The second-century date fixes the main contours of the New Testament about a hundred years before Constantine decriminalized Christianity in the Roman empire (A.D. 313). That is important in view of Barbara Herrnstein Smith's influential essay on canonization. She argues that the "test of time" as an indicator of the "classic" value of a text may be reinterpreted — fairly easily, it transpires — as masking the acts of "those with cultural power. . . . [T]he texts that are selected and preserved by 'time,'" she says, are really those that fit the "characteristic needs, interests, resources, and purposes . . . of the culturally dominant members of a community."[21] The new canon-makers like to make much of the eventual cultural dominance of the church, beginning in the fourth century, for it suggests a straightforward connection between the canon and cultural power, understood in sociopolitical, ideological categories. But the remarkable acceptance of most New Testament documents long before the fourth century, during the decades of harsh (if not widespread) persecution, makes the connection remarkably clumsy. During the first two centuries, Christians were a small minority in the empire. So alienated were they from its culture that they were accused of being antisocial. Although general persecution did not begin until the third century, many Christians of the first two centuries chose martyrdom over saying "Caesar is lord." Christians attacked many aspects of imperial culture as immoral, from its theatres and gladiatorial spectacles to its practices of infanticide and abortion. Perhaps most threatening to the cultural power of Rome, they refused to acknowledge its gods, and their writings condemned participation in its wars. Neither in its government nor in its religious life, neither in its entertainments nor in its armies, had the Christians any desire to wield cultural power in the empire during the crucial first two centuries when the canon of the New Testament assumed its shape. In fact, the historical record is almost exactly the opposite of what Smith's theory of cultural power posits.

Perhaps the "power" in question, however, should be more nar-

20. In general, the last books to gain widespread acceptance were Hebrews, James, 1 & 2 Peter, 2 & 3 John, Jude, and Revelation. Some places accepted them earlier, some later, as the letter from Jerome in A.D. 414 (noted earlier) makes clear.

21. Smith, "Contingencies of Value," 33.

rowly defined as the power of the bishops, or episcopal power within the church. This is the approach, for instance, of Elaine Pagels. Some of the earliest testimony about the New Testament books, or the contents of those books, comes from bishops in the first generations after the apostles themselves (c. 70-135), who are among the "apostolic fathers." Other testimony around the end of the second century comes from Irenaeus, bishop of Lyons (d. 202?). Should one read the earliest testimonies for the New Testament canon as anything other than an attempt to bolster episcopal power?

Before I turn to the historical evidence, however, I should note that the ideological approach also allows one to prove exactly the opposite of what Pagels and Bruns maintain — without even a glance at the record. One of the other figures present during the discovery of the Torah, along with Hilkiah, is Huldah the prophetess. If one believes that the allegorization of power relationships is the same as scholarship, the rare inclusion of a female prophet at the moment of the rediscovery of the canon could prove that the canon empowers females. Huldah's presence could show that "canon" is a category of inclusion, questioning the culturally accepted norms of power. The presence of women in many church leadership roles during the centuries of New Testament canonization could lead to the same conclusion. The point is that ideological criticism, coupled with an allegorical approach to history and literature, allows one to prove anything one wishes.

My own description of the major historical figures involved in New Testament canonization, below, will no doubt be partial as well. But I hope it does not suggest the need to assign the chief players the roles of heroes or villains in an allegorical story whose meaning may be accepted only by those who agree with my own view of the world.[22]

Irenaeus had sat at the feet of Polycarp, the bishop and martyr of Smyrna, who was thought to have had the disciples themselves as his

22. Origen and Jerome offer interesting examples. While Origen's evidence for the shape of the biblical canon is excellent, his allegorical hermeneutic is generally unacceptable in my view. Jerome's arguments for Hebrews and Revelation are significant, but his misogynistic views of sexuality and marriage are not true to the full teaching of Scripture. Calvin powerfully argued against Origen and Jerome on both matters, as I shall explain in the next chapter. These are complicated historical figures, not characters, good or bad, in a morality play.

teachers. His predecessor bishop in Lyons had been martyred, together with scores of his flock. By contrast, the gnostic Christians at Lyons remained safe due to their spiritualized conception of Christ's nature and death, as presented in their own gospels, and their consequently equivocal beliefs. "Over against the ever-shifting and contradictory opinions of the heretics," writes Metzger, "Irenaeus places the unchanging faith of the catholic [or universal] Church based on Scripture and tradition, and compacted together by the episcopal organization."[23] Irenaeus regards the four Gospels as the only valid ones, and although he designates Acts and twelve of the Pauline epistles as "Scriptures," he does not say whether he regards this latter portion of the New Testament closed as well. In any case, he sharply disputes the authority of the gnostic gospels.

Pagels suggests that the gnostic gospels' view of Christ has equal or greater validity than that of the apostolic testimony through Polycarp and Irenaeus. Irenaeus and others wrote "propaganda for martyrdom," as she calls it, and they urged their view of the Christian faith and Scriptures to increase their institutional power, even at the cost of their lives.[24]

It turns out, however, that some of the most important corroborating testimony of the New Testament writings comes from Christians who were not bishops or even priests, such as Justin Martyr, and from others, such as Tertullian and Origen, who had a great deal of trouble with bishops. It is worth noting that Samuel Johnson owned many volumes of the works of all three of these writers, in addition to the works of many others who testify to the early recognition of the New Testament writings.[25] Johnson was certainly familiar with arguments about the historical evidence for the New Testament canon, and as we shall see, he probably knew eighteenth-century arguments that proceeded by rationalistic deduction rather than historical induction as well.

23. Metzger, *The Canon of the New Testament,* 154.

24. Pagels, *The Gnostic Gospels,* 93, 120.

25. For instance, he owned works by Clement of Alexandria, Irenaeus, Eusebius, and Athanasius, as well as those by later fathers like Cyril, Basil, Jerome, and Augustine, whose testimony is also valuable for our knowledge of the canon. See Donald Greene, *Samuel Johnson's Library: An Annotated Guide* (Victoria, B.C.: University of Victoria, 1975).

Justin Martyr (c. 100–c. 165), one of the first defenders of the Christian faith, speaks of the contemporary practice of reading the " 'memoirs of the apostles,' " or " 'gospels' " alongside the Old Testament prophets during worship.[26] He is familiar with the traditions that came to be included in the later apocryphal gospels, but does not generally consider them authoritative, in the manner of the "memoirs." They are not read in Christian worship, as the "memoirs" are, because they are not "authorized witnesses to Jesus' life and teaching."[27] Killed in Rome for his faith in Christ, Justin and later martyrs were described as "morbid and misguided exhibitionists" by Marcus Aurelius (emperor from 161 to 180) — a description that Pagels offers sympathetically to her modern readers, along with the possibility that they were "neurotic masochists."[28]

According to Jerome, Tertullian (c. 160–c. 225) was a priest, but there is also evidence that he was a layman. In any case, this Carthaginian Christian was not a bishop, and his objections to a hierarchical priesthood were of long standing.[29] Tertullian is our source for the phrase "rule of faith," which gained acceptance as the theological criterion for canonicity. The rule of faith "signified the common fundamental belief of the Church," writes Metzger, "orally received by the churches from the apostles and orally transmitted from generation to generation as the baptismal creed."[30] Tertullian states the rule of faith three times, one of which is a form of the Apostles' Creed. It is perhaps significant, in light of the new canon-makers' emphasis on the role of episcopal power, that the widely accepted Apostles' Creed affirms the "holy catholic church" but not episcopal church government, and that the theological criterion of canonicity does not come to us from a bishop. As against the acceptance of only one gospel by the heretic Marcion, Tertullian defends all four Gospels as the work of either the apostles or their companions and disciples. He accepts a wider number

26. Metzger, *The Canon of the New Testament,* 145.

27. Metzger, *The Canon of the New Testament,* 148.

28. Pagels, *The Gnostic Gospels,* 81.

29. Boughton, "From Pious Legend to Feminist Fantasy," 375.

30. Metzger, *The Canon of the New Testament,* 158. The remainder of this paragraph is indebted to Metzger, 158-60.

of the Pauline epistles than Marcion, including the three letters to Timothy and Titus, which speak of the very offices in church government that gave him so much trouble. Unlike Marcion, Tertullian accepts the Old Testament as deserving inclusion, along with the four Gospels and apostolic epistles, in the church's Scriptures.

Origen of Alexandria (185–253/4) is particularly significant for evidence of the widespread acceptance of only certain New Testament writings, for his travels had brought him in contact with much of the church — in Palestine, Antioch, Ephesus, Athens, and Rome. He was appointed a teacher by Bishop Demetrius of Alexandria but was not ordained even to preach. When some bishops in Palestine ordained him for that purpose, Demetrius abrogated Origen's teaching authority and excommunicated him from the church. He moved to Palestine, where he opened a new school and continued to preach and teach. During the general persecution of the church in 250, he was tortured and died a few years later.[31] If anyone had motives to question the authority of bishops, it was Origen. Moreover, his residence in Alexandria, one of the homes of gnosticism, would have placed him in an excellent position to find intellectual and social support for a gnostic alternative to the Scriptures of the church. But exactly the opposite occurs: he affirms the four Gospels as "the only indisputable ones in the Church of God under heaven" and accepts all thirteen epistles of Paul (and Hebrews as well), along with Acts, 1 Peter, 1 John, Jude, and Revelation.

In light of the new canon-makers' emphasis on power, it is telling that so many of the key historical figures who recorded the acceptance of the New Testament had little or no power, cultural or ecclesiastical. Far from emphasizing the authority of the canon as such — as an authoritative collection established by some central authority, perhaps, at a particular time — the early Christian writers refer to the widespread and remarkably unanimous acceptance of certain individual writings over a long period of time. The "popular fallacy" that the New Testament was collected at a single moment by church authorities is hardly worth a footnote in Metzger's treatment.[32] Nevertheless, the related,

31. Metzger, *The Canon of the New Testament,* 135-36.
32. Metzger, *The Canon of the New Testament,* 189n.61.

anachronistic notion of a highly centralized "cult of orthodoxy" settling the canon by "fiat" and "the violence of political suppression" finds its way into influential feminist writing on the canon.[33] The testimony of the general acceptance of New Testament writings comes from bishops and laymen, from persons hostile to their surrounding culture like Tertullian, and from others like Justin who tried (and failed) to reconcile the Roman authorities to the new faith. It comes from theologians who may be described as "hyperorthodox," such as Lucifer of Calaris and others on the fringes of orthodoxy in some areas, like Origen.[34] The story of the acceptance of New Testament writings cannot be understood in the simplistic vocabulary of ideology. It requires the hard and fascinating labor of true academic inquiry.

The common acceptance of a New Testament writing by ordinary Christians and pastors worked together with the two other criteria for canonicity: its conformity with the apostolic rule of faith (which, without great distortion, may be said to be embodied in the Apostles' Creed), and its apostolic origin (real or attributed). In short, the theological authority of each New Testament book derived from its author and content, rather than from some authoritative, institutional pronouncement of absolute value.[35] In the Muratorian Fragment, one of the most important lists of New Testament books, probably dating from around the close of the second century, the tone is one of explaining a "more or less established condition of things," as Metzger says, rather than that of prescription.[36] Four books of the present New Testament are missing, and one difference of opinion continues to exist (regarding the Apocalypse of Peter). The "'primary theme'" of the Scriptures, however, is clear: it is Jesus as the Christ, and the fragmentist sees no place for works that teach views of Christ that are already widely regarded as heretical.[37]

One of the major difficulties in arguing against an ideological

33. Christine Froula, "When Eve Reads Milton: Undoing the Canonical Economy," in *Canons,* 154.

34. See Metzger, *The Canon of the New Testament,* 232.

35. This is true down to the early fourth century, as seen in the writings of Eusebius. See Metzger, *The Canon of the New Testament,* 202.

36. Ibid., 200.

37. Bruce, *The Canon of Scripture,* 160-61.

approach to the canon, however, is that any inductively proposed conclusions, such as Metzger's criteria for canonicity, may be retranslated into the preconceived "category of power" that is so attractive to the new canon-makers. All of the historical evidence that I have cited can doubtless be assimilated into some previously unexplained aspect of the ideological critique of the canon. But the critique continually diverts attention away from historical phenomena in order to save the appearances of its ideology. Epicycles can always be added to the Ptolemaic system, but how much understanding of the universe will be gained?

Perhaps an analogy will clarify how I believe the emphasis on "power" diverts attention from history and directs us instead to the superficially plausible categories of ideology. Suppose two thousand years from now someone wants to write on the twentieth-century novel. There is already an immense amount of scholarship on the subject, which would seem to discourage anyone in the fortieth century from trying to say anything new. It would even discourage most people from familiarizing themselves with what has already been said. At the same time, however, a revived radicalism has presented scholars with the prospect of raising questions about the social structures of their day. The account might go as follows:

> While earlier writers have tended to assume that twentieth-century narratives reflect the diverse modes of perception in the fragmented, post-Enlightenment world, modern scholarship has raised new challenges to the orthodox interpretation of history. While pretending to open up new ways of seeing, the novel actually controlled the perceptions of its readers. Perhaps an ideological homology from the history of the automobile will illuminate the subject. History, after all, is the story of the winners, and the automobile was indisputably one of the greatest hegemonic forces of the twentieth century. Moreover, the inventor of the mass-produced automobile, Henry Ford, said that "history is bunk" and yet built a park whose theme is American history — testimony to his wish to obscure his own historical role. Just as we would never account for the car on the basis of what its inventors, manufacturers, and consumers have said about it, likewise the novel must be related to the surrounding forces of culture. Rather than providing opportunities for dealing with the fragmentation of social life, the automobile actually functioned as a system of control. The need for steel and oil resulted in widespread

> ecological damage, made worse each year by exhaust fumes; in 1941 the need for petroleum supplies forced Japan to begin a war with America; in the United States alone, traffic fatalities each year approximated those of its most politically devastating war of the century. The car cannot be understood in the terms of transportation. The essence of the automobile was power, for its owners and manipulators attempted to control the planet ecologically and politically through the manufacture of the product itself and related products of petroleum and rubber. The seat belt may serve as an allegory of control, mystifying itself under the appearance of protection. The automobile, along with highway construction, anti-lock brakes, and the oil tanker, functioned to control national politics and the environment in the twentieth century. The history of the car cannot help but raise new questions about the systems of control in the literature of the period as well.[38]

The essay would be entitled something like "Breakdowns of the (Auto)nomous Story: Overhauling the Transmission of Narrative."

Every inquiry that adds to our knowledge of history is valuable. But presupposing that history is generally explained by the self-interested pursuit of power, residing in everyone other than oneself, raises questions about the foundations of ideological criticism.

New Testament Canonization, Johnson, and Samuel Clarke

One of the attractions of Samuel Johnson's life and writings is the underlying integrity that connects his work. True, there is distortion in his biography of his friend Richard Savage, but in general Johnson's work presents the picture of a man of great intelligence, religious commitment, and moral depth trying to register accurately his powerful emotional responses to literature. These responses and commitments cause tremendous inner conflicts, which are in turn the source of some of Johnson's most interesting observations. One is struck as well by the unity between his writings on the moral implications of literary or

38. One student told me that this account of the automobile is similar to what she was actually taught at a major university.

biographical subjects and his own life. At one moment, Johnson is seen extending his charity to the granddaughter of Milton, at the next to a blind poet who needs a home.

Unlike the ideological approach that sees all phenomena under the aspect of power, the unity in Johnson's work allows for authentic diversity as well. Religion and poetry both fulfill their deepest callings when they lead people to the truth in Johnson's view, but he typically distinguishes their manners of doing this. Poetry leads its readers by means of pleasure; religion by happiness. The two types of writing have much in common — so much, indeed, that Johnson uses the term "literature" to refer to virtually all types of writings that convey knowledge, sermons as well as poems, intellectual prose as well as fiction. But it remains true nevertheless that Johnson thought the believer gained "eternal happiness" from following the teachings of the New Testament. In contrast, he observed that the common readers of literature ordinarily gained pleasure from their experience of reading, and that they made pleasure their criterion for the books they continued to esteem. Johnson's task as a critic of literature was to ask why and how certain writings had generally pleased mankind. His criticism treats pleasure as a complex phenomenon, not easily accountable and certainly not reducible to an all-embracing, ideological category like "power." One of the chief pleasures of literature, he thought, was encountering accurate representations of human nature, and therefore the works that had long given pleasure would likely be the source of valuable knowledge — real knowledge — about human nature. The continual esteem in which the common reader held those works was probably due ultimately to that knowledge, thought Johnson, and it was his task to explain it.

The parallel between Johnson's procedure and the early church fathers is this: the fathers believed that the content of the twenty-seven New Testament books gave accurate knowledge of the rule of faith, which explained their widespread and long-attested (if not unanimous) acceptance — an acceptance that preceded the fathers themselves. The fathers' task, then, was to seek the ways in which those writings contributed to the knowledge of the "rule of faith."

By contrast, the new canon-makers are more like the gnostics who argued for different gospels, based on their own esoteric wisdom. Today's critics see the literary choices of generations of readers (like the widely accepted but limited number of New Testament writings) as somehow flawed or based upon power disguising itself as knowledge. Johnson's approach is far more humble: however much he dissented from the popular estimate of a writer, he was willing to consider that the disagreement came from a lack of understanding on his part.

Before considering Johnson's literary criticism, however, I should like to examine his view of the canon that he actually recognized — the canon of the Bible and the New Testament in particular — and the opinions of one of Johnson's chief influences, Samuel Clarke, on the canon.

I have already noted that Johnson's library contained the works of many of the earliest church fathers. These works attest to the church's recognition of the authority of particular New Testament writings, not the recognition of the collection as such, by some powerful church authority. It is helpful here to note Johnson's single definition of the word "canonize" in the *Dictionary* (1755): "to declare any man a saint." In other words, he acknowledges that the church assumes its authority in making saints, but he gives no other definition for the word. Specifically, he does not acknowledge any church authority for declaring certain biblical books to be authoritative — which is the way "canonize" is used by today's canon-makers. For them, "to canonize" means to *bestow* putative authority on *collections of texts.*

Johnson's definitions of "canon" are similarly revealing. His first definition, derived from the Greek cognate, is "a rule; a law," and the second, "the laws made by ecclesiastical councils." The third meaning is most important for my purposes: "the books of Holy Scripture; or the great rule," which Johnson illustrates with this quotation from John Ayliffe: "*Canon* also denotes those books of Scripture, which are received as inspired and canonical, to distinguish them from either profane, apocryphal or disputed books. . . ." Canonical literature is specifically distinguished from secular literature ("profane" here has the neutral meaning of "not sacred"). Furthermore, Ayliffe's language of "receiving" rather than "bestowing" or "declaring" is similar to that of the thirty-nine Articles of Religion of the Church of England: "All the Books of the New Testament, as they are commonly received, we do *receive,* and account them Canonical."[39] There is nothing in Ayliffe's

39. Article VI, emphasis added.

sentence, the Articles, or in Johnson's definitions to suggest that the canon of Scripture owed its authority to the magisterial authority of church councils or bishops. Instead, one finds the opposite emphasis, on common reception of the writings "accounted" canonical by the church at large.

More revealing than the books Johnson owned or the definitions he wrote, however, is his view and use of Scripture. The authenticity of Scripture had been attacked and defended vigorously in the Restoration and eighteenth century by writers Johnson knew well. One of the most well-known attacks came from David Hume, who denied the validity of scriptural evidence for inquiring into miracles or the problem of evil. Two leading scholars on Johnson and religion conclude that he examined the authenticity of the Scriptures before he acknowledged their authority. Chester Chapin writes, "[A]ll arguments in favor of theism, or 'natural religion,' . . . seemed to Johnson less important than those which tended to establish revelation itself as solidly grounded in the facts of history."[40] Hume's purely rational critique of a rationalistic "natural religion," then, carried less weight with Johnson than the confirmation of the historical truth of Christianity by the "number of great men" down through the ages.[41] Richard Schwartz explains the disagreement between Johnson and Hume this way: "[t]he problem is the authenticity of scripture. . . . If the authenticity is demonstrable, as Johnson believes it to be, then his low opinion of Hume's procedure [of disallowing scriptural evidence] is understandable. If it is not, then Johnson's faith is shaken. . . ."[42] As Schwartz goes on to note, however, Johnson did not believe that the "evidences" of the truth of Christianity, though compelling, were " 'irresistible' ": the Christian religion " 'was intended to induce, not to compel.' "[43] That is, the "historical evidences" are a necessary but not

40. Chester F. Chapin, *The Religious Thought of Samuel Johnson* (Ann Arbor: University of Michigan Press, 1968), 80.

41. Chapin, *The Religious Thought of Samuel Johnson,* 88-90; cf. James Boswell, *The Life of Samuel Johnson,* ed. G. B. Hill, rev. L. F. Powell, 2nd ed. (Oxford: Clarendon, 1964), 1:454.

42. Richard B. Schwartz, *Samuel Johnson and the Problem of Evil* (Madison: University of Wisconsin Press, 1975), 73.

43. Schwartz is quoting from p. 306 of Johnson's review of Soame Jenyns's *A Free Enquiry Into the Nature and Origin of Evil* (1757), which Schwartz usefully reprints

sufficient component of Johnson's faith. Without the evidence, Johnson would not have believed. But his faith reached far beyond mere assent to an acceptance of the historical reliability of the New Testament.

Another challenge to Scripture, and in particular to the canon of the New Testament, came from John Toland, well known as a satirical object of Swift and the author of a biography of Milton (1698) which Johnson had read. Toland questioned whether Charles I had actually written the *Eikon Basilike* (the meditations published in 1649 to which Milton had responded with *Eikonoklastes*), and he insinuated that a mistake on this point might suggest similar mistakes concerning the authenticity of early Christian writings: "'I cease to wonder any longer how so many suppositious [*sic*] pieces under the name of Christ, his Apostles, and other great Persons should be publish'd and approved in those primitive times.'"[44] After being attacked for these views, Toland wrote a response, *Amyntor* (1699), which declared "in so many words, that there is not one single book of the New Testament which was not refused by some of the ancient writers as being unjustly attributed to the apostles and as actually forged by their adversaries."[45]

It is significant that Toland, whose most well-known book is *Christianity Not Mysterious* (1696), seeks a purely rational (as opposed to historical) defense of the authority of Scripture. Any authority the Bible possesses depends upon its prior agreement with "natural reason," as Toland (in the tradition of Lord Herbert of Cherbury) understands that term. Toland made reason the "norm of revelation," which meant he reconciled any scriptural difficulties with "reason" — at the expense, of course, of Scripture.[46]

Among the respondents to Toland's *Amyntor* was Samuel Clarke, whom Johnson acknowledged as one of his most significant religious influences. Although he may have exaggerated, Johnson twice credited

---

in his own book (98-112). Johnson significantly acknowledges that a rational appreciation of the evidences for Christianity does not displace the need for faith, an acknowledgment found in Christian theologians generally, as Johnson says.

44. Gerard Reedy, S.J., *The Bible and Reason* (Philadelphia: University of Pennsylvania Press, 1985), 92-93; see also Metzger, *The Canon of the New Testament,* 12-13.

45. Metzger, *The Canon of the New Testament,* 13.

46. Reedy, *The Bible and Reason,* 27.

Clarke's sermons for his salvation.[47] Clarke was not orthodox on the Trinity: he overemphasized the superiority of the Father to the other two members, and he neglected the unity of the Godhead.[48] Johnson therefore refused to include him in the *Dictionary* citations or to recommend his sermons unequivocally. It is noteworthy, however, that Clarke's "little heresy," as Johnson called it, came from his reading of Scripture and not from a prior commitment to philosophical rationalism. Johnson valued Clarke highly for his explanations of the meaning of Christ's death, liberty and necessity, and Christian evidences, as well as for his immense learning and literary style. Clarke's view of Scripture, as Johnson found it in his sermons, was that the Bible's teachings are consistent with human reason, and contain a wisdom that supplements the deficiencies of reason — a view which is found in many of Johnson's own works.[49] An editor of Homer and a translator of Sir Isaac Newton, Clarke was "the most complete literary character that England ever produced," in Johnson's opinion.[50] Johnson owned two sets of Clarke's *Sermons* and read them over a period of many years.

The leading authority on Johnson's sermons, James Gray, summarizes the difference between Clarke and contemporary rationalists (such as Toland) thus: "[W]here Clarke differed from many of the deistical free-thinkers was in his emphasis on scriptural confirmation of the existence of the God that nature reveals to us, and in his insistence that there is no opposition between reason and revelation."[51] So far, however, no Johnsonian has written about Clarke's essay on the canon of the New Testament, which may have actually influenced Johnson's own views. The essay is certainly of greater historical importance to Johnson studies than modern, ideological theories of the canon. The ideological theories are more akin to Toland in their *a priori* assumptions than to Johnson's own thought and practice.

Clarke's essay answers the following question, raised by Toland:

47. James Gray, *Johnson's Sermons* (Oxford: Clarendon, 1972), 66.

48. Gray, *Johnson's Sermons,* 86, 88.

49. Gray, *Johnson's Sermons,* 75; see Samuel Johnson, *Lives of the English Poets,* ed. George Birbeck Hill, 3 vols. (Oxford: Clarendon, 1905), 1:179. Subsequent quotations from *Lives* are cited in the text with the abbreviation *L.*

50. Boswell, *The Life of Samuel Johnson,* 1:3n.2.

51. Gray, *Johnson's Sermons,* 67.

how can we be confident in the authority of the twenty-seven New Testament books, and only those twenty-seven, when some of them were written by the companions of the apostles rather than the apostles themselves? Why place the books of Mark and Luke in the New Testament when the writings of other companions of the apostles (e.g., the letters of Polycarp, Ignatius, Barnabas, and Clement, known as the "apostolic fathers") occupy a lower level?

Clarke answers Toland on three fronts, and each time his reasoning is historically based. First, Toland had charged that one may easily prove the works of the apostolic fathers, which attest to the New Testament writings, "spurious, and fraudulently imposed upon the Credulous," thereby calling into question the entire New Testament.[52] Clarke replies that, on the contrary, there is good reason to believe them genuine. Clarke takes the apostolic fathers one at a time and explains how *their* writings are attested by Clement of Alexandria, Irenaeus, Origen, Tertullian, and Eusebius — church fathers whose writings, as we have seen, were in Johnson's library. On this basis, Clarke says, it would be very difficult indeed to prove the apostolic fathers spurious. The apostolic fathers' attestation to the New Testament writings, Clarke concludes, is quite significant.

Second, Toland charges that the apostolic fathers were ignorant and superstitious, and their writings occasionally ridiculous. Presumably this could cast doubt upon the integrity of the early church as a whole. Clarke admits that these authors "were guilty of some Mistakes" and does not place their authority on a level with the apostles', but cites Eusebius and Irenaeus on the confidence with which the early church received the fathers' attestation of the New Testament writings.

The third point is the most significant. Toland had stated that anyone convinced of the authenticity of the writings of the apostolic fathers should

> receive them into the Canon of Scripture, since the reputed Authors of them were the Companions and Fellow-labourers of the Apostles,

52. Samuel Clarke, "Some Reflections on that Part of a Book called Amyntor, or The Defense of Milton's Life, which relates to the Writings of the Primitive Fathers and the Canon of the New Testament," in *Works* (1699; reprint, London, 1738), 3:917.

> as well as St. Mark, or St. Luke, which is the only reason he has ever heard of, why these two Evangelists are thought inspired. For to say that these Books ought not to be received now into the Canon, because the Ancients did not think fit to approve them, is but a mere Evasion; since many books now received as Canonical, were not approved by the Ancients; and some received by the Ancients, are now rejected by the Moderns. . . . And besides, no stress can be laid on the Testimony of the Fathers; since they not only contradict one another, but are often inconsistent with themselves in their relations of the very same Facts; [they use] reason precariously . . . and give hard Names to those who contemn such precarious reasoning.[53]

Notice how, for Toland, the authority of the New Testament depends upon its adherence to a straightforward, rationalistic procedure: if any companions of the apostles are accepted into the canon (Mark, Luke), *all* must be. If modern Christians accept any pronouncements of ancient Christians on the shape of the canon, the moderns must accept *all* of their pronouncements — perhaps Hebrews and Revelation should be cut from the present New Testament, for instance, since some of the ancients rejected one, while some rejected the other. Finally, if the church fathers reason inconsistently in some places, *all* of their testimony is worthless.

In some respects, Clarke's response to this third point does not go to the heart of this objection. Clarke responds to Toland by amassing testimony from the church fathers regarding the widespread acceptance of certain writings, their apostolic character, and the "Standard and Rule of Faith" found in them.[54] In other words, Clarke is so concerned with the way the early Christians actually came to value certain writings that he overlooks Toland's main point: that someone who is previously committed to an all-encompassing "system" of some sort — in Toland's case, a seamless system of natural reason — will never be able to acknowledge the authority of Scripture. Clarke's arguments are persuasive to other sorts of people, but they cannot shake someone whose presuppositions require that all data be classified into a monistic system.

53. Clark, "Some Reflections," 3:918.
54. Clark, "Some Reflections," 3:923, 924.

Clarke's procedure is logical, but a deductive system of purely natural reason — or, more powerful still, ideology — would appear more straightforward. There is no conflict between reason and revelation in Clarke, but a person determined to subordinate the historical evidence for an early canon to his or her own conception of "reason" would not find Clarke's arguments persuasive.

It is striking that one finds Metzger's three criteria, in slightly different form, in Clarke's essay. Clarke emphasizes "inspiration" a bit more, and he vaguely refers once to a "Council," but explanation of the criteria for New Testament canonicity is strikingly similar to the one Metzger describes.[55]

We know that Johnson held Clarke in the highest regard, in part for his writings on "Christian evidences." I cannot be sure that Johnson knew Clarke's response to Toland, although I think it unlikely that he remained ignorant of a controversy stemming from a Milton biography (which he knew well) and a respondent he esteemed highly.[56] Many of the ideas in Clarke's pamphlet, at any rate, are found in sermons by Clarke that Johnson did know. In the pamphlet, the authenticity of the Scriptures is attested by detailed, historical evidences, weighed by a discriminating, careful mind. Johnson found an argument like this — and perhaps this very argument — persuasive. Having been convinced of the historic authenticity of the Scriptures, he was ready to consider their authority and purpose for his own life.

55. The reference to a council (neither dated nor identified) occurs in the following sentence: "When we have made the best Judgment of things, that we can possibly at this distance of Time, we cannot after all but pay some Deference to the Judgment of the Antients, especially when assembled in a Council . . ." (924). The first council that issued a list that corresponds to the present canon of the New Testament was the Synod of Hippo Regius, in A.D. 393 (Metzger, *The Canon of the New Testament,* 314). Unlike this sentence, most of the referents in Clarke's pamphlet are precise, and no later than Eusebius (d. 340?).

56. Regrettably, the two sets of Clarke's sermons in Johnson's library, one in eight volumes, the other in ten, do not turn up much evidence either. Greene does not speculate on the eight-volume set, but he notes that a ten-volume edition of the sermons was published in 1730-31. This edition does not contain the response to Toland. In any event, the quality of the sale catalogue from Johnson's library makes speculation unwise: it can possibly "claim the distinction of being the worst book catalogue ever produced" (Greene, *Samuel Johnson's Library,* 5; see also 49).

"Happiness" and Samuel Johnson's Reading of the Bible

In Johnson's sermons, the purpose of Scripture is described as teaching the ethical life on earth and the way to eternal salvation in heaven.[57] Salvation and virtuous conduct are the two primary elements of "happiness," as the sermons describe it, and happiness, in turn, is the unifying subject in those works:

> The one constant theme pervading all Johnson's sermons, then, is the search for happiness, both in this world and in the next: that form of happiness which transcends the vanity of human wishes and the transitoriness of life, and which derives its promise and its strength both from the harmonious workings of society and from the message of the Christian faith.[58]

The prospect of death in particular shows the vanity of all merely human pleasures, and even the limits of reason itself, if reason is viewed from an entirely secular standpoint. Happiness and freedom from the anxiety of death can be obtained, writes Johnson in Sermon 14, only "by securing to [oneself] the protection of a Being mighty to save" — a phrase which echoes Isaiah 63:1 (*W* 14:154). The limits of worldly pleasures, including the pleasures of knowledge, are perhaps most strongly impressed in Sermon 25, which Johnson wrote on the occasion of his wife's death:

> To afford adequate consolations to the last hour, to chear the gloomy passage through the valley of the shadow of death . . . is the privilege only of revealed religion. All those to whom the supernatural light of heavenly doctrine has never been imparted, however formidable for power, or illustrious for wisdom, have wanted that knowledge of their future state, which alone can give comfort to misery. . . . (*W* 14:261-62)

The consolations of "revealed religion" are different in kind from those of even the most formidable earthly wisdom — presumably including the wisdom that could be gained from literature.

57. Samuel Johnson, *The Yale Edition of the Works of Samuel Johnson* (New Haven: Yale University Press, 1958), 14:83. Subsequent quotations from the Yale edition of Johnson's *Works* are cited in the text with the abbreviation *W.*

58. Gray, *Johnson's Sermons*, 182.

The limits of human wisdom are a prominent theme in Johnson's works. The often overlooked *Vision of Theodore, Hermit of Teneriffe* (published 1748) is an allegory of those limitations. In brief, the characters who follow "unassisted reason" (i.e., unsupported by religion) find themselves overwhelmed by passion or appetite. They ultimately give way to a host of vices, from avarice and indolence to tyranny and intemperance. Those who follow religion, by contrast, are able to overcome their temptations, which are chiefly those of "habit," and are "placed . . . in the direct path to the temple of Happiness" (*W* 16:208).

Johnson's greatest poem, "The Vanity of Human Wishes," includes scholarly pursuits among the vain ambitions that fail to satisfy human longings. Although the poem is an imitation of Juvenal's tenth satire, Johnson's final lines depart markedly from the sentiment of the Latin original. In place of urging stoical fortitude in the face of death, Johnson's poem recommends praying for "faith, that panting for a happier seat, / Counts death kind Nature's signal of retreat" (lines 363-64). That is, Johnson's Christianity takes him beyond the moral imagination of the pagan poet by promising a hope in eternal happiness after the grave. Equally significant are the final lines of the poem, which conclude a verse paragraph on the consolations of providence, obedient passions, a resigned will, love, patience, and faith:

These goods for man the laws of heaven ordain,
These goods He grants, who grants the power to gain;
With these celestial wisdom calms the mind,
And makes the *happiness* she does not find.

(lines 365-68, emphasis added)

The lines refer to the inability of the mind (the "she" of the last line) to find happiness on its own. As Johnson writes in Sermon 12, "Every man will readily enough confess, that . . . he has not yet been able, with all his labour, to make happiness, or, with all his enquiries, to find it" (*W* 14:127). Only God can make one happy, and there is no doubt that the poem (when viewed in the context of Johnson's entire work) refers to the God of the Scriptures and Christian experience. In his final prayer, written December 5, 1784, just eight days before his death, Johnson implores God, "by the Grace of thy Holy Spirit . . . [to] receive me, at my death, to everlasting happiness, for the Sake of Jesus Christ" (*W* 1:418).

Although Johnson viewed happiness from the prospect of eternity, he considered the ethical life on earth to be a necessary condition of happiness. In *Rambler* 54, for instance, he writes that at one's deathbed, the only thing to raise the spirits of the dying man is "the recollection of acts of goodness" (*W* 3:291). Riches, authority, and praise are transitory, "external goods" and of little account when compared with "piety and virtue." Two of Johnson's biographies seem to be motivated by their subjects' exemplary ethical behavior, combined with their intense piety and formidable intellect — his biographies of the Dutch physician Herman Boerhaave and the English hymnodist Isaac Watts. To Johnson, Boerhaave's character was exemplified in his earnest attentions to the sick, his sincere faith, and his scientific inquiries:

> He asserted, on all occasions, the divine authority and sacred efficacy of the holy scriptures; and maintained that they alone taught the way of salvation, and that they only could give peace of mind. . . . So far was this man from being made impious by philosophy, or vain by knowledge, or by virtue, that he ascribed all his ability to the bounty, and all his goodness to the grace of God. May his example extend its influence to his admirers and followers! May those who study his writings imitate his life![59]

This tone of reverence toward his biographical subject is comparable only to his treatment of Watts. Of the hymnodist, Johnson writes, "It was not only in his book but in his mind that orthodoxy was united with charity" (*L* 3:308). Imagining the reader of Watts's prose, Johnson says "he that sat down only to reason is on a sudden compelled to pray" and remarks that "[e]very man acquainted with the common principles of human action will look with veneration on the writer who is at one time combating Locke, and at another making a catechism for children in their fourth year" (*L* 3:309, 308).

As his particular emphasis on charitable acts might suggest, Johnson's theology is Arminian rather than Calvinist. That is, while he

59. Johnson, "Boerhaave," in *The Works of Samuel Johnson* (Troy, N.Y.: Pafraets Book Co., 1903), 14:182-83.

believes he is saved by grace, he also believes that humans must cooperate with grace by their free will. For Johnson, this includes an especially strong element of exercising his moral freedom to "be the soul [God wants him] to be," as Owen Chadwick has explained.[60] In particular, the person who practices charity, as Johnson writes in Sermon 4, is the one who "shall stand without fear, on the brink of life, and pass into eternity, with an humble confidence of finding that mercy which he has never denied" (*W* 14:45).

In summary, Johnson invests his thought and life with the authority of the New Testament writings not to legitimate an institutional value that is being threatened, to paraphrase Alvin Kernan's conclusion on the "history of canon-making,"[61] but rather to reaffirm the testimony of millions of ordinary believers, great thinkers, and exemplary saints who have commended themselves as witnesses to salvation and eternal happiness. Johnson and his mentor Samuel Clarke looked to historical testimony or "evidences" for the authenticity of the New Testament canon, and were skeptical of purely rationalistic, speculative theology. Johnson talked little about the canon as an authoritative collection; he talked and wrote much of the way the words and deeds of Jesus and his apostles had authority over his own life and works. In short, Johnson was a practical Christian, not a theorist of canons. In the next section, I shall argue that his practical literary criticism distinguishes his work, analogously, from the theories of the new canon-makers.

The Literary Pleasures of the Common Reader

In Boswell's *Life of Samuel Johnson,* Johnson is seen distinguishing happiness from pleasure on two occasions. In the first of these, Johnson tells Boswell that abstaining from wine has diminished his pleasures in life, but not his happiness. "There is more happiness in being rational. . . . When we talk of pleasure, we mean sensual pleasure. . . .

60. Owen Chadwick, "The Religion of Samuel Johnson," *Yale University Library Gazette* 60 (April 1986): 119-36.

61. Kernan, *Printing, Technology, Letters, and Samuel Johnson,* 161.

Philosophers tell you, that pleasure is *contrary* to happiness." Shortly after this conversation, Johnson criticizes Mandeville's *Fable of the Bees* because it "reckons among vices every thing that gives pleasure." Johnson goes on to defend innocent pleasures, such as the pleasure of a garden. "The happiness of Heaven will be," says Johnson, "that pleasure and virtue will be perfectly consistent."[62] A year later, Boswell records a third conversation which bears on this subject as well. In April 1779 Boswell had criticized Johnson's eulogy on his friend, the actor David Garrick. His death, wrote Johnson, "has eclipsed the gaiety of nations and impoverished the publick stock of harmless pleasure" (*L* 2:21). To Boswell's criticism that the phrase "harmless pleasure" was "very tame," Johnson replied,

> Nay, sir, harmless pleasure is the highest praise. Pleasure is a word of dubious import; pleasure is in general dangerous, and pernicious to virtue; to be able therefore to furnish pleasure that is harmless, pleasure pure and unalloyed, is as great a power as man can possess.[63]

In the *Dictionary* Johnson defines pleasure as "Delight; gratification of the mind or senses." This "gratification" can be harmful or harmless, virtuous or vicious, as the conversations in Boswell indicate. He defines "happiness" as "felicity," a word with overtones of greater permanence in Johnson's usage. More telling is the *Dictionary*'s illustrative quotation for "happiness" from Richard Hooker:

> *Happiness* is that estate whereby we attain, so far as possibly may be attained, the full possession of that which simply for itself is to be desired, and containeth in it after an eminent sort the contentation of our desires, the highest degree of all our perfection.

Johnson felt desires strongly and enjoyed his pleasures passionately. But as his religious essays, sermons, diaries, and prayers indicate, he felt that happiness — the highest degree of human perfection — would be found only in heaven. The pleasures of literature, while related, are of a different order.

62. Boswell, *The Life of Samuel Johnson,* 3:245-46, 291-92.
63. Boswell, *The Life of Samuel Johnson,* 3:388.

An underlying unity in Johnson's life and work is part of the attraction and permanent relevance of the man, and it is discovered in his uncompromising integrity and commitment to the pursuit of truth. But the unity of his life does not result in a monism that attempts to explain all reality from the standpoint of a single principle or from the commitment to a single system. On the contrary, it is significant that Johnson, unlike modern ideological critics, considers it important at times to prevent his deepest commitments (which are moral and religious) from overwhelming his literary criticism. He believes that the critic should proceed empirically, by noting which poems and plays have pleased many people over the years, and then asking why this is so, even if their pleasures are at odds with his own moral commitments. His procedure is in this way the reverse of the new canon-makers', and the reverse as well of the role of "literary dictator" which they imagine for Johnson as the paradigmatic critic. Indeed, a skeptic would ask whether the categories of dictatorial power express the ideologues' own aims rather than the actual performance of Samuel Johnson.

"The end of writing is to instruct," writes Johnson in the "Preface to Shakespeare," and "the end of poetry is to instruct by pleasing" (*W* 7:67). "Writing" suggests Johnson's broad conception of "literature" — sermons, history, oratory, memoir, travel literature, essays — as well as the imaginative literature that the term "poetry" suggests. "Pleasure," as many excellent Johnson scholars have explained, is one of the richest words in Johnson's critical lexicon.[64] In his life of Milton, Johnson writes, "Poetry is the art of uniting pleasure with truth, by calling imagination to the help of reason" (*L* 1:170). The linkage between pleasure and truth is a tense one for Johnson at times, and his conver-

64. Jean H. Hagstrum, *Samuel Johnson's Literary Criticism* (Chicago: University of Chicago Press, 1952), and Leopold Damrosch, *The Uses of Johnson's Criticism* (Charlottesville: University of Virginia Press, 1976), are particularly noteworthy in this regard, as are articles such as W. R. Keast, "The Theoretical Foundations of Johnson's Criticism," in *Critics and Criticism: Ancient and Modern,* ed. R. S. Crane (Chicago: University of Chicago Press, 1952), and Clarence Tracy, "Johnson and the Common Reader," *Dalhousie Review* 57 (1977): 405-23. Hagstrum's book inquires at length into Johnson's description of the "sources" of poetic pleasure, in beauty, sublimity, pathos, variety, wit, etc. Damrosch investigates the significance of pleasure for Johnson's criticism as a whole.

sations with Boswell show the contradictions he experienced between pleasure and rational happiness.

In his life of Milton, Johnson links pleasure with moral knowledge, explaining that the indispensable elements of education are moral, not technical: "Whether we provide for action or conversation, whether we wish to be useful or pleasing, the first requisite is the religious and moral knowledge of right and wrong" (*L* 1:99). While this passage refers to education in general, the phrase "useful or pleasing," with its echo of Horace and its context in the life of Milton, has particular applicability to the poet. The poet must attain a high degree of religious and moral knowledge, thinks Johnson, if his work is to please and benefit mankind.

If pleasure is often inconsistent with rational happiness, it is often inconsistent as well with virtue and truth. Yet even while he applies the same moral standards to poetry as to life in general, Johnson simultaneously remains committed to the principle that poetry must give pleasure.[65] Those commitments to both pleasure and morality produce a tension in Johnson's criticism that one does not find in the writings of the new canon-makers. Their obsession with power drives out "pleasure" except perhaps as one of the many mystifications used by the powerful to obscure their "real" interests. By contrast, Johnson's well-known passage on Falstaff preserves his uncertain negotiations between pleasure and morality in both style and substance:

> But Falstaff unimitated, unimitable Falstaff, how shall I describe thee? Thou compound of sense and vice; of sense which may be admired but not esteemed, of vice which may be despised, but hardly detested. Falstaff is a character loaded with faults, and with those faults which naturally produce contempt. . . . Yet the man thus corrupt, thus despicable, makes himself necessary to the prince that despises him, by the most pleasing of all qualities, perpetual gaiety, by an unfailing power of exciting laughter. . . .
>
> The moral to be drawn from this representation is, that no man is more dangerous than he that with a will to corrupt, hath the power to please; and that neither wit nor honesty ought to think themselves

65. See Damrosch, *The Uses of Johnson's Criticism*, 222-23.

> safe with such a companion when they see Henry seduced by Falstaff. (*W* 7:523-24)

Literary pleasure is complex and practical for Johnson, and it deserves to be rendered in complex and beautiful prose. Johnson's uncertainty in describing Falstaff is intensified as he balances Falstaff's "sense" with his "vice," which are, in turn, themselves balanced: his admirable sense is nevertheless not estimable; his despicable vice is nevertheless not detestable. The proximity of Johnson's pleasure to his moral disapprobation is evident in the very rhythms and alliterations of the contrasting words — admired/esteemed; despised/detested. Above all, Falstaff pleases Prince Hal — and Johnson — by "the most pleasing of all qualities." The moral that Johnson draws is not that Shakespeare's Henry plays should be cut from the canon, or that the canon should be "expanded" to include, say, Puritan sermons on "wit and honesty." The moral is not identical with the pleasure of the text, but it is to be found within that pleasure, by a mind, like Johnson's, educated with the "requisite religious and moral knowledge of right and wrong." Pleasure and instruction are a unity in Johnson's life and work, but they function in complex ways that correspond to the complexity of human nature. Johnson's style preserves both the pleasure and the moral interest of this complexity.

For the new canon-makers, by contrast, literary ideology is generally simplistic and theoretical, and it attracts complicated and ugly prose, as a sentence drawn almost at random will illustrate:

> One of the major effects of prohibiting or inhibiting explicit evaluation is to forestall the exhibition and obviate the possible acknowledgement of divergent systems of value and thus to ratify, by default, established evaluative authority.[66]

Smith goes on to criticize Northrop Frye for maintaining that Milton is a "more rewarding . . . poet to work with than [Richard] Blackmore," whose works Johnson had asked to be included in the series of his *Lives.* "Surely," writes Smith, "if one were concerned with a question such as the relation of canonical and noncanonical texts in the system of literary

66. Smith, "Contingencies of Value," 11.

value in eighteenth-century England, one would find Blackmore just as rewarding and suggestive *to work with* as Milton."[67] No doubt Smith would consider Blackmore and Milton equally rewarding, for her concern is with "the system." Johnson, like most ordinary readers, is concerned with literature.[68]

For Johnson, the question that commands attention is why certain literature has given pleasure over many generations to many readers. He views his critical task not as primarily forming a taste for the literature he likes most, but as attempting to explain the sources of pleasure for the literature that has actually won wide recognition. On the other hand, Johnson does believe that the most lasting and therefore the most valuable sources of pleasure are found in truest representations of human nature: "Nothing can please many, and please long," he writes in the "Preface to Shakespeare," "but just representations of general nature" (*W* 7:61). Even here a tension is present in Johnson's criticism, for he has two differing conceptions of "nature," as Jean Hagstrum explains:

> Nature as particular reality carries with it no principle of universal value or formal organization. But it is instructive in that it is sober and unfanciful and keeps one's feet firmly planted on the ground. . . . Nature as ordered reality introduces universal psychological truth, the uniform and unchanging constitution of man's mind and emotions, and also those radically simple but fundamental moral truths which must provide the subject matter of all permanent literary art.[69]

To use Johnson's own words, nature as particular reality refers to "exhibiting the real state of sublunary nature, which partakes of good and evil" (*W* 7:66). Nature as ordered reality, by contrast, attempts to

67. Smith, "Contingencies of Value," 12, her emphasis.

68. It is of course worth asking why Johnson wished to include Blackmore in the collection of poets he edited. In view of Johnson's requests to include Watts (probably because of his pious life) and Pomfret (probably because of the great popularity of his poem "The Choice"), it seems probable to me that he had some hopes of popularizing one of Blackmore's pious poems, *The Creation,* and that he believed Blackmore's virtuous character needed defending against the contempt he had suffered at the pens of the Pope, Gay, and others (see *Lives,* 2:242-43, 252-55).

69. Hagstrum, *Samuel Johnson's Literary Criticism,* 74.

arrange that good and evil with reference to a deeper, moral reality. An "ordered" representation is "just" in the sense that it shows humanity's fulfillment in the rational, virtuous life. Both types of representations give pleasure, and both types are found in Shakespeare, but Johnson is apprehensive when so pleasing a writer as Shakespeare stops with the first type, as he seems to do in the character of Falstaff. Shakespeare "sacrifices virtue to convenience, and is so much more careful to please than to instruct, that he seems to write without any moral purpose. . . . [H]e makes no just distribution of good or evil, nor is always careful to shew in the virtuous a disapprobation of the wicked" (*W* 7:71). Johnson's honesty permits him to deny neither the pleasure which Shakespeare has given him and generations of other readers, nor the conflict between Shakespeare's texts and his own moral foundations.

When Johnson expresses reservations about writings that enjoy such wide popularity as Shakespeare's, he often tests his own reactions against those of an imagined "common reader." The common reader is not merely an allegory for popular sentiment, for he or she is more thoughtful. In his life of Addison, for instance, Johnson writes "About things on which the public thinks long it commonly attains to think right" (*L* 2:132). The judgment of the common reader, then, is "attained" after "long thought." His or her judgment is more than an arbitrary vote, as Leopold Damrosch explains, or a kind of "referendum of history, but rather an accumulating series of individual judgments that are active (good or bad), not passive (sweet or sour). Each reader must be his own common reader, trusting his immediate, but not unreflecting, response to what he reads."[70]

To some degree the common reader is, as Damrosch says, an abstraction of Johnson's own experience, but it may be more precise to say that he or she is one whose pleasures are even more immediate than Johnson's. This means on the one hand that the common reader may respond with immediate favor to temporary literary fashions, such as the popular odes of Cowley (which Johnson criticizes), or the novels of Herman Hesse of recent memory. The common reader may then be persuaded by Johnson's critical intelligence to examine certain works more closely to see whether the pleasure they give can last. The common

70. Damrosch, *The Uses of Johnson's Criticism,* 54.

reader's responsiveness to pleasure also means, on the other hand, that his long-standing acceptance of, say, the hymns of Isaac Watts serves as a corrective — with Johnson's full acknowledgement — of Johnson's critical reservations.

The longest description of the common reader comes in Johnson's life of Gray, whose work he generally considers unoriginal. Of Gray's "Elegy in a Country Churchyard," however, Johnson writes,

> I rejoice to concur with the common reader; for by the common sense of readers uncorrupted with literary prejudices, after all the refinements of subtilty and the dogmatism of learning, must be finally decided all claim to poetical honours. The *Church-yard* abounds with images which find a mirrour in every mind, and with sentiments to which every bosom returns an echo. (*L* 3:441)

The common reader, then, is someone with common sense but without the "prejudices" that grow up inside the world of professional literary criticism. His or her acceptance of particular writings is the ultimate *test* of their worth, although it remains for the critic to try to explain *why* those writings are pleasing. The second sentence indicates still more about the common reader: he is representative of "general nature" in its intellectual ("every mind") and emotional ("every bosom") aspects.

The common reader's favorable judgments of particular works over time suggest, empirically, that these works may have the most to teach about human nature. The common reader makes the choice; the critic is obliged as a teacher to explain why the choice was made. The common reader's choice gives the critic the opportunity to advance our knowledge of human nature — emotional, intellectual, and moral — by uncovering the permanent appeal of these works. Johnson admits that his knowledge and method of inquiry are inexact. He distinguishes his efforts as a literary critic from those of a scientist in the "Preface to Shakespeare":

> To works . . . of which the excellence is not absolute and definite, but gradual and comparative; to works not raised upon principles demonstrative and scientifick, but appealing wholly to observation and experience, no other test can be applied than length of duration and continuance of esteem. What mankind have long possessed they

have often examined and compared, and if they persist to value the possession, it is because frequent comparisons have confirmed opinion in its favour. (*W* 7:59-60)

Once again, "duration and continuance of esteem" is an empirical test of the continuing pleasure and likely value of a work, not an explanation of *why* it is valuable. Johnson's critical role is to take those works and examine them for himself, to see if he can give some rational account of their pleasure-giving powers. Note how different Johnson's words are from the interpretation of his words by Alvin Kernan:

> What is essentially at stake in the device of the fictional audience is the interpretative will, the power to control the meaning of a work by defining its audience and their response. . . .
>
> . . . From our vantage point in time, we can see that the poetics Johnson constructed out of and around his common reader is rickety as a philosophic system and fundamentally contradictory in its root assumptions that poetry tells truths about a "general nature" that is at the same time known to be too vast and metamorphic for human comprehension or accurate description. Furthermore, Johnson's poetics, for all its pretense of absolute empiricism, is no less historically determined than the neoclassical criticism it displaced. . . .
>
> . . . [T]he critical question [Johnson's *Lives*] most obviously answered was, put crudely, who owns poetry, or, more circumspectly, where does poetry originate and what determines its nature? . . . Not the king, not the nobles, not the booksellers and printers, not even the audience of common readers — though they are flattered into thinking themselves all-powerful even while they are being cleverly instructed — but the writer is the basic fact of letters.[71]

Kernan's words bear little resemblance to Johnson's critical practice. Johnson talks rarely about the "meaning" of a work. He takes works that have pleased, and especially works like Pope's *Rape of the Lock* that have pleased "readers of every class, from the critick to the waiting maid," and "[inquires] from what sources the power of pleasing is derived" (*L* 3:232). Johnson does not want to "control" the interpreta-

71. Kernan, *Printing, Technology, Letters, and Samuel Johnson*, 233, 239, 272-73.

tion or acceptance of literary texts, and in *Idler* 61 he satirizes his fictional critic, Dick Minim, for that very failing: Minim "has formed a plan for an academy of criticism, where every work of imagination may be read before it is printed, and which shall authoritatively direct the theatres what pieces to receive or reject, to exclude or to revive" (*W* 2:190). Johnson's poetics is not a "system"; it is a mode of inquiry, and differs from systems in the same way that all traditional academic inquiry differs from ideologies, as I have argued in the introduction. Johnson's immense interest in the book trade, particularly evident in the *Lives of the Poets,* is complex and detailed; it cannot be reduced to the simplistic categories of "owning" poetry (or owning "culture," as Kaplan puts it),[72] as if the relations between literature and economics were straightforward. Johnson is indeed interested in human nature, and he believes strongly that the literature valued by the common reader has pleased, in part, because it tells him something valuable about himself. If one takes the opposite point of view, that the *Rape of the Lock* tells us nothing about human nature, or that human nature is too "vast and metamorphic" for comprehension by poets, why should anyone read poetry? In fact, I believe this is the common sense conclusion of many students today, as attested by the historic decline in humanities majors: since their teachers no longer believe poems teach them about human nature, why bother with a course in poetry? To listen to a literature professor develop his or her own, idiosyncratic critique of the "systems" of culture?

This is the continental divide between the new canon-makers and critics like Johnson. In a 1988 essay for the *Bulletin* of the Associated Departments of English — a useful journal with regard to trends in literary studies — Cyrena Pondrom asks, "is politics the chief determinant in the debate about . . . the canon," specifically with regard to feminist criticism of the canon?[73] Her answer is, well, yes: either your entire worldview must undergo a "paradigm shift" on a parallel with Thomas Kuhn's familiar (and, as here, often misapplied) methodological shift during a legitimate scientific revolution; or you will be viewed

72. Kaplan and Rose, *The Canon and the Common Reader,* xix.

73. Cyrena Pondrom, "Gender and (Re)formation of the Canon: Is Politics All?" *ADE Bulletin* (Winter 1988): 21-27.

as the political enemy of the new canon-makers. To writers like Pondrom and Kernan, convinced that a rational system can overcome the uncertain and conflicting elements within empirical criticism like Johnson's, the "Preface to the *Dictionary*" is particularly apropos, even if Johnson's explicit subject is the uncertain senses of words rather than the uncertainties of literary evaluation:

> [T]his uncertainty is not to be imputed to me, who do not form but register the language; who do not teach men how they should think, but relate how they have hitherto expressed their thoughts. . . . [T]o enchain syllables and to lash the wind are equally the undertakings of pride, unwilling to measure its desires by its strength.[74]

As Johnson "registers" rather than "forms" the language in the *Dictionary*, so his criticism accepts rather than "owns" the poetry that actually pleases himself and others. To fix literary criticism within an ideological system would have struck him as an undertaking of pride.

Johnson was well aware of the temptations to pride that particularly afflict the literary world (in Johnson's broad sense of "literature"). In Sermon 8, he writes:

> There is perhaps no class of men, to whom the precept given by the Apostle to his converts against too great confidence in their understandings, may be more properly inculcated, than those who are dedicated to the profession of literature. . . .
>
> With [manual laborers], . . . a man of learning has such frequent opportunities of comparing himself; and is so strongly incited, by that comparison, to indulge the contemplation of his own superiority; that it is not to be considered as wonderful, that vanity creeps in upon him. . . . (*W* 14:88)

In place of such pride, Johnson recommends that the scholar acquire the very qualities that are needed today: "patience in enquiry; eagerness of knowledge; and willingness to be instructed; a due submission to greater abilities and longer experience" (*W* 14:90).

74. Samuel Johnson, "Preface to *A Dictionary of the English Language*," in *Samuel Johnson: Selected Poetry and Prose,* ed. Frank Brady and W. K. Wimsatt (Berkeley: University of California Press, 1977), 292, 294.

To the extent that the new canon-makers present their views as an ideological critique of the past, it seems that one must choose between their presuppositions and Johnson's own explanation of why certain books continue to be read. To my knowledge, none of them takes seriously the element that Johnson considered crucial to the experience of reading, namely, pleasure. As Clarence Tracy writes in his excellent essay, Johnson thought of the author as a "kind of public servant whose job it is to bring pleasure of the most valuable kind to a wide range of readers."[75] Johnson had harsh words for criticism that ignored pleasure: "the purpose of a writer is to be read, and the criticism which would destroy the power of pleasing must be blown aside" (*L* 3:240). Let us ask: have the recent disputes over "the canon" tended to increase or diminish literature's "power of pleasing"?

The Limits to Literary Criticism as "Canonization"

The parallels between Johnson's criticism and the history of the New Testament canon can now be assessed more precisely. First, the widespread acceptance of certain secular writings commends them to Johnson's attention as a critic, similar to the way the acceptance of certain New Testament writings commended themselves to the early fathers. Second, the remarkable unanimity of the early church's New Testament canon is parallel to the remarkably consistent (but by no means unanimous) recognition of certain literary works by Johnson's "common reader." Neither the early Christians nor Johnson's common reader acknowledged a controlling authority that dictated their choice of texts.

After recognizing the common reader's pleasure in certain texts, Johnson's task as a critic begins. He must inquire into "what sources the power of pleasing is derived." Johnson tries to find a critical vocabulary ("nature," "newness," "virtue," "beauty," "pathos," "sublimity," etc.) that will account for the pleasures of particular writings. A passage from Johnson's *Lives,* attempting to define the "wit" that is lacking in Cowley, illustrates this second step:

75. Tracy, "Johnson and the Common Reader," 422.

> If by a more noble and more adequate conception that be considered as Wit which is at once natural and new, that which though not obvious is, upon its first production, acknowledged to be just; if it be that, which he that never found it, wonders how he missed; to wit of this kind the metaphysical poets have seldom risen. (*L* 1:19-20)

In trying to account for the relative permanence of some poems and the gradual rejection of others, Johnson's procedure is somewhat similar, in a very limited sense, to the way the early fathers expected to find the "rule of faith" in any writing that deserved the name of Scripture. Already the parallel between Johnson's criticism and the canon is quite shaky though, for where the fathers used the "rule of faith" as a criterion for canonicity, Johnson largely accepts the judgments of the past and merely tries to account for them. The passage on "wit" attempts to explain why the common reader of his day had rejected so much metaphysical poetry. It does not attempt to establish a particular definition of wit as a criterion of future poetry. In this case, his critical vocabulary asks how a particular kind of poetry produces pleasure or new (or rediscovered) knowledge of human nature.

Johnson's critical terms, then, are not criteria at all, in the sense of ruling poems in or out of a canon, but rather the very tools that begin to make literary study into academic inquiry. Indeed, when Johnson finds his terms beginning to function as criteria for dictating how an author "should" write, he takes a self-critical backward step to "nature" or to "pleasure." For instance, of Pope's *Essay on Man,* Johnson first writes, "never were penury of knowledge and vulgarity of sentiment so happily disguised" (*L* 3:243). But shortly afterward he concludes:

> The vigorous contraction of some thoughts, the luxuriant amplification of others, the incidental illustrations, and sometimes the dignity, sometimes the softness of the verses, enchain philosophy, suspend criticism, and oppress judgment by overpowering pleasure. (*L* 3:244)

Johnson is interested in learning why Pope's *Essay on Man* retains its hold on readers, and his first five phrases give five different explanations. He is not interested in dictating its place in or out of a supposed canon of English poetry. To be sure, Johnson is highly critical of the poem's superficial intellectual basis: "the poet was not sufficiently master of his subject," says Johnson tersely, and we know how much he detested the rationalistic, "natural religion" of the poem (*L* 3:242). But since a couple of generations of readers had found pleasure in the poem, Johnson seeks a vocabulary to account for it. Terms like "vigorous," "luxuriant," and "dignity" may always be questioned, to see whether they actually account for pleasure in the experience of the common reader. Moreover, the pleasure may vary in different generations of readers, as the history of the metaphysical poets indicates, or be lost altogether. Johnson found pleasure in novels and poems by women writers. He would no doubt favor any tendency to increase literary pleasure by reading the works of a wider variety of authors — if the emphasis of such tendencies remained on finding genuine enjoyment. Johnson's emphasis is on literary pleasure. He does not emphasize — or even mention — an unchanging collection of authors whose authority must be legitimated by a dominant intellectual class wielding arbitrary criteria.

Disagreement with previous critics or with the common reader, and questions over the value of particular poems call for rational discussion in Johnson. Perhaps this is similar to questions over particular books in the New Testament. But neither the early fathers nor Johnson imagine an authoritative council or academy issuing "fiats," to use Christine Froula's word, to control their audience. The early fathers were concerned with the contents of particular writings, and Johnson is concerned with the qualities of particular poems, but neither he nor they are interested in an authoritative *collection,* as such, of writings or writers.

The early fathers gradually came to recognize twenty-seven books, no more and no less, as the authentic witness to the gospel of Jesus Christ, but here the parallel to Johnson's criticism completely breaks down. Perhaps the example of Homer can illustrate the point. Homer's hold on the public depends upon the availability of a pleasing English translation for each age, which is the basis for Johnson's praise of Pope's *Iliad.* But if a generation or two goes by without a pleasing translation, Homer will drop out of favor for a while. This Johnson would lament, for he knows the power of the original. If other works drop out of the reading public's favor, as Otway's plays have, and others return, such as the poems of the metaphysicals, Johnson would not be surprised. He would want to know why, but he would not treat the loss of Otway in any sense like the loss of, say, the Gospel according to St. John, or the recovery of Donne like the recovery of a third letter to the Corinthians. In fact, Johnson's manner of recounting a portion of Pope's life seems almost insouciant about the possible loss of some of his major poetry. Pope had threatened to quit writing altogether in 1732 because of his treatment by literary critics. This prompts Johnson to comment:

> Pope had been flattered till he thought himself one of the moving powers in the system of life. When he talked of laying down his pen, those who sat round him intreated and implored, and self-love did not suffer him to suspect that they went away and laughed. (*L* 3:154)

But Johnson laughed. His gesture seems to laugh away the revised *Dunciad*, the "Epistle to Dr. Arbuthnot," and the Horatian Satires. Johnson's laughter is moved by Pope's pretentious self-estimate, which suggested that his works called the "system of life" into being. Pope is not a "moving power" like God, and his writings are not "canonical." To speak of literature as a "canon," however, comes very close to presupposing that the author speaks with something like the voice of God. Johnson's response to an analogous instance of self-inflation is laughter.

The use of "canon" to refer to secular in addition to sacred texts was introduced into English in 1768 by David Ruhnken. He was translating the Greek word *pinakes* (not the Greek cognate word *kanones*), which more accurately means "list" or "index." Ruhnken found the word was used by Alexandrian literary critics of the third and second centuries B.C. to refer to lists of the best poets in various categories.[76] Homer heads the list of four heroic poets, and various other poets are named in iambic, elegiac, and other poetic genres:

> [T]he chief responsibility for drawing up the lists was that of the two editors of Homer already mentioned, Aristarchus and Aris-

76. W. D. Davies, "Reflections about the Use of the Old Testament in the New in Its Historical Context," *Jewish Quarterly Review* 74, no. 2 (1983): 122-23.

> tophanes. . . . [T]he former especially did not reveal the kind of reverence before unchangeable texts which we associate with the scribes of Israel, and . . . the interests of both were mainly textual, lexicographical, and literary. Such men are unlikely to have been moved by the deep religious concerns which govern Jews in fixing their canon. By literary discrimination *(krisis, enkrinein),* they were primarily concerned to confirm the fame of the great authors of their people's past and not to provide a literature to govern their people in all the details of their lives in the present. The textual and so-called "canonical" intentions in Alexandria are perhaps not to be entirely distinguished from those of Judaism and Christianity, but they certainly do not share the same dimensions as in both the latter.[77]

The parallel between these lists and the biblical writings (here, the Hebrew Scriptures) originates in a simple lexicographical error. In the view of the eminent biblical scholar W. D. Davies, the parallel is a very weak one.

Johnson had no canon of English literature in the sense in which that term is used by the new canon-makers, as an authoritative collection of writings.[78] He did indeed have a canon — the canon of the Bible — and the possession of a real canon and a real religious faith, practically speaking, changed his perspective on all other writings.

Johnson's criticism suggests that a "biblical poetics" will not equate poetry with the Bible or vice versa. The literary curriculum can never function as the canon, nor would anyone who accepts very much of Johnson's literary criticism wish it to. Johnson returns us to pleasure, and if so devout a Christian as Johnson can found his literary study in pleasure, perhaps a biblical poetics can learn from his example. As I shall explain in the next chapter, *Paradise Lost* will offer a large opportunity to explore the significance of pleasure.

To Johnson, who believed in the Anglican Articles of Religion, Scripture is different in kind from all other writings because it alone

77. Davies, "Reflections," 124.

78. In perhaps the best general article on the current debates over "canonicity," Wendell V. Harris argues, "The processes by which specific collections of Jewish and Christian writings became closed canons . . . are largely irrelevant to the question of the literary canon" ("Canonicity," *PMLA* 106 [1991]: 110).

teaches the way of salvation. He illustrates this in some diary entries, not unusual in themselves, but significant in that they were recorded in 1779, when he was hard at work on the *Lives of the Poets:*

> EASTER EVE. APR. 3. 11 P.M. This is the time of my annual review, and annual resolution. The review is comfortless. Little done. Part of the life of Dryden, and the Life of Milton have been written; but my mind has neither been improved nor enlarged. . . .
> EASTER DAY. Transc. 1779.
> Purposes Apr 4.
>
> 1 To rise at eight, or as soon as I can
> 2 To read the scriptures
> 3 To study Religion.
>
> (*W* 1:295, 297)

These are not the reflections of a man who is trying to control his audience by establishing a canon of secular literature. Viewed from the perspective of eternal happiness, the intellectual progress he made in writing the lives of Dryden and Milton is of no account, and the twenty-two prefaces published that spring are not even mentioned. Indeed, what is remarkable in view of Johnson's religious intensity here (and throughout the *Diaries*) is that he is capable of taking such unaffected and prodigious pleasure in literature in the first place.

If one didn't know better, one might attribute Johnson's diary reflections to a man who hardly cared for literature. Hogarth comes close to this view of Johnson when he remarks, "That man . . . is not contented with believing the Bible, but he fairly resolves, I think, to believe nothing *but* the Bible."[79] A pointed illustration of a sensibility like Johnson's comes from the life of another critic, C. S. Lewis, who shares many of Johnson's critical and religious characteristics. The words are those of John Wain, a student of Lewis and an excellent Johnsonian in his own right:

> [F. R.] Leavis once said to someone that Lewis "hated literature."

79. George Birbeck Hill, ed., *Johnson Miscellanies* (Oxford: Clarendon, 1897), 1:241.

> When I first heard this, I thought it merely an absurd remark to make about someone so devotedly literate, so seldom found without a book in his hands, as Lewis. But of course from Leavis's own specialized point of view it is a meaningful judgment; it means, basically, that Lewis was content to enjoy literature and take it as he found it, without trying to make literary study into a priestcraft. . . . To a humanist like Leavis or myself, great literature will inevitably come to occupy something like a body of scripture — a record of what mankind has found worth living and worth dying for. . . .[80]

This chapter has suggested that if there really is such a thing as "Scripture," then no other writing is very much like it. Many of those who are most earnest today about reshaping our concept of older literature use the term "canon" a great deal, without knowing or caring very much about how Scripture actually came to be accepted, or how it continues to make its claims on the believer. Secular literature cannot become a "canon," but it can become an idol in the hands of a self-appointed priestcraft.

In *Towards a Christian Poetics,* Michael Edwards notes that in Northrop Frye's taxonomy each literary category has its complement in a "demonic parody" of itself.[81] Thus the social renewal that one finds at the end of an authentic tragic cycle, like that of the *Oresteia,* has its complement in the parody of social renewal in *Sejanus,* where the fall of the political tyrant issues in even greater cruelties than before. The new canon-makers write as if literature, sacred and secular, has been valued by believers and by readers because it enabled them to exert power over others. If they succeed in persuading large numbers of literature teachers, their position will be "correct" in the parodic sense that they will no doubt exert power over the choice and interpretations of texts. But there is also power in literary pleasure that "blows aside" the distortions of ideology. It is refreshing, then, in a day like ours, to return to Samuel Johnson. He reminds us to read for pleasure again,

80. Joseph Epstein, ed., *Masters: Portraits of Great Teachers* (New York: Basic Books, 1981), 249, 250.

81. Michael Edwards, *Towards a Christian Poetics* (Grand Rapids, Mich.: Wm. B. Eerdmans, 1984), 31-34.

even as he reminds us of the limits of pleasure when viewed from the perspective of eternal happiness.

As we shall see in the next chapter, Milton's choice of locating the origins of language in the pleasures of Eden goes to the very root of current ideological criticism and offers a powerful alternative beginning point for literary study.

CHAPTER 3

Blessing and Naming in Genesis and Paradise Lost

A Biblical Poetics as an Alternative to Ideological Feminism

THE STRONG implication of Johnson's criticism is that no other writing can truly resemble Scripture. The uniqueness of God's word is the first half of a biblical poetics. From very early times, however, Jewish and Christian authors have tried to discern the significance of the biblical word for their own words. In so doing, they encountered all of the problems of our current ideologies, often failing, sometimes succeeding brilliantly, as John Milton does.

The more successful of these authors begin (like Johnson) with a firm sense of the uniqueness of God's word, combined with a conviction of both the goodness of creation and the prevalence of sin. An overemphasis on sin, however, sometimes leads them to reject all secular culture, including all works of literature, or to regard them as so tainted by sin as to be useful only as negative examples. The way of rejection is seen in Tertullian's famous rhetorical question, "What hath Athens to do with Jerusalem?" and in Jerome's agonized dream in which God says, "Thou art a Ciceronian and not a Christian." An overemphasis on the goodness of creation, by contrast, sometimes leads them to accept virtually all pagan writings, read very inadequately through the lenses of allegory, fabricated history, and harmonizations of mythology and

Scripture. Justin Martyr tried to make the gospel palatable to the Roman elite, for instance, by drawing parallels between Zeus and God the father, and between the Mercury as the "word" of the gods and Jesus as the word incarnate. The Alexandrian Jew Philo and some of the early church fathers went so far as to suppose that the Greeks got their ideas from Moses — a parallel to the Afrocentrist ideology that the Greeks stole their ideas from Egypt, as I shall note in the next chapter. Because they believed that all truth proceeded directly and immediately from the one true God, Justin and Philo presupposed that all good poets and philosophers must, on some level, ratify biblical revelation. Starting with similar presuppositions, the medieval allegorizers associated with the *Ovide moralisé* rewrote classical myths to make them compatible with Christian revelation.[1]

Both the ways of extreme rejection and extreme acceptance have parallels to current ideological criticism. In recent writing on *Paradise Lost,* extreme feminists go out of their way to reject scholarship that highlights Milton's description of the mutuality between husband and wife, and to demystify his extraordinarily exalted portrait of Eve. In rejecting Joseph Wittreich's description of Milton as a "potent ally" of feminism, Mary Crane reproves his attempt to preserve Milton as a "political, cultural, and literary authority."[2] From within the pure ideology of feminism, of course, Crane is correct: anyone who represents and commends "authority" from the past represents an unacceptable "sexual politics." At the opposite extreme, *Paradise Lost* continually inspires ingenious, but partial, feminist readings that accept the poem

1. Rosemond Tuve treats this issue in *Allegorical Imagery: Some Mediaeval Books and Their Posterity* (Princeton: Princeton University Press, 1966), especially chapter 4, "Imposed Allegory," pp. 219-333. I do not mean to suggest that the history of allegoresis is void of solid achievement, beginning with the several allegorical readings in the New Testament (Gal. 4:24-25; 1 Cor. 10:4; 1 Tim. 5:18) and continuing through (for instance) the allegorization of Song of Songs into a poem of divine love. Like the medieval allegorizers, current ideologues distort older literature largely out of a laudable desire to find contemporary significance in it. My contention, as I shall explain, is that the difference between true exegesis and the allegorizing of imagery (biblical or classical) is parallel to the difference between true literary study and ideological criticism.

2. Mary Thomas Crane, "Milton's Gaze," *Review* 11 (1989): 289-300.

by allegorizing certain portions and harmonizing others with feminism. Adam's narrative of Eve's creation, for instance, is turned into an allegory that "dramatizes an archetypal womb envy as constitutive of male identity."[3] In a related way, the ideologically difficult fact that Eve narrates the story of her creation before Adam does[4] is harmonized with feminism by suggesting that the woman must first articulate her own subjectivity and autonomy so that the patriarchal order can later come along and teach her the values of submission.[5] Whether *Paradise Lost* is rejected as incompatible with feminism or accepted through some allegorical interpretation, in neither case does ideological criticism allow the poem an integrity of its own.

There is a third, intermediate range of options that Christians have used to relate the biblical word to human words — or, more broadly, to relate Christ and culture.[6] This range of options between outright acceptance and outright rejection considers how Christ transforms or acts in dialectical tension with human culture. Milton's relation to culture is to be found here. His disposition toward cultural forms and products, past and present, is linked to the complex notion of "pleasure" (as Johnson will use that word in the eighteenth century), or more precisely, to the biblical language of "blessing." Following John Calvin in many of his attitudes towards culture, Milton sees himself as a "warfaring Christian," in the words of the *Areopagitica,* in transforming the area of human endeavor that God has given him. He transforms

3. Christine Froula, "When Eve Reads Milton: Undoing the Canonical Economy," in *Canons,* ed. Robert von Hallberg (Chicago: University of Chicago Press, 1984), 149-75.

4. John Milton, *Paradise Lost,* 4.440-91; hereafter abbreviated as *PL.*

5. Mary Nyquist, "Gynesis, Genesis, Milton's Eve," in *Cannibals, Witches, and Divorce: Estranging the Renaissance,* ed. Marjorie Garber (Baltimore: Johns Hopkins University Press, 1987), 147-208.

6. A full treatment of this subject may be found in H. Richard Niebuhr, *Christ and Culture* (New York: Harper, 1951). For the general topic of a biblical poetics from late antiquity through the Middle Ages, see Ernst R. Curtius, *European Literature and the Latin Middle Ages,* trans. Willard R. Trask (Princeton: Princeton University Press, 1953), especially pp. 39-48, 72-75, 203-46, 362-64, 446-67. Barbara Lewalski studies the topic with regard to the lyric poetry of Milton's contemporaries in *Protestant Poetics and the Seventeenth-Century Religious Lyric* (Princeton: Princeton University Press, 1979).

the available genres — heroic epic in *Paradise Lost,* classical elegy in "Lycidas," tragedy in *Samson Agonistes,* and many smaller genres within these poems.[7] He transforms the heroic ideal from that of a martial hero, like Achilles, to that of the self-sacrificing Christ. He adds his voice to the transformation of the ideal relation between man and woman from courtly lovers to married couple, spiritual friends, and vocational partners.

In all of his transforming acts, Milton maintains a critical relationship to the pagan literature of the past: it potentially bears the traces of God's blessing in creation, most obviously through the "light of nature," natural law, and conscience, which God bestowed on pagan as well as Jewish and Christian peoples; yet pagan culture also bears the deep traces of sin, and Milton's task is to transform the very tools of literary creation along with its content. In his own poetic acts he must discipline his art to "the Word" — to the incarnate word, Jesus Christ, as described in the written word of Scripture, and as present in the author through the Holy Spirit.

The significance of this procedure is not isolated to Milton's poetry. It also suggests a critical way of reading literature beyond Milton's own verse, a way that lies between the outright acceptance and outright rejection of past literature. This way differs fundamentally from the method of allegorizing literature so that it ratifies all of one's prior beliefs, for while it relates the act of reading to ultimate values, it also requires one to refrain from translating the text in such a way that it confirms those values in every significant instance.

This intermediate range of critical options does not exist in ideological criticism, whether feminist, Marxist, or any other variety. At first glance, the ideologies seem to attempt the transformation of literature in the way I have described. But this would presuppose seeing something good, something really good, in the culture of the past, and especially in the culture whose primary commitments are different from one's own. Even Jerome, who maintained that he rejected pagan literature for himself, was at least troubled by his sincere love for Cicero's writing, and went so far as to recommend pagan literature for apologetic

7. See Barbara K. Lewalski, *"Paradise Lost" and the Rhetoric of Literary Forms* (Princeton: Princeton University Press, 1985).

and other purposes.[8] For Calvin and Milton, the transformation of culture presupposed seeing something good in pagan culture — and they did. For the ideologues, it would presuppose seeing something good in "traditional" culture, and more particularly in the Western culture of the past — but they do not.

For the current ideologues, Milton and other commonly taught authors are "good" only insofar as they allow an allegoresis on their texts — which, of course, every text will do in the hands of a clever reader. For Christine Froula, Eve is read as an empowering allegory of female subjective authority, and she extends an evangelistic invitation to her critical respondent, Edward Pechter, to convert: "His gender need not constitute an insuperable impediment to his reading and writing feminist criticism. . . . [A woman speaking] does not demand that men be silent; she only asks that men cease speaking in such a way as to silence her."[9] It transpires, however, that all approaches that fall short of feminist ideology (to say nothing of approaches critical of that ideology) do speak in these forbidden ways: after all, "'Humanist,' 'universal' culture," says Froula earlier, has been criticized by many others — presumably by the ideological allies of feminism — for its being "white, male, ruling class, and ethnocentric."[10] Similarly, Mary Nyquist sees in Milton the allegorical embodiment of "English literature's paradigmatic patriarch,"[11] whose texts she can then proceed to "interrogate." But "interrogating the text" is fundamentally different from allowing the text to speak to the reader. In the first instance, the reader places the text beneath the lamp of the investigating officer, as it were, under suspicion of racism, classism, and sexism. In the second instance, allowing the text to speak to the reader assumes that it has something new to say, to recall one of Johnson's criteria for literary excellence, and that the reader would be the poorer for not listening. For the ideologue, then, the only excellence of *Paradise Lost* is its

8. For Jerome's complex relationship to pagan literature, see Curtius, *European Literature and the Latin Middle Ages.*

9. Christine Froula, "Pechter's Specter: Milton's Bogey Writ Small; or, Why Is He Afraid of Virginia Woolf?" *Critical Inquiry* 11 (September 1984): 178.

10. Froula, "Pechter's Specter," 174-75.

11. Nyquist, "Gynesis, Genesis, Milton's Eve," 167.

symbolic, "paradigmatic" status, whose use lies in the possibility of placing Milton in odd, comparative relationships with writers like Richard Blackmore (Smith), Isak Dinesen (Froula), and Mary Astell.[12]

The intermediate range of options for a biblical poetics, between outright acceptance or rejection of culture, is rather parallel to traditional, humanistic literary study. Reading Milton does not convert most people to Christianity, any more than reading Homer converts them to paganism. Nor does *Paradise Lost* convert Catholic readers to Protestantism, or royalists to republicanism. Instead, most readers adopt a critical attitude to the poem, finding its attraction in myriad ways. Here are two examples: Noting the initial attraction of Satan and his subsequent repulsiveness, contrasted with the initial coldness of God and his later ability to inspire joy, Edward Pechter remarks the general critical "recognition that the tremendous power of the poem lies in its capacity to involve its readers in its material in contradictory ways that demand action and choice."[13] Regarding Milton's treatment of marriage, Joan Webber remarks, "For [Milton] it is the basic, central figure of the way the world is, and of the way it could be — sometimes in a pattern of higher and lower status, sometimes in a balance of equals, sometimes stressing the separateness of the partners and sometimes their unity."[14] Neither author displays an uncritical attitude toward Milton's religious, domestic, or political views. But both do find in his poetry something good, something worth knowing about human actions and human relationships.

By contrast, "interrogating" and "problematizing" Milton, to use the language of the ideological critics, is closer to what the Christian allegorists do to Virgil and Ovid: they interpret the text against the backdrop of the one, true critique and find that critique (by examples positive and negative) in the text. In addition, their procedure, like

12. Nyquist uses Astell in a different version of the essay to which I refer in this chapter, printed in *Re-membering Milton,* ed. Mary Nyquist and Margaret W. Ferguson (New York: Methuen, 1987), 123-24.

13. Edward Pechter, "When Pechter Reads Froula Pretending She's Eve Reading Milton: or, New Feminist Is But Old Priest Writ Large," *Critical Inquiry* 11 (September 1984): 165.

14. Joan Webber, "The Politics of Poetry: Feminism and *Paradise Lost,*" *Milton Studies* 14 (1980): 15.

that of the medieval allegorists, has made the poetry largely inaccessible to great numbers of teachers and students. While specialists know the errors and partial readings of current ideological criticism, for many others, Milton has no existence apart from his "well-known misogyny."[15] To overcome these partial readings, an immense amount of distinguished, humane scholarship, mostly by women, has been produced.[16] These scholars have argued that a full reading of Milton commends gender relations which, while hierarchical, are based not on power, but on complementarity, common purpose, reason, and holiness. Milton believes in the spiritual equality of the sexes, they point out, and rejects the double standard of sexual conduct. He praises domestic virtues over traditionally male, martial virtues and sees roles for women beyond matrimony. Along with contemporary Reformation figures, he endorses marriage as the source of civic virtue, rather than seeing it as a necessary evil or primarily as a means of controlling sexual passion. The rational capacities of Milton's Lady in *Comus,* for example, are above those of her male tempter. The intellectual range of Eve is far greater than that of any future male, and she listens with understanding to an angel describe their conditional residence in Paradise, the fall of Satan, and the creation of the world (*PL* 5.469–7.640). In writing about many of these roles and capacities, Milton was at the forefront of advancing women's opportunities and status; in some of them, he was unique. Except among specialists, however, the effect of pointing out these aspects of Milton has been

15. Sandra Gilbert, "Patriarchal Poetry and Women Readers: Reflections on Milton's Bogey," *PMLA* 93 (1978): 375.

16. In particular, works already mentioned by Joan Webber and Barbara Lewalski, as well as Diane McColley, *Milton's Eve* (Urbana: University of Illinois Press, 1983); Anne Ferry, "Milton's Creation of Eve," *Studies in English Literature* 28 (1988): 113-32; Mary Ann Radzinowicz, *Milton's Epics and the Book of Psalms* (Princeton: Princeton University Press, 1989); and Kathleen Swaim, *Before and after the Fall: Contrasting Modes in "Paradise Lost"* (Amherst: University of Massachusetts Press, 1986). Additional important books and articles on this subject are Philip Gallagher, *Milton, Misogyny, and the Bible* (Columbia: University of Missouri Press, 1990); Joseph Wittreich, *Feminist Milton* (Ithaca: Cornell University Press, 1987); and William Shullenberger, "Wrestling with the Angel: *Paradise Lost* and Feminist Criticism," *Milton Quarterly* 20, no. 3 (1986): 69-85.

quite minimal, as the following representative comment from *College English* suggests:

> Any contemporary course in Milton that does not acknowledge and address the ways in which Milton's *Paradise Lost* is implicated in the ongoing oppression of women in our society is, as I see it, condemned to reaffirm that oppression.[17]

Those who love poetry, including the poetry of Milton, sometimes seem exasperated at their inability to make any headway at correcting these misreadings. Diane McColley, impatient with the politicized reading of Milton, has this sharp comment:

> If we are to read Milton's poem with pleasure we need to get rid of Satan's dreary habit of thinking himself impaired by another's goodness. . . . Some censure the slight imparity of perfections of Eve and Adam without lamenting our general inferiority to them both. Some think Eve unfree who do not protest the massive oppression of psychological theories that put each person and all action and affection into a few sexual categories and locate the genesis of all creativity in the vicinity of that portion of the male body on which 'Adam sat.' Some denounce Milton's fidelity to the scriptural idea of the family who accept the stupendous repression of spirit with which much criticism ignores the wellspring of holiness from which all value issues in *Paradise Lost.*[18]

In a more general critique of recent feminist works, Helen Vendler remarks that such criticism "has never been strong on delight, while art is."[19]

Rather than attempt yet once more to argue Milton's worth in terms acceptable to our time, I believe a biblical poetics can place the debate in a new perspective. This perspective will help to explain both

17. Ronald Strickland, "Confrontational Pedagogy and Traditional Literary Studies," *College English* 52, no. 3 (1990): 297.

18. Dennis Danielson, ed., *The Cambridge Companion to Milton* (Cambridge: Cambridge University Press, 1989), 159-60, 163.

19. Helen Vendler, "Feminism and Literature," *New York Review of Books,* 31 May 1990, 20.

the intractability of the feminist critique of Milton and the frustration of his defenders. More important, it can lead to new insight into Milton. The source of this poetics is in two words that flow almost unnoticed from the pens of McColley and Vendler, but which are central to a biblical poetics, to Johnson, and to Milton: "pleasure" and "delight."

Both sides in the debate about Milton recognize that the central dispute is over his view of marriage, especially marriage before the fall. What has not been recognized is that Milton's poetic descriptions of marriage in particular and cultural institutions in general are most accurately understood through the biblical language of "blessing." This language is central to the "common expositors" of Genesis whom Milton had read and to whose interpretations he responded in the divorce tracts. Moreover, "blessing" and related concepts provided Milton with a way of distinguishing what is essential for the salvation of the elect, from that which extends the blessings of God to mankind generally. The language of blessing enabled Milton, his contemporaries, and his Protestant forebears (such as Calvin) to arrive at a critical appreciation of pagan literature and secular culture, including its pleasures.[20] In so doing, they provided a realm of limited autonomy for culture without severing its link to Christian understanding.

This chapter will build on the work of Mary Ann Radzinowicz, who has shown how Milton's epics reflect his discovery of a "poesis" in the genres, themes, and styles of the Psalms. It will build as well on the work of Georgia Christopher, who has illustrated how the Reformed doctrine of "the word" is a crucial source of poetic energy in Milton. But in addition to filling out the historical background of Milton's verse, I will argue that the language of blessing can provide the terms for a nonideological approach to Milton, and for literary criticism in general, by establishing a realm of true autonomy for the study and advancement of culture.

20. "Secular" in my usage describes any realm with an authentic existence outside the church. *Paradise Lost* is therefore a secular poem, while the *Magnificat* is not. The vocation of poet (like that of a farmer or an astronomer) is a sacred one, as Milton believes, but its institutions, sciences, and products are secular. The word "pagan" describes anyone who has never heard the message of the Old or New Testaments. Neither "secular" nor "pagan" has negative connotations.

In feminism and ideological criticism generally, by contrast, there is no such realm of autonomy. All statements and all cultural artifacts are part of either the structure of oppression or the effort of liberation. "The critique of patriarchal/canonical authority," writes Froula, "assumes that literary authority is a mode of social authority and that literary value is inseparable from ideology."[21] To use the parallel theological terms, everything is a matter of deliverance from sin. There is no realm of blessing, no area of pleasure. Most nonideological students find this approach to literature very tiresome, but that doesn't explain or answer it. In fact, student complaints about the tedium of politicized education is reinterpreted as "resistance" by certain feminists, and has even become something of a mark of distinction.[22]

More broadly, ideology is fundamentally incapable of building a culture or tradition, because the act of building (as opposed to criticizing and revolting) presupposes that the oppression has, in some very important senses, ended, and that individuals are free to create. There can be no "history" or tradition or culture if every act is one of deliverance from oppression. The feminist Cyrena Pondrom puts it this way: until "the consequence of this [feminist] revolution in discourse becomes clear and the values it portends become the possible possession of us all . . . the sense in which politics is all will be particularly acute. . . ."[23] That moment — the eschatological "until" — will never occur, and therefore her classroom will always be politicized; nor, I would suggest, will even a normal form of politics be possible. Every essay that seriously questions the conclusions or methods of feminism prevents the new discourse from becoming the "possible possession of us all." The need to place each utterance in the categories of deliverance — oppression or liberation — will be permanent in any ideological structure, like that of feminism, which cannot acknowledge a realm of autonomy where the blessings of culture can give delight and pleasure. There will be a continual need for rage, a continual need for "revolution in discourse."

21. Froula, "When Eve Reads Milton," 164.

22. Dale M. Bauer, "The Other 'F' Word: The Feminist in the Classroom," *College English* 52, no. 4 (1990): 385.

23. Cyrena N. Pondrom, "Gender and the (Re)formation of the Canon: Is Politics All?" *ADE Bulletin,* no. 91 (Winter 1988): 26.

A biblical poetics that takes seriously the language of "blessing" helps one to understand the monism of ideology. It places *Paradise Lost*'s treatment of marriage, naming, and culture in a historically accurate perspective. It provides an area for the enjoyment of culture without compromising one's largest commitments. It acknowledges oppression and liberation without locating every cultural gesture with respect to those terms. It provides a relative autonomy for the secular study of literature. Unlike current ideological approaches, it is capable of embracing a wide diversity of opinion, including many opinions that derive from fundamentally different philosophical commitments. Finally, a poetics rooted in the biblical language of blessing provides a way of helping to reconstruct our conversations about literature, among various readers, whether or not those readers accept the "discourse" of biblical faith.

I. Humanistic Responses to Recent Feminist Criticism of Milton

William Shullenberger has summarized the feminist critique of Milton in four categories:

1. Milton's God, "patriarch of patriarchs," institutes a rule of masculine authority which is static, closed, and oppressive, especially to women, who are "excluded from heaven" and subordinated on earth. . . .
2. The structure of the bourgeois family determines Milton's representation of Adam and Eve's roles in Paradise. The security of Eden depends upon the bourgeois values of sexual restraint, a male-dominated gender hierarchy, and absolute submissiveness to the will of the Father. . . .
3. Eve, archetypal woman, is necessarily devalued by such a system. Her potentially sinister sexuality is domesticated by the institution of marriage, and her creativity, her voice, is silenced as she is impressed with the need to submit to and articulate the imperatives of the patriarchal voice. . . .
4. Since Eve's creative energies and identity are neutralized by

> the order of the Father, her deepest sympathies are with the revolutionary artist and Romantic hero of the poem, Satan. Satan provides women with an example of an energetic, defiant, self-created identity and assertive sexuality. . . .[24]

Like the other humanistic scholars I have mentioned, Shullenberger responds to these charges serially, showing how they rest on partial readings, or on readings that follow fairly directly from the presuppositions of the critic's own ideology.

Milton's God, he writes, is not a figure who validates the claims of kings and fathers in an abstract realm of patriarchal authority.[25] Rather, the Father and the Son respond to the actual events of the poem — most notably, the fall — with love, grace, self-sacrifice, and compassion.

Eve fills roles far beyond those of the bourgeois housewife, cultivating and harvesting the garden and making decisions (with Adam) crucial to their very existence.[26] As Diane McColley writes, Adam and Eve's "sexual bliss is matched by the spiritual intimacy of their prayers; and these set to music, along with their work and conversation, represent all wholesome arts and sciences. It is hard to think of anything worth doing that Adam and Eve do not, both, actually or tropologically do."[27] Adam and Eve's relationship depoliticizes itself through love and work, writes Shullenberger, and suggests

> a possibility of what human life might be when labor does not mean one thing for a man and another for a woman because labor is not divided from love; when each partner enriches the life of the other because imagination and feeling, reason and desire, the life of the spirit and the life of the senses, are not categorically isolated according to gender. . . .[28]

The use of Satan as a feminist hero, the last of the four typical lines of approach, has met with especially sharp criticism from Mil-

24. Shullenberger, "Wrestling with the Angel," 71.
25. Shullenberger, "Wrestling with the Angel," 72-73.
26. Shullenberger, "Wrestling with the Angel," 73.
27. Danielson, *The Cambridge Companion to Milton,* 162.
28. Shullenberger, "Wrestling with the Angel," 78.

tonists. Sandra Gilbert's influential essay on "Milton's Bogey" has often been criticized for characterizing — and accepting — Satan as a sexually attractive "Byronic hero" and an aristocratic egalitarian who is concerned "with liberty and justice for all."[29] "Of Satan's sexual appeal," comments Shullenberger, ". . . I will hazard no comment other than that it seems perilous to think that the archetypal model for seduction and betrayal is a figure to whom women can trust their fate."[30] Nor is Satan a dependable guide to justice, as Gilbert's lame allusion to the Pledge of Allegiance suggests. Tyrants typically begin by asserting their concern for liberty and for justice on behalf of the oppressed — in Satan's case the fallen angels. Gilbert's inability to discern the inchoate tyranny in Satan's character merely repeats Satan's own determined techniques of misreading.

Shullenberger is surprised that "no feminist critic has yet seen fit to complicate or challenge the assertion by . . . Sandra Gilbert that Milton 'wars upon women with a barrage of angry words.'"[31] But given the character of pure ideology, the silence is perfectly understandable. There is endless quarrelling over the exact formulation of correct feminist ideology, as I shall point out, but there can be no disagreement about the main task of destroying the authority represented by Milton.

* * * * *

Of all the passages in *Paradise Lost* that have offended feminist critics, the last four lines below are probably the most noteworthy:

> Two of far nobler shape erect and tall,
> Godlike erect, with native Honor clad
> In naked Majesty seem'd Lords of all,
> And worthy seem'd, for in thir looks divine
> The image of thir glorious Maker shone,
> Truth, Wisdom, Sanctitude sever and pure,
> Severe, but in true filial freedom plac't;

29. Gilbert, "Patriarchal Poetry and Women Readers," 375.
30. Shullenberger, "Wrestling with the Angel," 78.
31. Shullenberger, "Wrestling with the Angel," 74.

Whence true autority in men; though both
Not equal, as thir sex not equal seem'd;
For contemplation hee and valor form'd,
For softness shee and sweet attractive Grace,
Hee for God only, shee for God in him.

(4.288-99)

The first eight lines speak of Adam and Eve together, as human beings. The last four speak of them as male and female. Milton's detractors have failed to deal seriously with the first eight lines, concentrating only on the last four. The passage clearly sees true authority for both males and females in their fulfillment of the divine image, and both of them are capable of exercising authority. Like Calvin, Milton believed that the words of Genesis 1:27, on creating Adam "in the Image of God," applied as well to Eve.[32]

There is no getting around the fact, however, that the poem attributes greater authority and dominion to Adam than to Eve. Her charms are "submissive," for instance, while his love is "superior." But even the final lines of this passage would have been heard differently in the Renaissance than today. The typical Renaissance ear, writes McColley, would likely have expected not "shee for God in him" but simply "she for him."[33] "[T]his distinction is so vital," she continues, "that Milton's whole characterization of Eve may be referred to it. She is in the right as long as she serves not just Adam but 'God in him.' . . ." However foreign to modern sensibilities, McColley argues, subordination is not inferiority in *Paradise Lost,* for it is reflected throughout the entire cosmos, and even in the Godhead itself.[34] Many traditional readers, who are willing to enter the world of the literature they read, will find McColley's words persuasive. For the ideological feminist, however, "God" is simply one more reification of the patriarchal structure. Moreover, by displacing Eve's obedience to God rather than to

32. John Calvin, *Commentaries on the First Book of Moses, Called Genesis,* trans. John King (Grand Rapids, Mich.: Wm. B. Eerdmans, 1948), 1:128-30; hereafter referred to as *Genesis.*

33. McColley, *Milton's Eve,* 42.

34. McColley, *Milton's Eve,* 35, 52-54.

Adam alone, a level of mystification is inserted, which enforces Eve's acquiescence in paternal submission all the more. But the "willing suspension of disbelief" assumed by traditional literary study is impossible for a true feminist reading, as Christine Froula's reply to the criticism of Edward Pechter demonstrates: "Mr. Pechter apparently imagines that I take the Holy Spirit to be an actual entity. While he may find this belief useful in reading the poem, he should be made aware that many women readers are more likely to remark the peculiar translation of the mother in that parody of the family, 'Father, Son, and Holy Ghost.'"[35] "God," whether in Milton or the Bible, can be viewed in only one way, Froula assumes, namely as a projection of human relations and aspirations in an oppressive, patriarchal culture.

Protestant interpreters, such as Calvin, the editors of the Geneva Bible, and Milton himself, did not read the Bible as a projection of human reality or aspirations. Their hermeneutic attempted to recover the true meaning of the Scripture by beginning with the literal, even grammatical level. Their interpretations frequently conflicted with church traditions by emphasizing the spiritual equality of the sexes and mutuality in marriage. Calvin's commentary on Genesis 2:18 argues that God's announced intention for creating the woman ("I will make him an helpe meet for him") demonstrates the greater importance of the social union of husband and wife over the sexual.[36] "Moses intended to note some equality" between male and female in this verse, comments Calvin, and the social and spiritual significance of marriage "extends to all parts and usages of life." Milton constantly reiterates these and related themes in the divorce tracts; in *Paradise Lost,* the priority of rational and spiritual union over a purely sexual basis for matrimony could hardly be clearer.

While accepting that the woman reflects God's image "in the second degree," Calvin goes out of his way, in his commentary on Genesis 2:18, to attack three elements of the structure of misogyny: (1) the arguments of Jerome and others that "hallowed wedlock [is] both hateful and infamous" (which he calls "wicked suggestions of Satan"); (2) that human

35. Froula, "Pechter's Specter," 173.

36. In this chapter, all quotations from the Bible are from the translation used most by Milton, the 1611 Authorized Version (reprint, New York: Oxford University Press, 1911).

nature is fulfilled in the male alone, while the female is but an imperfect reflection (to which he replies, "What was said in the creation of the man belongs to the female sex"); (3) that women and wives are but a necessary evil for the reproduction of the race (to which he replies that "woman is given to be a companion and an associate to the man, to assist him to live well"). Calvin mentions the "blessing" of marriage twice in his comments on Genesis 2:18: first, to indicate how little it may be perceived in our present corrupted state; second, to affirm that despite our corruption, the blessing "which God has once sanctioned by his word . . . [was not capable of being] utterly abolished and extinguished."[37] It is significant as well, for the larger cultural context of "blessing," that Calvin mentions pagan authors — Plato "and others of the sounder class of philosophers" — as having perceived that marriage is primarily a provision for the social nature of mankind. Finally, Calvin says that both husband *and* wife should "cultivate a holy, as well as friendly and peaceful intercourse." God's blessing extends to the husband through the wife, and to the wife through the husband, and it is available to all mankind.

Among feminist critics, Mary Nyquist has discussed the background of biblical commentary in Calvin, but she omits all of the antimisogynist portions of Calvin's exegesis. Her primary purpose in quoting Calvin, it transpires, is to argue against the influential position of feminist theologian Phyllis Trible that, up to the creation of the woman in Genesis 2:22, Adam is an "ungendered earth creature." It is crucial for the feminist project, as Nyquist sees it, that Adam be "gendered" before that point *and* that he not be considered (by current readers) a "generic" human, regardless of what Calvin or Milton thought the Bible taught.[38] That way, nothing good that pertains to Adam in Genesis 1–2 can apply to Eve. The feminist critique of Milton, as Nyquist understands it, must maintain that, according to the Bible,

37. "Fateor quidem in corrupto hoc generis humani statu non perspici nec vigere, quae hic describitur, Dei *benedictionem*. . . . Quanquam non potuit adeo vitiari coniugium hominum pravitate, ut in totum abolita sit et exstincta *benedictio* quam semel Dominus verbo sui sancivit" (emphasis added). The Latin quotations are from Calvin's original text, as printed in *Opera Exegetica Et Homiletica*, vol. 23 of *Ioannis Calvini Opera Quae Supersunt Omnia*, vol. 51 in *Corpus Reformatorum*, ed. G. Baum, E. Cunitz, and E. Reuss (Brunswick, 1882).

38. Nyquist, "Gynesis, Genesis, Milton's Eve," 180.

the male alone is created in God's image, and that marriage is ordained for the benefit of males alone — even if Milton and Calvin deny both of these biblical interpretations.[39] Moreover, even the exalting of non-sexual relations over sexual ones, in Calvin's and Milton's views of Adam and Eve, can be explained away by feminist ideology as "a bipolar and hierarchical ordering of the spiritual and physical dimensions of experience, [which] structures many of Milton's exegetical moves in these [divorce] tracts." Because of this "bipolar and hierarchical ordering," Nyquist concludes that the hermeneutic of Milton and Calvin is structurally "phallocratic."[40]

Discovering the way in which one's opponents are "implicated in phallogocentrism" is the Holy Grail of feminist criticism, and like medieval allegory the main requirement for success is a pure faith that enables one to read the signs correctly. Reading the signs requires cleverness, but because the outcome is known in advance, the signs themselves are of little importance. Commenting on a similar tendency in the anthropological critic of literature, C. S. Lewis writes,

> It is also a quest story, but it is he, not Perceval or Gawain, that is on the quest. The forests are not those of Broceliande but those of . . . theory. It is he himself who quivers at the surmise that everything he meets may be more important, and other, than it seemed. . . .
>
> He gets in the end an experience qualitatively not unlike the experience the romancers meant to give. The process is very roundabout. He rejects the fiction as it was actually written. He can respond to it only indirectly, only when it is mirrored in a second fiction, which he mistakes for reality. . . . [But is the critic] himself quite sure that the allegory Fulgentius found in Virgil, or the philosophy Chapman found in Homer, were really there?[41]

The "humanistic" response to Nyquist and Froula would be to continue pointing out the merely local deficiencies of such readings: the ways Calvin and contemporary Protestant interpreters have been

39. Nyquist, "Gynesis, Genesis, Milton's Eve," 192, 179.

40. Nyquist, "Gynesis, Genesis, Milton's Eve," 176, 181.

41. C. S. Lewis, *Selected Literary Essays,* ed. Walter Hooper (London: Cambridge University Press, 1969), 310-11.

misrepresented by selective readings, and the failure to read *Paradise Lost* whole and in the context of Milton's other poetry and prose. But these responses will fail to move the true ideologue for the reason suggested in a comment by Froula: "The patriarchal authority Milton establishes in *Paradise Lost* is not mere precondition for his story; it *is* that story."[42] She can only respond to *Paradise Lost,* that is to say, when it is mirrored in her second, ideological fiction. For Nyquist, the goal is a reading that combines feminist and Marxist belief, so that even in Milton's assertions of mutuality one sees "the self-consistent outcome of the deeply patriarchal assumptions at work in Milton's articulation of a radically bourgeois view of marriage."[43]

Absent a realm of some autonomy for culture, such critics are committed to read in every story an allegory of ideology, similar in form to the one Lewis criticizes, with its predictable structure of oppression and liberation. More urgent than another humanistic response, therefore, is the discovery — or rediscovery — of a foundation for literary study that provides for some autonomy for literature, while yet allowing the reader to interpret the work with respect to his or her deepest values. I will therefore leave both the critique of ideology and the humanistic alternatives to ideology. Instead, I will turn the discussion to a deeper question: how can we grant literature an integrity of its own? Milton himself can help provide such a foundation.

II. Blessing and Human Culture in Genesis, Calvin, and Milton

Several discussions of Milton's view of women refer to John Calvin, but they usually begin and end with his commentaries on the biblical texts where marriage is discussed. By so doing, they fail to put marriage in its proper biblical context, as an area of human culture available to mankind generally, and not restricted to Jews and Christians, God's "covenant" peoples. This area, named "common grace" by Calvinists in the nineteenth century, is founded upon the distinction between the

42. Froula, "When Eve Reads Milton," 167.
43. Nyquist, "Gynesis, Genesis, Milton's Eve," 176.

blessings given to all humanity and those set apart solely for the chosen people. Calvin and his English followers, such as those who wrote the Geneva Bible (a copy of which was owned by Milton's third wife), were well aware of the distinction between the gifts of God to all and those reserved for the elect.[44] The distinction is apparent in their treatment of the "light of nature" and the existence of "natural law" potentially available to all peoples. It is apparent in Milton's description of "conscience" as God's "Umpire," placed within all people (*PL* 3.185-97). It is apparent as well in Calvin's positive remarks about the cultural achievements of pagans and his endorsement of the secular realm of culture as the area where most Christians exercise their vocations.

Among modern biblical scholars, Claus Westermann has done the most to locate the different biblical emphases on "blessing" and "deliverance," which are fundamental to this distinction. The distinction begins in the opening chapters of Genesis, where male and female are created, and where marriage and work are first mentioned.

The contrast is between God's saving acts (of deliverance) and the acts (of blessing) that produce a state of well-being.[45] God's saving acts,

44. Elizabeth Minshull, whom Milton married in 1663, owned a Geneva Bible (printed 1588), which bears a 1664 autograph. Milton's usual reliance upon the Authorized Version of the Bible, however, is well known. The leading authority on Milton's use of the Bible concludes that there is no direct evidence of Milton's use of the Geneva Bible in his poetry (James H. Sims, *The Bible in Milton's Epics* [Gainesville: University of Florida Press, 1962], 4). I will point out, however, that the marginal notes to the Geneva Bible's translation of Gen. 1:27 are extremely close to *Paradise Lost* 4.292-94, and (more generally) that its marginal glosses on marriage are reflected in the thinking behind the poem. See George Wesley Whiting, *Milton and This Pendant World* (Austin: University of Texas Press, 1958) for a fuller estimate of the significance of the Geneva Bible on Milton's thought.

45. Claus Westermann's *Blessing in the Bible and the Life of the Church,* trans. Keith Crim (Philadelphia: Fortress Press, 1978), provides the basis for this and the following paragraph. I will deal primarily with Westermann's remarks on the treatment of blessing by the Yahwist and the Priestly writers, who are thought to be responsible for the early chapters of Genesis. The portions of Genesis usually ascribed to "J" are far more concerned with civilization than those ascribed to "P," but the Priestly writer's words in 1:26, 28 provide the context for the consideration of human achievements as a whole. Westermann considers their accounts complementary. The Deuteronomist sees blessing as conditional upon obedience, a view which the book of Job and Psalm 73 address. See Westermann, *Genesis 1-11: A Commentary,* trans. John J. Scullion,

such as the exodus and the crucifixion, are interventions into human history, whereas his blessings are continuous. The Old Testament speaks of gratitude as a response to blessing; faith, by contrast, is more properly the response to God's saving acts.

Blessing seems specifically excluded only from activities that are regarded as sinful, such as idolatry and the killing of other human beings. Foreign gods are never "blessed" in the Bible.[46] Regarding killing, the covenant with which God "blesses" Noah specifically warns that "Who so sheddeth mans blood, by man shall his blood be shed: for in the image of God made he man. And you, be ye fruitfull, and multiply . . ." (Gen. 9:6-7). It is noteworthy that the language of this covenant recalls the original creation and blessing (". . . be fruitfull") of humanity. It suggests that, despite its limitations after the fall, the blessing still remains and that this early legal code itself is part of the blessing. Consistent with this suggestion, Paul seems to consider a secular legal code among God's blessings when he counts himself fortunate to gain a legal hearing before Agrippa (Acts 26:2).

Apart from the exclusion of sinful activities, blessing has a wide range of meaning in the Bible. In Genesis, blessing is the next "speech-act" God undertakes after creation, first with sentient creatures, then with human beings (Gen. 1:22, 28). By his blessing, God establishes

---

S. J. (Minneapolis: Augsburg, 1984), 61-62, and *Blessing,* 62. Against Westermann's general thesis, Christopher Wright Mitchell argues that "blessing and deliverance are closely intertwined," but he nevertheless grants that there "are large differences both in the range of meaning and in the range of application between *brk* (bless) and the words of deliverance." See *The Meaning of* BRK *"To Bless" in the Old Testament* (Atlanta: Scholars Press, 1987), 178. Westermann's critics are correct, I think, to emphasize that the Old Testament does not limit "blessing" to nature and creation, and to see it extending to the history of Israel (G. Johannes Botterweck and Helmer Ringgren, eds., *Theological Dictionary of the Old Testament,* trans. John T. Willis [Grand Rapids, Mich.: Wm. B. Eerdmans, 1974-], 2:306; hereafter abbreviated as *TDOT*). But while the two activities intersect, they are not coterminous. Until the final renewal of creation, in the eschatological reunion of all things with God, the distinction between God's activities of blessing and deliverance will remain valid, for the former extends throughout creation while the latter applies to God's particular mode of bringing about that ultimate restoration.

46. Botterweck and Ringgren, *TDOT,* 2:295.

both the creature's relationship to God and an area of existence outside of God. Blessing is God's way of establishing and upholding the creature's attachment to him, while yet placing the creature in the created world. While blessing originates in God and establishes the creature's relationship to God, it also places the creature in its own, authentic realm.

In contrast with many contemporary Mesopotamian stories, the opening chapters of Genesis locate human culture outside the creative activities of God himself — and instead, under God's blessing. As Westermann writes, human endeavor and culture are desacralized; human achievements are not themselves divine.[47] They are neither gifts from God (like fire from Prometheus) nor the results of conflicts within the Godhead (like metal work in some ancient Near Eastern myths). Nor are they bestowed ready-made on mankind. Still, the products of culture are linked to God by his blessing at creation. The God-given capacities that result from blessing enable humanity to fulfill God's commands to be fruitful and to exercise dominion as responsible stewards of the earth. Nevertheless, the blessings of Genesis 1–11 — family, agriculture, viticulture, metal-working, music, and so on — are not closely linked to faith in God or even knowledge of God. They are secular, human products.

Creation and its effects, especially fertility, marriage, and Adam and Eve's work in the garden, are aspects of God's blessing. Creation itself is not an act of deliverance, nor is there any need for deliverance until after the fall. There is, however, need for blessing from the very beginning of sentient life on earth, which occurs on the fifth day with the creatures of water and air. "And God blessed them, saying, 'Be fruitful and multiply and fill the waters in the Seas, and let foule multiply in the earth'" (Gen. 1:22). Blessing is related first of all, then, to the fertility of all living creatures, which suggests that blessing is an even wider concept than "culture." Indeed, the ultimate scope of blessing extends to God's Sabbath rest after creation ("And God blessed the seventh day and sanctified it: because that in it he had rested from all his worke, which God created and made" [Gen. 2:3]).

When human beings are created in Genesis 1:27-28, blessing

47. Westermann, *Genesis 1-11,* 60-62, 67.

again includes the element of fertility, which is now placed in the context of humanity's share in God's image. Blessing is the framework as well for humanity's relationship to creation:

> 27 So God created man in his owne Image, in the Image of God created hee him; male and female created hee them.
> 28 And God blessed them, and God said unto them, Be fruitfull, and multiply, and replenish the earth, and subdue it, and have dominion over the fish of the sea, and over the foule of the aire, and over every living thing that mooveth upon the earth.

The blessing in verse 28, remarks Westermann, means that as long as mankind exists, God will remain effectively at work in it because of this original blessing.[48]

In the next chapter, the second account of human creation provides a fuller account of the human relationships to creation (through work and naming) and, even more important, to another human being in the society of marriage:

> 15 And the Lord God tooke the man, and put him into the garden of Eden, to dresse it, and to keepe it. . . .
> 18 And the Lord God said, It is not good that the man should be alone: I will make him an helpe meet for him.
> 19 And out of the ground the Lord God formed every beast of the field, and every foule of the aire, and brought them unto Adam, to see what he would call them: and whatsoever Adam called every living creature, that was the name thereof.
> 20 And Adam gave names to all cattell, and to the foule of the aire, and to every beast of the fielde: but for Adam there was not found an helpe meete for him.
> 21 And the Lord God caused a deepe sleepe to fall upon Adam, and hee slept; and he tooke one of his ribs, and closed up the flesh in stead thereof.
> 22 And the rib which the Lord God had taken from man, made hee a woman, & brought her unto the man.

48. Westermann, *Genesis 1-11,* 161.

23 And Adam said, This is now bone of my bones, and flesh of my flesh: she shalbe called woman, because shee was taken out of man.
24 Therefore shall a man leave his father and his mother, and shall cleave unto his wife: and they shalbe one flesh.

There is no question that Milton locates marriage among God's blessings, and (following Calvin's commentary on Genesis 2:18) that its highest benefits were spiritual and rational, rather than physical. In *The Doctrine and Discipline of Divorce* he calls the institution itself a "blessing," and says its greatest advantages are to the mind, especially when one partner supplements the deficiencies of the other: the "dignity & blessing of mariage is plac't rather in the mutual enjoyment of that which the wanting soul needfully seeks," he writes.[49] In *Tetrachordon* he speaks of marriage as a "mystical and blessed unity" (*YP* 2:622). That these blessings extended beyond the fall is especially evident in the Geneva Bible's comment on Genesis 4:1, where Eve conceives Cain: "Man's nature, the state of marriage, & God's *blessing* were not utterly abolished through sinne, but the qualitie or condition thereof was changed . . ." (emphasis added). Marriage, understood through the language of blessing, remains available to all mankind, not just to the line of the covenant people, who were traced through Seth rather than Cain.

Because Milton refers to Calvin's commentary on Genesis in *Doctrine and Discipline of Divorce,* Calvin's remarks on culture there are particularly noteworthy. The phrase "keepe and dresse" (vs. 15) was taken by Protestant commentators such as Calvin to incorporate human vocations under the blessing of God. The heaviest part of our labors, admits Calvin, comes from God's curse.[50] But before the fall, "Adam's labor, truly, was pleasant, and full of delight," remarks Calvin on Genesis 2:15 *(Erat quidem iucundus hic plenusque oblectationis labor);*

49. John Milton, *Complete Prose Works of John Milton,* ed. Donald W. Wolfe et al. (New Haven: Yale University Press, 1953-82), 2:235, 246, 252. Subsequent quotations from this source are cited in the text with the abbreviation *YP.*

50. John Calvin, *Commentaries,* ed. Joseph Haroutunian and Louise Pettibone Smith, Library of Christian Classics 23 (Philadelphia: Westminster Press, n.d.), 340, on Ps. 127:1-2.

it teaches us true economy by encouraging improvements to cultivation, he writes, moderation in consumption, and faithfulness in the stewardship of God's "good things" *(bonis).*

Words like "pleasant," "delight," and "good things" are part of the biblical language of blessing. Like Calvin, Milton's Adam uses the word "pleasant" in connection with their labors in Eden. The word "Eden" itself is derived from the Hebrew verb for "delight." That this language extends beyond the fall, even to the cultural achievements of those outside the chosen race, is made clear by Calvin's comments on Genesis 4:20. Calvin here considers the surprising fact that the Bible records the invention of the arts by the sinful family of Cain. Calvin explicitly locates their achievements under God's blessing and distinguishes it from the regenerating work of salvation:

> Clearly, here Moses is celebrating what was left of God's blessing *(Residuam vero Dei benedictionem Moses diserte . . . commendat),* in a people we should otherwise regard as sterile and devoid of every other good.
>
> We must therefore recognize that, although the sons of Cain were deprived of the spirit of regeneration, they were blessed with endowments far from negligible *(praediti fuerint non contemnendis dotibus).* In fact, the experience of all ages shows us how many rays of divine light have always beamed among unbelieving nations, and have contributed to the improvement of our present life. And today we see glorious gifts of the Spirit spread throughout the whole human race. For the liberal and industrial arts and the sciences have come to us from profane men. Astronomy and other branches of philosophy, medicine, political science — we must admit that we have learned all these from them. Although the invention of the lyre and of other musical instruments serves our enjoyment and our pleasures rather than our needs, it ought not on that account to be judged of no value; still less should it be condemned. Pleasure is to be condemned only when it is not combined with reverence for God and not related to the common welfare of society. But music by its nature is adapted to rouse our devotion to God and to aid the well-being of man; we need only avoid enticements to shame, and empty entertainments which keep men from better employments and are simply a waste of time.

> However, even if you think the invention of the lyre does not in itself deserve much praise, everyone knows how long and how widely people have valued the carpenter's skill.[51]

This passage is highly significant for the contemporary Protestant culture of which Milton was a part. Calvin sees all of the gifts of civilization as coming ultimately from God, but he sees them as human rather than divine achievements: they are neither the direct gifts of God, nor of conflicts among the gods, as in the mythology of the ancient Near East. Moreover, these are secular achievements, secured by human skills acquired in the world, rather than through any magical, priestly, or ecclesiastical agency. Calvin explicitly notes that the blessing of God, though deformed, continues after the fall, even among the "sons of Cain," people regarded as outside the covenant of grace.[52] Man's original sin does not negate God's original blessing. Calvin suggests the limits to "blessing" in his principle that cultural endeavors should raise the common welfare of society without encouraging idleness or temptation, but within those limits the passage embraces a wide area of autonomy. He indicates as well that cultural achievements are not acts of regeneration, and therefore a Calvinist should never confuse education with holiness, or the analogous forms of deliverance that are envisioned in much recent ideological pedagogy. Calvin recognizes authentic achievement by persons far removed from Jewish or Christian faith, and endorses scientific advances and aesthetic pleasures in addition to pragmatic achievements.

An even more pointed endorsement of certain attainments of pagan culture occurs in Calvin's commentary on Titus, where he refers to Paul's use of Greek poetry and expresses impatience with Christians who refuse to have anything to do with classical culture:

51. Calvin, *Commentaries,* 354-55. Calvin's Latin is supplied from the *Corpus Reformatorum.*

52. Many modern readers are surprised at Calvin's high view of pagan culture because they misunderstand his doctrine of "total depravity," which refers to the inability of man to do anything to save himself — even to decide to turn toward God when salvation is offered. The doctrine does not mean that the literary and scientific achievements of non-Christians are worthless. See also Calvin's comments on Genesis 1:16, on astronomy.

> From this passage we may infer that those persons are superstitious, who do not venture to borrow anything from heathen authors. All truth is from God; and consequently, if wicked men have said anything that is true and just, we ought not to reject it; for it has come from God. Besides, all things are of God; and, therefore, why should it not be lawful to dedicate to his glory everything that can properly be employed for such a purpose? But on this subject the reader may consult Basil's discourse [to the young men].[53]

The reference to Basil's discourse locates Calvin's thought within the tradition of biblical poetics of which Milton too is a part. Milton quotes a homily of Basil's in his *Commonplace Book* on the purpose of poetry as a gift of God "to rouse in human souls the love of virtue."[54] Milton refers twice in the *Areopagitica* to the same discourse to which Calvin alludes, the "Address to Young Men on the Right Use of Greek Literature." Milton there deemphasizes the asceticism of Basil's address to make two points: first, to remind Parliament that Moses and Daniel had attained skill in the learning of the Egyptians and Chaldeans (*YP* 2:507); and second, to suggest that however Jerome may have rejected Cicero, Basil recommends the reading of Homer (*YP* 2:510-11).

Calvin's phrase "dedicate to [God's] glory" captures perfectly Milton's use and enjoyment of culture, and his ambitions for his own poetry. There are true and useful achievements by Greeks and Romans that have advanced "the common welfare of society." These achievements cannot be accepted in place of the kingdom of God, which is why Jesus Christ, whose particular vocation is to restore the kingdom, must decline Greek learning in *Paradise Regained.* The way of total acceptance must be refused. But neither should these achievements be totally rejected, as Calvin's "superstitious persons" have done, for they can be used to glorify God.

The language of "blessing" is, I believe, the most useful domain

53. John Calvin, *Commentaries on the Epistles to Timothy, Titus, and Philemon,* trans. William Pringle (Grand Rapids, Mich.: Wm. B. Eerdmans, 1948), 309-10, on Titus 1:12.

54. John Milton, *The Works of John Milton,* gen. ed. Frank Allen Patterson (New York: Columbia University Press, 1931-38), 18:139. Subsequent quotations from this source are cited in the text with the abbreviation *CE.*

in which a biblical poetics may locate culture, even though this language goes beyond even so broad a realm as culture. For Paul, blessing embraces secular, cultural concerns, such as the wisdom and achievements of pagan nations, but the New Testament writers generally go beyond human culture to associate blessing with the religious joy of the believer on sharing in the kingdom of God.[55] Christ's last act, before his ascension in Luke 24:50, is a blessing that has a particularly evangelistic purpose.

Moreover, the final goal of blessing, as described in Genesis 1–2:4, lies not in cultural advance, but in the Sabbath rest of the creator, as implied by God's blessing and hallowing of the seventh day (Gen. 2:3). Blessing is therefore particularly associated with Sabbath worship at certain places in the Old Testament. Blessing is universal in the Sabbath rest of Genesis 2:3, and it will be universal again when history is fulfilled, as suggested by the apocalyptic use of "blessing" in Isaiah (chapters 11, 65) and in Revelation.[56] To conclude, the biblical language of blessing embraces human cultural achievement, but points beyond it.

In *Paradise Lost,* Milton shows an awareness of all of these significances. The concept of "rest," for instance, which provides part of the poem's structural foundations, is closely related to the initial blessing of creation and its return to a higher level at the end of time. In 1.66 hell is spoken of as a place where "rest can never dwell," and its restlessness is expressed in physical, intellectual, and emotional dissatisfaction. After the end of creation, we read that the

Author and end of all things . . .
Now *resting,* bless'd and hallow'd the Sev'nth day,
As *resting* on that day from all his work,
But not in silence holy kept; the Harp
Had work and *rested* not, the solemn Pipe,
And Dulcimer, all Organs of sweet stop. . . .

(7.591-96, emphasis added)

55. Gerhard Kittel, ed., *Theological Dictionary of the New Testament,* trans. and ed. Geoffrey W. Bromiley (Grand Rapids, Mich.: Wm. B. Eerdmans, 1964-76), 4:365-67; hereafter abbreviated as *TDNT.*

56. Westermann, *Blessing,* 30, 63.

These lines suggests that certain aspects of human culture (music, and the poetry that the angels later sing) are especially fit for the enjoyment of God, both in the sense that his creatures enjoy them and that God enjoys their use. In this case, music and poetry are used in worship by the angels in response to God's creation. By contrast, when Satan reports the fall and invites the other devils to "enter now into full bliss" of their reign on earth, the response is "[a] dismal universal hiss" (10.503, 508). Outside of worship, in the secular world, Milton associates "rest" with the continued blessing upon Adam and Eve as they leave Paradise in the final lines of the poem. "The World was all before them, where to choose / Thir place of rest, and Providence thir guide . . ." (12.646-47). Adam and Eve do not set out for a new place of work, primarily, nor to a chamber of self-denial and asceticism, nor even to a temple or place of sacrifice. They seek a place of rest under the guidance of Providence, for their ultimate destiny is to rest in God's love. But this "rest" will be the active life of the "warfaring Christian," for their "chief end," as the Westminster Catechism put it in 1648, is to "glorify God and enjoy him forever."

Avoiding the Extreme of Rejection: Wisdom and Education as Secular Blessings in Milton's Works before Paradise Lost

While marriage may be the most obvious of the general biblical blessings, perhaps more relevant to a biblical poetics is the spectrum of human acquisitions, education, and "wisdom," which are seen as universally beneficent. The Bible is fully aware of the human tendency to pass beyond the limits of blessing in the acquisition of technological progress, as in the account of the Tower of Babel. But the acquisitions themselves derive from a good source, not a merely neutral one.

In the Bible, wisdom is more properly associated with the universal blessing of God than with his acts of deliverance or salvation. Westermann notes that, like blessing (in its connection with creation), wisdom is associated with growth and maturation. Wisdom is therefore associated with the growth of the whole person and is particularly found among the elderly.[57] It is not the preserve of the Jews only, but may be

57. Westermann, *Blessing,* 37-38.

borrowed from the Egyptians and others. While a true, saving knowledge of God arises out of his grace, bestowed on his chosen people, the Old Testament also sanctions a secular wisdom that arises out of God's universal blessing.[58] Indeed, the entire Old Testament genre of "wisdom literature" would probably not have survived in the canon if Judaism and Christianity had rejected the achievements that believers held in common with nonbelievers. Similarly, the New Testament term for "blessed" (or "happy"), *makarios,* has a very wide degree of usage in Greek outside the Bible. It can mean a godlike happiness that comes from enjoying a life beyond earthly cares. Or it can be restricted to the happiness that comes from earthly blessings: children, prosperity, honor, fame, virtue.[59] Christ's blessing of the children suggests that the New Testament writers saw no need to exclude some of these wider connotations from the Christian understanding of blessing (Matt. 19:14).

Milton's writings on wisdom and education reflect the two types of knowledge in the Bible: the saving knowledge of God and the secular knowledge crucial for human endeavor. Both come ultimately from God, and the ultimate purpose of both is the love of God, as Milton's opening sentence in *Of Education* indicates: "no purpose or respect should sooner move us, then simply the love of God and of mankinde" (*YP* 2:362). But while the ultimate "end" or purpose of learning "is to repair the ruins of our first parents by regaining to know God aright," as Milton says in the next paragraph of that work, a definite hierarchy exists in the kinds of knowledge. The knowledge of "naturall causes and dimensions" is a "lower wisdom" than the knowledge of God (*YP* 1:801). This "lower wisdom" cannot save anyone, but it is nevertheless true wisdom. Its purpose is the acquisition of truth, and secular education has the potential to accomplish this task, within its limits, as Milton makes clear in the *Areopagitica.* He recounts the Egyptian myth in which the allegorical body of Truth is hewn to pieces, after which her "sad friends" make a "carefull search . . . gathering up limb by limb still as they could find them. We have not found them all . . . nor ever shall doe, till her Masters second comming" (*YP* 2:549).

Milton's definition of education is derived largely from pagan sources and is secular in most of its significance: "I call therefore a

58. Westermann, *Blessing,* 38-39.
59. Kittel, *TDNT,* 4:363.

[illegible] Education that which fits a man to perform [illegible]ously all the offices both private and [illegible] *YP* 2:377-79). "All the offices" would [illegible]d there is no doubt about the religious [illegible]tion in Milton's eyes. But there is likewise [illegible]ed of education as fitting one for under- [illegible] world" as it was and is. Education is a [illegible] Irene Samuel has written, "living provides [illegible]r learning" in Milton, from the early *Of Education* [illegible] *Lost.*[60]

Milton's approval of pagan culture and his remarks on the secular scope of education make it clear that he cannot endorse the way of rejection, as represented by Tertullian and by the ideologue's typical rejection of the past as the embodiment of oppression. In *Areopagitica,* Milton criticizes some of the radical Reformers for rejecting everything but Protestant achievements since Luther: Englishmen should not be "for ever staring on" the "light" of the Reformation, to the exclusion of "things more remote from our [present] knowledge" (*YP* 2:550). He refers to Paul's use of "the sentences of three Greek Poets," noting that the dispute in the primitive church over whether to use pagan learning was decided emphatically in the affirmative (*YP* 2:508). He believes that the pursuit of a proper education is among the items on which he will be asked to "give an account to God" (*YP* 2:374). Milton is perhaps thinking of God's judgment upon the "works" of those who are saved: "[A]nd the fire shall trie every mans worke of what sort it is. If any mans worke abide which he hath built thereupon, he shal receive a reward. if any mans worke shall bee burnt, he shall suffer losse; but he himselfe shall be saved: yet so, as by fire" (1 Cor. 3:13-15). He is almost certainly thinking of his favorite parable, the parable of the talents (Matt. 25:14-31). Talent is a universal blessing, writes Milton, and God "requires the improvment of these his entrusted gifts" (*YP* 1:801).

For one to reject all learning except the knowledge of salvation, thinks Milton, would be a burying of one's talent, and such a person would have to answer to God for it. The talents of poets, to take the

60. Irene Samuel, "Milton on Learning and Wisdom," *PMLA* 64 (1949): 710.

most pertinent example, "wheresoever they be found, are the inspired guift of God rarely bestow'd, but yet to some (though most abuse) in every Nation: and are of power beside the office of a pulpit, to imbreed and cherish in a great people the seeds of vertu, and publick civility, to allay the perturbations of the mind . . ." (*YP* 1:816). Gifts, talents, and wisdom are part of the biblical language of blessing as it relates to the cultural achievements of all peoples. Nevertheless, the second option, the way of outright acceptance of every cultural achievement, is not open to Milton either, as his poetry makes clear.

Avoiding the Extreme of Acceptance: The Limits to Human Culture in Paradise Lost *and After*

Throughout his writings, Milton recognizes that everything good can be twisted into something bad. Moreover, there is no earthly security, no secular authority, and no ecclesiastical power that can guarantee the continuance or growth of these good gifts. The blessings of marriage, sexuality, liberty, and wisdom itself may all turn into demonic parodies of themselves, as Milton explores in his work from *Comus* to *Samson Agonistes.* In *Samson,* Manoa uses the word "blessing" to refer to the birth of his son (line 357). But then he goes on to ask why God's "gifts desirable," for which we pray, contain a "Scorpion's tail behind" (358-60). Samson is quick to correct Manoa's misunderstanding — more pagan than Jewish — of answered prayer: "Appoint not heavenly disposition, Father, / Nothing of all these evils hath befall'n me / But justly" (372-74). As Milton suggests here and elsewhere, the blessings are good in themselves, and their deformation is due to human and demonic evil, not to a Janus-like nature in God himself.

Before the fall, Adam and Eve are able to use the blessing of natural reason to increase their knowledge of God. It is no accident, therefore, that Eve's first words on eating of the tree of knowledge reflect a perversion of knowledge as a blessing: "O Sovran, virtuous, precious of all Trees / In Paradise, of operation blest / To Sapience, hitherto obscur'd . . . thou op'n'st Wisdom's way . . . (*PL* 9.795-97, 809). " 'Obedience and love are always the best guides to knowledge,' " Irene Samuel quotes Milton as saying, "evidently meaning that they lead to the knowledge that can be absorbed into the way of life."[61] But obedience and love cannot be guaranteed from one moment to the next, and they cannot be turned into a formula.

The most difficult crux in Milton's treatment of pagan culture is the rejection of Greek learning by Jesus in the second temptation of *Paradise Regained.* The temptation to assume cultural power is higher than the first, the physical temptation of bread, and lower than the third, the spiritual temptation of religious power. Pagan culture is seen both positively and negatively in *Paradise Regained.* The amorous poetry of Ovid is criticized, while allusions to Plutarch commend the authentic achievements of pagan literature. Jesus credits the Roman worthies for their government over the inner man, but condemns the present state of the empire (2.455-77; 4.131-45). He uses Socrates as an example of one who suffers death for the sake of truth, but places pagan wisdom, "though granted true," as "little else but dreams" compared to the truths of Scripture (3.96-98; 4.285-364).

Satan cannot understand the distinction. "All knowledge is not couch't in Moses' Law," he correctly says, trying to force Jesus into accepting the kingdoms of this world. But when Jesus rejects the offer, Satan petulantly accuses Jesus of having adopted the way of absolute rejection:

> Since neither wealth, nor honor, arms nor arts,
> Kingdom nor Empire pleases thee, nor aught
> By me propos'd in life contemplative,
> Or active, tended on by glory, or fame,
> What dost thou in this World? The Wilderness
> For thee is fittest place.
>
> (4.368-73)

Satan's temptation and reaction indicate two crucial misperceptions. First, Christ's particular vocation — bringing the gospel to his people and dying on their behalf — is unique, and he can therefore never assume the cultural role that Satan suggests. Still, that need not prevent

61. Samuel, "Milton on Learning and Wisdom," 712; cf. Milton, *YP,* 6:129.

the followers of Christ from cultivating various kinds of cultural excellence, appropriate to *their* particular vocations. Most obviously, it does not prevent John Milton, poet, from learning as much as he can from pagan culture, within the limits of obedience and love, for fulfilling his poetic vocation.

Second, Satan depends upon obscuring the hierarchy, evident in Milton's prose, between the knowledge of God and the "lower wisdom" of "naturall causes." Within that order, there is the widest conceivable freedom to pursue knowledge and advance culture, as Milton's entire *oeuvre* suggests. But once that order is upset and knowledge is no longer oriented properly, the advance of knowledge is replaced by intellectual restlessness and confusion. This restlessness is nowhere more apparent than in the fruitless speculations of the devils in *Paradise Lost* "in wand'ring mazes lost":

> Of good and evil much they argu'd then,
> Of happiness and final misery,
> Passion and Apathy, and glory and shame,
> Vain wisdom all, and false Philosophy.
>
> (2.561-65)

A "plaine unlearned man" is far wiser than a "learned foole" or hypocrite, as Milton writes in *Animadversions:* the first "lives well by that light which he has, is better, and wiser, and edifies others more towards a godly and happy life then he: The other is still using his sophisticated arts and bending all his studies how to make his insatiate avarice, & ambition seem pious . . ." (*YP* 1:720). A great many human words are folly, as both Milton and the biblical writers knew: nothing can guarantee that one's words will become the wisdom of the ages rather than "vanitie of vanities."

Descending from Milton's treatment of "wisdom" to more concrete aspects of human culture, certain scenes in books 11 and 12 of *Paradise Lost* suggest the scope and limits of human civilization, all of which are consistent with the biblical understanding of blessing after the fall. In his portrait of the sons of Seth, the angel Michael recounts their many achievements in agriculture, iron- and brass-working, and music:

. . . By thir guise
Just men they seem'd, and all thir study bent
To worship God aright, and know his works
Not hid, nor those things last which might preserve
Freedom and Peace to men.

(11.576-80)

Up to this point, their cultural achievements bestow only benefits, but even in this description the possibility of evil is present in the layers of meaning beneath "guise," "seem'd," and "bent." In the next line, they see the daughters of Cain, and the warning signals in Milton's verse increase — their eyes "rove[d] without rein" over the women in their "wanton dress." Still, they proceeded to "marriage," and the fallen Adam thinks all is well. Not so, as Michael explains. Although the men appear "studious . . . Of Arts that polish Life," they are — or perhaps they become — "Unmindful of thir Maker" (11.609-11). They are deficient of the one universally required response to blessing, namely gratitude: "they his gifts acknowledg'd none" (11.612). Michael is not saying that human achievements are worthless. Quite the contrary. Their musical pursuits are common to the angels, and their agriculture could be part of a restored, georgic life, reflecting harmony between human farming and the divine order. All of these blessings are good in themselves, but the capacities they imply and the pleasures they bring must be exercised and enjoyed within the limits of blessing.

In the opening of book 12, which picks up sacred history after Noah, a picture of human harmony emerges in these lines:

This second source of Men, while yet but few,
And while the dread of judgment past remains
Fresh in thir minds, fearing the Deity,
With some regard to what is just and right
Shall lead thir lives, and multiply apace,
Laboring the soil, and reaping plenteous crop,
Corn, wine and oil; and from the herd or flock,
Oft sacrificing Bullock, Lamb, or Kid,
With large Wine-offerings pour'd, and sacred Feast,

Shall spend thir days in joy unblam'd, and dwell
Long time in peace by Families and Tribes
Under paternal rule. . . .

(12.13-24)

The achievement of mankind in these lines is seen as a good thing, without any need for qualification. Because it is lived in accordance with "what is just and right," their civilization flourishes within the limits of peace, prosperity, and family concord. Their cultural achievements are consciously related to God through grateful sacrifice, but these achievements are not seen as direct service to God. Rather, their civilization fulfills God's original blessing by their labor, fertility, and family concord. Their cultural achievements are not seen as a means of deliverance; rather, these accomplishments produce "joy" — yet another word associated with "pleasure" and "delight" as Milton and Johnson use those terms. Their peace is then interrupted by the despotic rise of Nimrod, whose usurpation is said to dispossess the "law of Nature from the Earth."

Michael condemns Nimrod on three grounds: his warlike nature, his ambition and discontent with "fair equality, fraternal state," and his insistence on "second sovranty" — second to God, but too godlike. Now of these, only the third is based specifically upon revelation. The first two grounds are universally comprehensible, as stemming from Nimrod's violations of the "law of Nature." Though based ultimately on a belief in a common creation (like blessing itself), many agnostic thinkers could share Milton's condemnation of this tyrant and his endorsement of the earlier society of the sons of Noah.

Turning from human achievement as a whole to his own literary practice, Milton's use of classical literary forms is perhaps the most obvious example of his activity in the transformation of culture and its fundamental difference from the outright acceptance or rejection of past culture. This immense topic has been studied by many Milton scholars, most recently by Barbara Lewalski (in Paradise Lost *and the Rhetoric of Literary Forms*) and Georgia Christopher (in *Milton and the Science of the Saints*). Lewalski writes that "ancient and Renaissance tradition recognized the Bible as epiclike in its comprehension of all history, all subject matters, and many genres — law, history, prophecy, heroic poetry, psalm, allegory, proverb, hymn, epistle, tragedy, tragicomedy, and more."[62] *Paradise Lost* likewise incorporates a complete spectrum of literary forms and kinds, from eclogue to classical epic, from lyric to soliloquy.[63] But the drift of her study, like that of Christopher, shows that Milton's practice is very different from the ancients and medievals who sought allegories of Christian revelation in classical myth. Even when he writes of classical analogues that are quite close to the plots and images of *Paradise Lost,* as in the lines that parallel Mulciber and Mammon, or the golden apples of the Hesperides and the fruit of Eden, Milton does not try to syncretize classical myth and Christian truth. Milton criticizes and corrects, he restores and reconstructs. "To be sure," writes Lewalski,

> these lines supply a correction to the classical fables. But the important point in both cases is that the Bard can only imagine and render his ineffable truths by recalling those fables, and that the reader is also led by these fables to imagine truths that transcend them.[64]

I do not mean to suggest that the difference between allegory and other types of significance is always easy to discern. Indeed, Milton's (and Calvin's) use of classical literature may be considered "allegorical" in the moral sense described in the famous passage in Dante's "Letter to Can Grande." Dante there distinguishes the literal level of Scripture from the moral, typological, and anagogical levels. The latter three are all "allegorical," Dante says, in that they take the significance of the passage beyond its literal meaning. But the moral significance of a work is part of its contemporary, human meaning for any succeeding age. The Protestant Reformers, in fact, worked to *recover* this level of meaning by restraining the exegetical license that had obscured it in much previous biblical and literary interpretation, and Milton was even stricter than many of the Reformers.

In his study of Milton's view of the Bible's figurative language, H. R. MacCallum concludes that Milton "upholds the Protestant rejection of multiple meanings, rejects allegory as an instrument of exegesis, permits a compound sense [of Scriptural meanings] but prefers

62. Lewalski, *"Paradise Lost" and the Rhetoric of Literary Forms,* 5.

63. Lewalski, *"Paradise Lost" and the Rhetoric of Literary Forms,* 5.

64. Lewalski, *"Paradise Lost" and the Rhetoric of Literary Forms,* 8.

types clearly established by the New Testament. . . ."[65] Like the Reformers, of course, Milton accepted the typological interpretation of the Old Testament as found in the New Testament:

> Each passage of scripture has only a single sense, though in the Old Testament this sense is often a combination of the historical and the typological, take Hosea xi.1, for example, compared with Matt. ii.15: *I have called my son out of Egypt.* This can be read correctly in two senses, as a reference both to the people of Israel and to Christ in his infancy. (*YP* 6:581)

As MacCallum notes, this passage shows Milton's hostility to the multiplicity of meanings, common to allegorical exegesis, while yet acknowledging a combination of historical and typological senses.[66] It also shows that Milton tends to restrain the typological reading of the Old Testament by the examples of the New Testament, rather than use the typological method to license an unrestrained allegorical hermeneutic.

The point is that Milton suggests a way of reading that is aware of the multiple meanings of a text, while yet differing from allegoresis. This way of reading Scripture is different as well from allegorizing any secular poetry — including Milton's own — so that it will harmonize with ideology. For Milton, these approaches divorce the contemporary senses of the text from its literal meaning.

In the Reformers' view, this is precisely what allegorical interpreters, beginning with Origen, had done. In his exegesis of 2 Corinthians 3:6 ("for the letter killeth, but the spirit giveth life"), Origen had interpreted "letter" as "the grammatical and genuine meaning of Scripture," writes Calvin, "or as they say, the literal."[67] Origen interpreted "spirit" as the allegorical meaning. The allegorical meaning of Scripture was then associated with life, and the literal with spiritual death. "This error," Calvin continues, "became a source of much evil":

> It not only gave license for corrupting the true meaning of Scripture, but also led to the notion that the more unprincipled the allegorizer,

65. MacCallum, "Milton and Figurative Interpretation of the Bible," *University of Toronto Quarterly* 31 (July 1962): 409.

66. MacCallum, "Milton and Figurative Interpretation of the Bible," 404-5.

67. Calvin, *Commentaries,* 107.

> the more expert he was as interpreter of scripture. So, many of the ancients threw the sacred Word of God around as though it were a tennis ball. . . . Now, anybody could do anything, and many did; there was no madness so absurd or so great but it could be practiced in the name of some allegory. Even good people were caught, and invented many false notions, because they were deceived by their fondness for allegory.[68]

The exegetical restraint that Calvin recommends is evident in his refusal to accept the traditional interpretation of Genesis 3:15 — the prophecy that the seed of the woman would bruise the serpent's head — as the first announcement of the gospel of Christ. "Seed" is a collective noun, says Calvin, and therefore it must refer to the victory of the church as a whole over Satan. Paul alludes to the verse in this manner, Calvin notes, where Paul proclaims that the church will shortly "bruise" Satan under its feet.[69] In this case, Calvin is rejecting a typological interpretation — one quite important to *Paradise Lost* and accepted by many contemporary Protestants — on two grounds: the grammatical sense of the words and the witness of the Scriptures as a whole. Elsewhere, he has harsh words for those who attempt to erect entire doctrines on allegories by "departing from the literal sense."[70] In the *Institutes* Calvin severely criticizes the allegorization of the story of the Good Samaritan, in which the traveler is left "half dead" on the road (poorly translated *semivivus,* half alive, in the Vulgate).[71] Previous allegorical writers had interpreted *semivivus* to mean that the human race, though disfigured by sin, is still "half alive." Calvin rejects such interpretations for departing from the ordinary sense of the words, and for using allegorical interpretation as the basis for Christian doctrine.

Milton too rejected allegorical exegesis as a means of establishing Christian doctrine. The doctrine of baptism, for instance, should not be built on "shaky analogies" to circumcision, "but to the Lord's own

68. Calvin, *Commentaries,* 108.

69. Rom. 16:20; see Calvin, *Genesis,* 171.

70. Calvin, *Genesis,* 114.

71. See John Calvin, *Institutes of the Christian Religion,* ed. John T. McNeill, trans. Ford Lewis Battles, Library of Christian Classics (Philadelphia: Westminster Press, 1960), 2.5.19.

institution. . . . Even the theologians who oppose me [concerning infant baptism]," says Milton, "agree in this" (*YP* 6:549). Milton's exegetical restraint is evident in his characteristic use of the Old Testament to point to the moral and spiritual life of the individual Christian, rather than as typological pointers to Christ.[72]

The ultimate danger of allegorical exegesis may be seen in Calvin's comments on Exodus 4:2-4 (where Moses' rod is transformed into a serpent), which was used in contemporary defenses of transubstantiation: "it has no relevance to the present case," says Calvin tersely, going on with these words: "These adversaries of ours would hold that Christ's body was allegorically affixed to the wood of the cross."[73] The danger, then, is the divorce between faith and history. By treating words as if they are "tennis balls," many "good people" may be deceived into thinking their faith never had a historical basis in the past, and therefore it never needs to be tested against present reality. In *Milton and the Christian Tradition,* C. A. Patrides writes that Calvin's criticism of allegorical interpretation "testifies to the ever-present Christian concern lest the allegorical approach to the Bible should deprive Christianity of its uniquely historical character, reducing it to a mere philosophy, or, worse, an aggregate of myths."[74] By divorcing meaning from the text, one risks divorcing faith from history. At that point, allegoresis becomes fundamentally different from exegesis. In her study of "imposed allegory," Rosemond Tuve describes two principles that can prevent the allegorically minded reader from abusing a text: his or her reading should not require that "large portions of a work have to be covered with blotting paper" while directing the reader to the "correct" meaning in what is left; and it should not ignore the main direction of flow in the original work.[75] Her conclusion on the allegorical approach of Christine de Pisan is analogous to the difference between literary study and ideological criticism: "The whole attempt is outstandingly different from serious religious exegesis, which is concerned to find and read the

72. See MacCallum, "Milton and Figurative Interpretation of the Bible," 407-8.

73. Calvin, *Institutes,* 4.17.15.

74. C. A. Patrides, *Milton and the Christian Tradition* (Oxford: Clarendon, 1966), 27.

75. Tuve, *Allegorical Imagery,* 234, 235, 291.

meanings indubitably *in* the history read; [exegesis] would only be hampered by this multiplication of vessels to carry the same meaning in different and clever ways. . . ."[76]

The tensions between faith and history will always be felt by interpreters like Milton and Calvin, who refuse to syncretize the significance of each by interpreting one solely with reference to the other. In ideological criticism, by contrast, the parallel tension between literal, textual appearance and true, ideological reality is overcome by interpreting each text with reference to ideology.[77] The literal appearance of mutuality in much of Milton's writing, for instance, can be reinterpreted by Mary Nyquist as the outcome of Milton's deeply patriarchal assumptions, for there is no longer any tension between her ideological faith and the historical reality of Milton's text. The appearance that both Adam and Eve learn from one another in *Paradise Lost* can be reinterpreted by Christine Froula as merely the first stage in the patriarchal domestication of female subjectivity and autonomy. As history is divorced from faith in the allegorical hermeneutic, so experience is divorced from text in ideological criticism. It does no good whatever to point out that feminist ideology must frequently depart from a full reading of Milton's text to reach the level, within the "multiplicity of meanings," that is consistent with pure feminism. It does no good to argue that the ideological mode uses this allegorical approach to establish or confirm doctrines already affirmed by prior ideological commitments. The ideologue will respond with some version of "for the letter killeth but the spirit giveth life." Calvin can talk all he wants about words turning into tennis balls, and Milton can issue injunctions against "shaky analogies," but the ideologue can always respond that the restrictions urged by their critics treat "literature as pointless but very fine writing," as we have seen earlier in Berubé's essay.[78] For such persons, the "pointless" letter that kills is the interpretation that seeks,

76. Tuve, *Allegorical Imagery*, 302.

77. See Kenneth Minogue, *Alien Powers: The Pure Theory of Ideology* (New York: St. Martin's Press, 1985), 101-17.

78. Michael Berubé, "Public Image Limited: Political Correctness and the Media's Big Lie," in *Debating P. C.: The Controversy over Political Correctness on College Campuses*, ed. Paul Berman (New York: Dell, 1992), 148.

naively, to comprehend what the text is trying to say; the spirit that gives life is the reader's ideology. Lacking Milton's language of "blessing" or some parallel notion of a common humanity, they cannot receive a word that has a merely "human" significance. Every word must be translated into its allegorical, ideological place.

III. Naming in Genesis and *Paradise Lost*

The ideological approach to *Paradise Lost* has been especially harmful in its interpretation of another area of human endeavor with wide cultural significance — naming. There are two apparently contradictory feminist exegetical positions on naming in Genesis 2, and both have implications for *Paradise Lost:* the first is the widely popular position of Phyllis Trible that Adam's words in Genesis 2:23 do not constitute a "naming": "And Adam said, This is now bone of my bones, and flesh of my flesh: she shalbe called woman, because shee was taken out of man." The other position is that Adam does indeed name the woman, and this is but the first act of "instituting male dominance over language, nature, and woman."[79] Common to both positions — and more fundamental for the ideologue than the exegetical truth of Genesis 2:23 — is that the Old Testament naming formulas establish the very type of power relationship that is the essential object of ideological criticism.[80]

Trible's philological argument hinges on her assertion that the Hebrew in 2:23 is "strikingly" different from the Old Testament naming formulas because it does not join the noun "name" to the verb "call."[81] Although the woman is named "Eve" before the fall in *Paradise Lost* — one of Milton's more important interpretive maneuvers — she is not so named in Genesis. In the Bible she is named after the fall, in Genesis 3:20. Before the fall she is "called woman," which Trible takes to be a

79. Froula, "When Eve Reads Milton," 160.

80. Casey Miller and Kate Swift, *Words and Women* (London: Victor Gollancz, 1977), 16; and Phyllis Trible, *God and the Rhetoric of Sexuality* (Philadelphia: Fortress Press, 1978), 99.

81. Trible, *God and the Rhetoric of Sexuality,* 100.

"recognition of sexuality" rather than a sign of power; it is therefore dissimilar to the naming of the animals. The Hebrew for "woman" "itself is not a name," she says. "It is a common noun, not a proper noun" and suggests merely differentiation from the man without any suggestion of derivation or subordination.[82] When the naming formula does occur in Genesis 3:20, after the fall ("And Adam called his wives name Eve, because she was the mother of all living"), Trible finds the language of 3:20 radically different from that of 2:23: "in effect, the man reduces the woman to the status of an animal by calling her a name."[83]

Although I am not competent to judge the philological argument, Trible's position has been seriously challenged by George W. Ramsey, who studies a very large number of Old Testament naming formulas that lack Trible's rigid structure of "call" plus "name." Ramsey concludes that the man does name the woman in Genesis 2:23, using one of a number of possible variants of the formula. He believes, however, that Trible is correct to reject any chauvinist inferences from that act. "The exclamation in Genesis 2:23 is a cry of discovery, of recognition . . . it is an act of discernment rather than an act of domination."[84]

The important ideological point, however, concerns the feminist understanding of naming, in the Old Testament, in Milton, and elsewhere: is naming primarily to be understood as an assertion of power, as feminists believe? Is it an attempt to shape the essence of the other by imposing an identity upon it?[85] If this were true, of course, Adam could have bestowed names on the animals that would have made them a "helpe meete for him" — but he does not.[86] Naming has a very wide range of significances within the Old Testament, but not every act of naming implies authority over what is named. Even in those instances where naming is associated with authority, authority does not always connote control. Hagar "called the name of the LORD. . . . Thou God

82. Trible, *God and the Rhetoric of Sexuality*, 100-101.

83. Trible, *God and the Rhetoric of Sexuality*, 133.

84. George W. Ramsey, "Is Name-Giving an Act of Domination in Genesis 2:23 and Elsewhere?" *Catholic Biblical Quarterly* 50 (1988): 35.

85. Miller and Swift, *Words and Women*, 15-16.

86. This observation (and the rest of this paragraph) is indebted to Ramsey, "Name-Giving," 32-35.

seest me" (Gen. 16:13), because of her marvelous encounter with God, not to exercise control over him. When parents name their children in the Old Testament, they are filling their role — natural and conventional — but not attempting to control their children's character or destiny. Naming in the Old Testament, concludes Ramsey, signifies the "quality of discernment" in the name-giver, as in Jacob's naming of Bethel and Peniel: Jacob recognized God's activity in these places; he did not attempt to control God.

The older position of biblical scholars, of seeing an almost magical potency in Old Testament naming similar to the function of naming in primitive myth and ritual, is giving way to the understanding of naming that Ramsey suggests. The naming of the animals is an exercise of the limited human autonomy God gives to mankind, male and female, in his blessing in Genesis 1:26. The naming of the animals in Genesis 2:19-20 establishes a relationship with them, but the Bible says nothing about subjecting the animals to the service of humanity, as the popular feminist book *Words and Women* asserts.[87] In the context of Genesis 1:26, where God gives mankind dominion over the beasts, the naming is properly an act of dominion, but its primary sense is not that of "exploiting" the animal kingdom, even for purposes consistent with the vegetarian human society that seems to exist up to Genesis 9:3-4. As biblical scholar Claus Westermann writes:

> The creator has formed the animals; the man can do nothing about this, but must accept them as God presents them to him. This is the point where the man begins to exercise his capabilities. . . . The meaning is not, as most interpreters think, that the man acquires power over the animals by naming them. . . . But rather that the man gives the animals their names and thereby puts them into a place in his world.
>
> This is not a question of magic, but basically a rational procedure. Animals simply as creatures have no name. It is only the giving of the name that creates the world of humankind. . . . By naming the animals the man opens up, determines and orders his world and

87. Miller and Swift, *Words and Women,* 16.

> incorporates them into his life. The world becomes human only through language. The act of naming is directed not to things but to the animals, to living beings. . . .[88]

An ideologue could never accept this, for it suggests a realm of human activity that is outside both ideology and the "master-subject relationship."[89] It suggests that "dominion" in an unfallen Eden is fundamentally different from "domination" and "control," as ideology understands those terms. That is, the exegesis — the attempt to discover the meaning of the text — conflicts with the ideological enterprise as a whole.

Leaving aside ideology and turning to Milton, Adam's naming of the animals in *Paradise Lost* has two purposes: to exercise his rational faculties, and to teach him his own inadequacy apart from Eve. It is his first trial and his first educational step in coming closer to God: "As thus [God] spake," says Adam,

> each Bird and Beast behold
> Approaching two and two, These cow'ring low
> With blandishment, each Bird stoop'd on his wing.
> I nam'd them, as they pass'd, and understood
> Thir Nature, with such knowledge God endu'd
> My sudden apprehension: but in these
> I found not what methought I wanted still.
>
> (8.349-55)

Giving names to the animals, says Milton, was a sign of Adam's "very great intelligence," for these names corresponded "to their properties" (*YP* 6:324; 2:602). It is significant that this exercise of dominion is not, in Milton's view, understood in the ideological terms of control or exploitation, although the passage makes clear the animals' inferiority to Adam.

According to Milton's *Christian Doctrine,* the naming follows from Adam's creation in God's image, particularly his being "endowed with

88. Westermann, *Genesis 1-11,* 228-29.
89. Miller and Swift, *Words and Women,* 16.

natural wisdom, holiness, and righteousness" (*YP* 6:324). Milton's language about God's image here is similar to that of *Paradise Lost:*

> . . . for in thir looks divine
> The image of thir glorious Maker shone,
> Truth, Wisdom, Sanctitude sever and pure,
> Severe, but in true filial freedom plac't;
> Whence true autority in men . . .
>
> (4.291-95)

Rather than control, then, the naming indicates Adam's discernment, both of the animals' nature and (as the dialogue later indicates) of his own quite different nature as well. Naming is Adam's way of establishing his relations with the world and with himself. In the process, he learns that his solitude cannot be overcome by the animals, nor do they contribute to his social happiness:

> Among unequals what society
> Can sort, what harmony or true delight?
> Which must be mutual, in proportion due
> Giv'n and receiv'd; but in disparity
> The one intense, the other still remiss
> Cannot well suit with either, but soon prove
> Tedious alike: Of fellowship I speak
> Such as I seek, fit to participate
> All rational delight, wherein the brute
> Cannot be human consort. . . .
>
> (8.383-92)

This passage should remind the reader of Satan's threat of 4.375-76: "League with you I seek / And mutual amity so strait. . . ." But far stronger is the passage's anticipation of the creation of Eve, who will provide exactly the mutual society, fellowship, and delight that Adam cannot find among the beasts. She will provide the almost musical "harmony," "proportion due," and "consort" present in the imagery here. It is noteworthy, in view of the feminist critique of 4.297, where Adam is said to be formed for "contemplation," that Adam sees his need for an equal, and that the passage specifically anticipates the "*rational* delight" he will find in Eve.

Before God supplies this need, he asks Adam why he cannot find pleasure in inferiors since God himself must "hold converse" with inferiors. Adam's response is an extraordinary instance of his learning in "natural theology":

> Thou in thyself art perfet, and in thee
> Is no deficience found; not so is Man,
> But in degree, the cause of his desire
> By conversation with his like to help,
> Or solace his defects.
>
> (8.415-20)

Milton's language here is similar to the note of the Geneva Bible on Genesis 2:22, where the commentators remark on the insufficiency of the male by himself: the creation of the woman from Adam's rib, they say, "signif[ies] that mankinde was perfit, when the woman was created, which before was like an unperfit buylding." Even in their unfallen state, Adam and Eve are imperfect. Both need to learn the nature of the world, of God, and of their need for the other.

In his response, God commends Adam's naming of the animals both for the accuracy of the names and for the self-knowledge Adam has attained:

> Thus far to try thee, Adam, I was pleas'd,
> And find thee knowing not of Beasts alone,
> Which thou hast rightly nam'd, but of thyself,
> Expressing well the spirit within thee free,
> My Image, not imparted to the Brute,
> Whose fellowship therefore unmeet for thee
> Good reason was thou freely shouldst dislike.
>
> (8.437-43)

The "free spirit" of Adam is his autonomy, rightly used in the acquisition of natural knowledge and in his discernment (through the process of naming) of his own inadequacy. The whole process flows directly from his creation in God's image and God's blessing upon him.

Eve, too, exercises the intellectual aspect of the blessing in the naming of the flowers, to which she refers with regret after the fall:

> Must I thus leave thee Paradise? thus leave
> Thee Native Soil, these happy Walks and Shades,
> Fit haunt of Gods? . . .
> . . . O flow'rs
> That never will in other Climate grow,
> My early visitation, and my last
> At Ev'n, which I bred up with tender hand
> From the first op'ning bud, and gave ye Names.
>
> (11.269-77)

Milton's interest in Eve as a giver of names was unprecedented.[90] It is one of Milton's illustrations of her creation in the image of God, which both Calvin and the Geneva commentators believed she shared with Adam. But it does not sit well with feminist criticism of Milton, for, without diminishing the differences between Adam and Eve, it suggests their mutuality and the ability of each to share in the particular excellences of the other. What is more, the passage occurs in the chief work of "English literature's paradigmatic patriarch."[91] The only solution, for feminism, is to harmonize this passage with its prior ideological commitments. Nyquist comments that Eve's naming of the flowers is "revealed only incidentally" in her lament for the garden. The naming "seems never to have had the precise status of an event." Instead, her naming "becomes associated not with rational insight and dominion but rather with the act of lyrical utterance, and therefore with the affective responsibilities of the domestic sphere into which her subjectivity has always already fallen."[92] The sharp separation of their

90. John Leonard, *Naming in Paradise: Milton and the Language of Adam and Eve* (Oxford: Clarendon, 1990), 21.

91. Nyquist, "Gynesis, Genesis, Milton's Eve," 167.

92. Margaret Ferguson and Mary Nyquist, eds., *Re-membering Milton* (New York: Methuen, 1987), 100.

"spheres," however, is a presupposition of the feminist critique, not of the poem. While it is true, as Diane McColley writes, that Eve's naming is "subordinate on the scale of nature to Adam's charge, the 'bright consummate floure' which 'spirits odorous breathes' is Raphael's epitome of the process by which all forms of life become 'more refin'd, more spiritous, and pure.' "[93] Flowers are a figure for the process of sanctification in *Paradise Lost.* Eve's solitary work among her "fruits and flow'rs" is an example of her rightful exercise of autonomy in the garden's overall "economy," in the older and fuller sense of that term (8.44-47; see 9.233).

To assign Eve's naming and labors to a restricted, stratified sphere is a good example of how ideological requirements lead away from the text of the poem, as allegorical exegesis led away from the text of the Bible and classical literature. Naming is the first step in acquiring wisdom in *Paradise Lost,* and like the development of conscience, it contributes to a universal human civilization. Naming is a blessed human capacity, available before and after the fall, and available to everyone, for locating oneself rationally and relationally in the universe.

The cultural institution that is most obviously available to all persons through God's blessing is, of course, marriage. Marriage is prior to all the other cultural manifestations of blessing because it constitutes the first society and because of its association with fertility (*YP* 2:598-614). The language of blessing will enable us to understand the view of marriage in *Paradise Lost.* This language puts the poem's discussion of marriage in its proper, larger context and may help to redirect the current debate away from its narrow focus on Milton's view of women.

"Blessing" and Marriage in Paradise Lost

The blessing of Adam and Eve is first associated with the bond between them and its promise of offspring. Following the language of Genesis 1, Raphael tells Adam and Eve:

93. Milton, *PL,* 5.475-81; McColley, *Milton's Eve,* 113.

> Male he created thee, but thy consort
> Female for Race; then bless'd Mankind, and said,
> Be fruitful, multiply, and fill the Earth,
> Subdue it, and throughout Dominion hold. . . .
>
> (7.529-32)

Adam and Eve are referred to as the "blest pair" in the narrator's description of their unfallen love (4.774). In common with English speakers before and since his time, Milton typically uses the word "bliss" to describe the blessings of harmony between husband and wife, or between God and humanity. In their joint hymn of praise to God, Adam and Eve give thanks for their day of work, which they "Have finish't happy in our mutual help / And mutual love, the Crown of all our bliss" (4.727-28). "Blessing" is etymologically distinct from "bliss." According to the Oxford English Dictionary, the Anglo-Saxons used the antecedents of "bless" to render the Latin *benedicere* and Greek *eulogein.* (These words, earlier, had themselves been chosen to render the Hebrew *brk.*) "Bliss," by contrast, was originally a synonym for earthly "blitheness." "At a very early date," the OED states, "the popular etymological consciousness began to associate this verb [bless] with the substantive *bliss* . . . which affected the use of both words . . ." (OED, under "bless"). "Bliss" gradually lost most of its secular connotations, say the OED editors, and gained heavenly ones. Milton's use of "blithe" suggests that he is unaware of the etymologically distinct origins of the two words. It is no accident, however, that Milton generally restricts "bliss" to heavenly or marital blessings. The sexual component of bliss is understood in Milton solely with reference to marriage, in marked contrast to the courtly and Petrarchan love poetry that preceded *Paradise Lost,* as well as to the Cavalier poetry contemporary with the composition of Milton's epics.

For Milton, sexual bliss implies marital harmony, which in turn implies a rational "conversation," both spoken and acted, between husband and wife. "Love . . . hath his seat / In Reason," says Raphael (8.589-91). In *Comus* the Lady overpowers the seductive rhetoric of Comus with a rational defense of temperance. She specifically says that "Nature's full *blessings*" could be fully enjoyed by all — if only all were temperate in their enjoyment (lines 756-99). In *Paradise Lost,* when Adam joins the "sweet intercourse / Of looks and smiles" to their joint cultivation of the garden, he adds that "smiles from Reason flow" (9.239). Wedded love is, for Milton, the true habitation of sexual joy:

> Here Love his golden shafts imploys, here lights
> His constant Lamp, and waves his purple wings,
> Reigns here and revels; not in the bought smile
> Of Harlots, loveless, joyless, unendeared,
> Casual fruition, nor in Court Amours,
> Mixt Dance, or wanton Mask, or Midnight Ball,
> Or Serenate, which the starv'd Lover sings.
>
> (4.763-69)

The joint labor of Adam and Eve is "delight to Reason join'd," as Adam says, and their delight follows naturally from their sexual, marital, rational, and spiritual harmony.

In its spiritual significance, "bliss," like "rest," is related to the entire structure of the poem. The first sentence of *Paradise Lost* announces that the poem's subject is the disobedience that resulted in the "loss of Eden, till one greater Man / Restore us, and regain the blissful seat." At the end of the poem, Michael's apocalyptic new heaven and new earth carry the promise of bringing "forth fruits Joy and eternal Bliss" (12.551). Like the New Testament writers, Milton sees the ultimate blessing of God in the kind of joy the believer receives from harmonious union with God. That blessing is symbolized by the marriage between Christ and his church (Eph. 5:25), in which all Christians are metaphorically female and respond to Christ's initiative of grace (see, for instance, *YP* 2:465). In this image, the union of Christ and his church does at least as much to explain human marriage as human marriage explains that union.

One therefore needs to qualify even Joan Webber's statement that, in *Paradise Lost,* marriage is the "central figure of the way the world is." The relation of Christ to the church is not to be understood as a projection of human marriage any more than the biblical metaphors of "Father" and "Son" are projections of human fathers and sons.

The projectionist theory of religion is an assumption of much recent feminist criticism of Milton: "God is a *perfected* image of Adam," writes Christine Froula, "an all-powerful male Creator who soothes Adam's fears of female power by Himself claiming credit for the original creation of the world."[94] This statement follows directly from Froula's ideology, but it is not how Milton understands the workings of biblical language. It used to be a commonplace of Milton criticism to note the doctrine, common to Aquinas, Calvin, and Milton, of the "accommodated language" of Scripture, which contrasts sharply with Froula's presupposed projectionism. Milton's view, expressed in *Christian Doctrine,* is that accommodated language makes God comprehensible in human terms while yet limiting human speculation:

> It is safest for us to form an image of God in our minds which corresponds to his representation and description of himself in the sacred writings. Admittedly, God is always described or outlined not as he really is but in such a way as will make him conceivable to us. Nevertheless, we ought to form just such a mental image of him as he, in bringing himself within the limits of our understanding, wishes us to form. Indeed he has brought himself down to our level expressly to prevent our being carried beyond the reach of human comprehension, and outside the written authority of scripture, into the vague subtleties of speculation. (*YP* 6:133-34)

This means that the male imagery for God is not to be taken in an ontological sense. On the contrary, God's fatherhood is understood primarily with reference to his relation to the Son, and the sonship of Christ is understood primarily with reference to his relation to the Father — particularly his voluntary act of emptying himself and dying for God's people.[95] This act is the very reverse of the kind of patriarchy that many current feminists assume the Bible represents. Neither the first nor the second person of the Trinity is a projection of human fathers and sons. *Paradise Lost* fully reflects a biblical understanding of

94. Froula, "When Eve Reads Milton," 160.

95. Garrett Green, "The Gender of God and the Theology of Metaphor," in *Speaking the Christian God: The Holy Trinity and the Challenge of Feminism,* ed. Alvin F. Kimel Jr. (Grand Rapids, Mich.: Wm. B. Eerdmans, 1992), 58-64.

metaphor, while its detractors often assume the truth of the projectionist understanding — and apply it to Milton.

Similarly, the human institution of marriage (like "fatherhood" and "sonship") is stretched far beyond its worldly significance, for in this case the tenor, unity with Christ, does more to explain the vehicle, marriage, than vice versa.[96] In *Tetrachordon,* for instance, Milton says that "mariage . . . is the neerest resemblance of our union with Christ," which puts marriage in the position of resembling the believer's unity with Christ, even if Milton's usage diminishes somewhat the distinction between tenor and vehicle (*YP* 2:606). Marriage takes on a cosmic significance, therefore, not so much because everything in the universe should resemble human marriage, but because the fulfillment of God's blessing will result in the harmonious union of everything with God. Marriage is the "sum of earthly bliss," says Adam to Raphael (*PL* 8.522). That "bliss" is twisted by both Adam and Eve during their temptation and fall (9.831, 879, 916), not to be fully restored until the fulfillment of the Son's words to the Father: "All my redeem'd may dwell in joy and bliss, / Made one with me as I with thee am one" (11.43-44). The harmony between Adam and Eve, though enjoyed after the fall, will only be perfected at the end of time, when human marriage will be subsumed in the community of the saints with Christ.

* * * * *

96. On the general point of biblical metaphor as it relates to current feminism, see Roland Frye, "Language for God and Feminist Language," in *Speaking the Christian God,* 17-43. In the same collection of essays, Garrett Green discusses the projectionist theory of religion, originating in Feuerbach, which is paradoxically at the basis of both feminist critiques of God the Father and patriarchal misuse of this metaphor: both "share a common proposition: that the function of divinity is to provide a model for humanity," a corollary of Feuerbach's notion that " 'God is the mirror of man' " (54, 47). In his article "Milton and Figurative Interpretation of the Bible," H. R. MacCallum states that Milton's doctrine of accommodation eliminates "any distinction between the 'tenor' and 'vehicle' " (403). Perhaps that statement should be qualified, but MacCallum's emphasis is in the right direction, namely away from explaining God with reference to human and natural phenomena.

Virtually every reader of *Paradise Lost* sees that the descriptions of Adam stress his rationality and strength, while those of Eve stress her subjectivity. A common feminist critique is that Eve's subjectivity gives her an autonomous power that Adam fears and must subject to the patriarchal rule of "reason." It is true that Eve's subjectivity gives her an autonomy that Adam recognizes. But it is likewise true that Adam's rationality gives him an autonomy that Eve recognizes. Each of them must come to value the autonomy of the other rightly — neither overvaluing nor undervaluing it — and each must come to a true estimate of his or her individual excellences and deficiencies. Their growth through this process, which is fraught with all the dangers and possibilities of true liberty, is similar to what happens in any good marriage.

I have already noted Adam's perception of his need for an "other" in his account of the naming of the animals. Adam also comes to realize that Eve helps teach him the very virtues (wisdom, strength) that the feminist critique associates solely with masculinity in Milton:

> I from the influence of thy looks receive
> Access in every Virtue, in thy sight
> More wise, more watchful, stronger, if need were
> Of outward strength. . . .
>
> (9.309-12)

At this point in the separation scene, Adam is arguing that Satan's temptation will have less force if they meet him together. But before he suggests that Eve may need him, he says that he needs her. He needs her for the growth of *every* virtue, not just for her expression of the "feminine" ones. By sharing God's image, both Adam and Eve have access to "'Truth, Wisdom, Sanctitude sever and pure" (4.293). Milton's choice of words in that line is almost precisely parallel to the marginal gloss on Genesis 1:27 in the Geneva Bible: "this image and licknes of God in man is expounded Ephes. 4,24; where it is written, that man was created after God in righteousness & true holines, meaning by these two wordes all perfection, as wisdome, trueth, innocencie, power, &c." Two of the words (wisdom and truth) are identical in Milton and the Geneva Bible's comment; the others are closely parallel: sanctitude to holiness, pure to innocence, severe to power. It is correct to note that Milton goes on to say that Adam is particularly formed "for contemplation" (4.297), but by book 9, Adam has come to realize that Eve is a help for him in the pursuit of wisdom as well as in other ways.

"Domestic Adam," as he is described at this point in the separation scene, goes on to respond to Eve's charge that he mistrusts her faith by urging her against solitary labor: "Not then mistrust, but tender love enjoins, / That I should mind thee oft, and mind thou me" (9.357-58). "Mind" here means "remind" in the sense of reminding the other, especially of his or her rational duties to God: "For God left free the Will," Adam has just said, "for what obeys / Reason, is free, and Reason he made right . . ." (9.351-52). Both of them have access to this capacity. While correcting Adam's unqualified notion that Eve "seems . . . in herself complete" and urging him to fill his "just and right" position as her "Head," Raphael has earlier taught Adam that his spouse "sees when thou art seen least wise" (8.578). He has taught Adam that he will do well to "mind" Eve. Her wisdom is not completely autonomous; nor is Adam's. Nor is their wisdom identical. Each needs to learn that the blessing of marriage is a balance of autonomy and dependence. Each member grows toward God and toward the other, through the virtues that the other member brings to remembrance, while yet retaining his or her own individuality.

Adam's very first lesson in his life with Eve is perhaps his most important. John Leonard has sensitively put together the two accounts of the naming of Eve in books 4 and 8, and shown the significance of the chronology for their relationship.[97] When Adam first sees Eve, he exclaims for joy:

> I now see
> Bone of my bone, Flesh of my Flesh, my Self
> Before me; Woman is her Name, of Man
> Extracted.
>
> (8.494-97)

97. Leonard, *Naming in Paradise,* 35-40.

Although he names her "woman," however, Eve does not immediately turn to Adam. In her account, Eve reminds Adam that she turned away from him until "Thou following cri'd'st aloud, Return fair *Eve* . . ." (4.481). It is significant, first of all, that Milton departs from the biblical chronology in granting her the name before the fall. This means that the association of "Eve" with "evil" is a postlapsarian one — it is a pun of Adam's fallen imagination, similar to the debased punning of the devils (6.558-627).[98] Eve's name has a positive significance for Milton, unlike most contemporary expositors of Genesis.

Beyond this, however, the account of book 4 shows the significance of the identity of "Eve" for their relationship. Putting Eve's own account together with that of Adam's, Leonard writes,

> Not content to be "Woman," Eve wants a name all of her own — and to her undying credit she gets one. . . . Only now does Eve approve Adam's "pleaded reason" (8.510) and permit him to lead her to their bower.[99]

This naming is no doubt an exercise of Adam's "headship," as Milton conceives it. But it also implies discernment on the part of the namer, Adam, like biblical naming generally. Adam has learned his need for an "other," and Eve's naming is a recognition that their relationship will supply that need. Adam's naming also recognizes that Eve has a very particular identity — and a proper recognition of this identity must precede their sexual union. He has to follow her, literally, as she turns away from him. He must realize that she is his "individual solace," where "individual" means both that she is inseparable from him and that she is a separate human being. He learns that Eve "would be woo'd, and not unsought be won" (8.503). None of this is consistent with

98. When double meanings occur at other, more innocent points in *Paradise Lost,* as Leonard, Stanley Fish, Arnold Stein, and others have shown, they often make one imagine, with regret, the augmented, uncorrupted power of prelapsarian language. Milton's use of "error" is perhaps the most famous example (Leonard, *Naming in Paradise,* 233f.). A similar, well-known example is the double meaning of "individual" in 4.486, which is important for my argument below. The punning of the devils, by contrast, "establishes a clearly definable antipoetic," as Kathleen Swaim says, to that of the divine powers in the poem. See Swaim, *Before and after the Fall,* 186.

99. Leonard, *Naming in Paradise,* 40.

sexual ideology, whether patriarchal or feminist. It can, of course, be harmonized by a clever interpreter, by seeing Adam's "following," perhaps, as producing diffidence and rage in him, or by seeing his "wooing" as a mystification of sexual domination.

Eve's account of her creation and naming stresses her subjectivity, especially in the pleasure she takes in her own reflection in the lake:

> As I bent down to look, just opposite,
> A Shape within the wat'ry gleam appear'd
> Bending to look on me, I started back,
> It started back, but pleas'd I soon return'd,
> Pleas'd it return'd as soon with answering looks
> Of sympathy and love; there I had fixt
> Mine eyes till now, and pin'd with vain desire,
> Had not a voice thus warn'd me.
>
> (4.460-67)

Like Adam's capacity for reason, Eve's subjectivity is good but imperfect. Without instruction from above and exercise of their natural reason, each of these capacities would lead them astray: Adam to faulty speculation, Eve to narcissistic sterility. Each would betray the blessing they received at creation. The warning voice has to repeat its opening phrase to get Eve's attention:

> What thou seest,
> What there thou seest fair Creature is thyself,
> With thee it came and goes: but follow me,
> And I will bring thee where no shadow stays
> Thy coming, and thy soft imbraces, hee
> Whose image thou art, him thou shalt enjoy
> Inseparably thine, to him shalt bear
> Multitudes like thyself, and thence be call'd
> Mother of human Race.
>
> (4.467-75)

The voice does not condemn her subjectivity as wicked, any more than Raphael condemns Adam's curiosity in itself. The voice joins her subjectivity to the blessing of fertility, promising "multitudes *like thyself*," and linking that fertility to her identity as "mother of human race." "What could I do," recalls Eve, "But follow straight, invisibly thus led?" (4.475-76). Eve could have done many things, of course. She could have stayed, or she could have walked elsewhere, just as Adam could have decided that the animals were sufficient for his social needs. Instead, she exercises her freedom in obedience and love.

Earlier in this speech, Eve had given a false, overly inflated estimate of Adam's position: "thou / Like consort to thyself canst nowhere find" (4.447-48). Like Adam's partially mistaken estimate of Eve at 8.534-59, this phrase comes amid many valid complimentary statements. But Adam's very next words to Eve correct her misapprehension in the gentlest possible way. He addresses her as "Fair Consort" (4.610). It is typical of a newly married couple, is it not, that their early knowledge of each other should be faulty, and that they should err on the side of attributing too much good, rather than too little, to their mate. Would that all our defects were such, and that they could be overcome by compliments to and from our spouses.

Adam continues his speech by indicating that they must rise early the next day to accomplish the labor that awaits them in the garden. Eve's response is another passage that grates on modern sensibilities:

> My Author and Disposer, what thou bidd'st
> Unargu'd I obey; so God ordains,
> God is thy Law, thou mine: to know no more
> Is woman's happiest knowledge and her praise.
> With thee conversing I forget all time,
> All seasons and their change, all please alike.
>
> (4.635-40)

Even here, however, Eve's words are not easily assimilable to a feminist critique. Eve does not say to Adam that "whatsoe'er" thou bidd'st, she obeys. She says "what" thou bidd'st. The "what" refers not just to Adam speaking, but to the content of what Adam has spoken above, namely the need for "pleasant labor, to reform" the garden. Moreover, "So God ordains" refers not just to Adam's position as "author and disposer" but also to Eve's intellectual assent to what Adam has said: namely, that God ordained them to reform the garden. In fact, she is more committed to the "economics" of the garden than Adam: it is this very conviction of their vocation to tend the garden that leads to her argument with Adam — not bad in itself — that they should work separately in order to accomplish more work. There is no doubt that Milton saw a hierarchy in marriage. But Eve's acceptance of it, here and elsewhere, is due to her rational assent to Adam's perception of their spiritual and economic duties.

When Eve's interests lie outside of Adam's, she feels free to pursue them on her own. For instance, she listens "attentive" (7.51) to the story Raphael tells her and Adam, from the middle of book 5 through the end of book 7. But at the beginning of book 8, when Adam's questions lead to "studious thoughts abstruse" regarding the planetary motions, Eve departs (8.44). Milton is careful to add that Eve was fully capable of understanding Raphael's discourse and deriving pleasure from it, but she preferred to hear the discourse as retold in Adam's words, later (8.48-57). More important, she departs in order to attend to her fruits and flowers,

> To visit how they prosper'd, bud and bloom,
> Her Nursery; they at her coming sprung
> And toucht by her fair tendance gladlier grew.
>
> (8.45-47)

Eve has already lent an attentive ear to the creation of the heavenly bodies, and Adam has already worked in the garden. Her solitary gardening is a rational enjoyment and fulfillment of her original blessing, just as Adam's pursuit of knowledge is a rational fulfillment of his. The fact that they are solitary is not, for Milton, an indictment. Their separate labors have an appropriate autonomy, under the blessing of God, for accomplishing their worldly tasks.

Conclusion

Several criticisms of feminist ideology have noted that the ideologue tends to adopt the perspective or technique of Satan in *Paradise Lost.* Adopting Satan as hero is only the most obvious of these. Diane

McColley implies that "Satan's dreary habit of thinking himself impaired by another's goodness" is a source of the politically oriented reader's displeasure with Milton.[100] William Shullenberger worries lest the current feminist misreadings of Milton result in the same kind of "eternal enmity [that] we can see in the archetypal misreader, Satan."[101] It hardly needs to be added that the readers they criticize share Satan's perspective on Eden, who "Saw undelighted all delight" (4.286). The tendency to use lame or insulting puns is another characteristic such readers share with the fallen angels, as in a book entitled *Re-membering Milton* or in turning "father . . . into a fat-her."[102]

Many of the humanistic readings of Milton, such as those by McColley, Shullenberger, and Joan Webber, express dismay over such tendencies. They see in Milton's entire work, and especially in *Paradise Lost,* an ability to "grasp the essentials of a problem," such as the tensions between liberty and virtue, the conflicting claims of autonomy and obedience, and relations between the genders.[103] I doubt, however, that the humanistic readings will succeed in overcoming the ideological objections to Milton.[104] My doubt stems ultimately from the nature of ideology. By failing to recognize any autonomous realm for culture, the ideologue must, perforce, oppose the figure of Milton root and branch. The fact is, however, that the ideological readings cannot succeed either: the attempt to understand Milton — or cultural achievements generally — from within ideological criticism will fail, ending (again, like Milton's Satan) in a combination of rage and self-parody.[105]

100. Danielson, *The Cambridge Companion to Milton,* 159-60.

101. Shullenberger, "Wrestling with the Angel," 81.

102. Susan Gubar and Sandra Gilbert, *The War of the Words,* vol. 1 of *No Man's Land: The Place of the Woman Writer in the Twentieth Century* (New Haven: Yale University Press, 1988), 182.

103. Webber, "The Politics of Poetry," 21.

104. A 1993 teaching guide for the most popular American anthology of British literature largely repeats the ideological arguments, without acknowledging the recent humanistic readings that are critical of them. See Alfred David, *Teaching with "The Norton Anthology of English Literature"* (New York: W. W. Norton, 1993), 129-30.

105. For a full treatment of how feminist readings of Milton, beginning with Wollstonecraft, have reproduced the very structures of oppression they intend to

Like Calvin and the writers of the Old Testament, Milton realized that every good blessing may be constructive or perverse: sexuality may be expressed in marriage and family, or in lust and bastardy; law may foster liberty or tyranny; the quest for knowledge may lead one toward God or the devil; marriage may be a blessing or a misery (*YP* 2:278). The difference in orientation is the crucial issue: does the person acknowledge that right relations with God are ordered by obedience? that human liberty requires the "strenuous" exertion of virtue, as Samson says? that sexual relations need to be established within some kind of rational and spiritual order? At its most general, does the person see that, by virtue of our common humanity — by sharing in the image of "Truth, Wisdom, Sanctitude sever and pure" — each person has the authority and freedom to contribute to the common labor of his or her civilization?

For the ideologue all of these questions are attempts to mystify the essential truth, which is the oppressiveness of society; such questions merely retard the deliverance sought by the ideologue. Far from seeing the ultimate significance of education in "delight," as *Paradise Lost* understands that term, the feminist begins "with the assumption that [she] should train students to be discontented with a culture that tolerates and perpetuates oppression."[106]

For the reader of Milton, by contrast, there is a realm of blessing, expressed in marriage, work, song, and knowledge, that welcomes and requires one's most resolute endeavors. The ultimate outcome of those endeavors issues in delight, not discontent. Milton hardly denies the need for deliverance — indeed, the treatment of this need in *Paradise Lost* is far more profound than that of any ideology — but deliverance (in the world of the poem) takes place for the purpose of reconstructing true pleasure under the blessing of God.

---

subvert, see Steven Blakemore, "Rebellious Reading: The Doubleness of Wollstonecraft's Subversion of *Paradise Lost*," *Texas Studies in Literature and Language* 34, no. 4 (1992): 451-80.

106. Barbara Frey Waxman, "Feminist Theory, Literary Canons, and the Construction of Textual Meanings," in *Practicing Theory in Introductory College Literature Courses*, ed. James M. Calahan and David B. Downing (Urbana, Ill.: National Council of Teachers of English, 1991), 149.

I have tried to suggest in this chapter a way of providing a relatively autonomous realm for culture. I believe this way offers the most secure beginning point for a biblical poetics. It is consistent with the deepest convictions of Jews and Christians without demanding that others share them. To take an analogy from political history, American constitutional democracy has provided the basis for politics among citizens who do not accept each others' deepest convictions. Nor did the framers of the constitution demand from each other an identical set of fundamental convictions before they engaged in real political activity. Nevertheless, they did provide the foundation for such activity.

My hope is that I have suggested a way of reading that is both self-conscious about its own assumptions and capable of accepting the genuine achievements of critics (like the many excellent scholars I have cited) who may base their work on different assumptions altogether. I hope to have contributed to a common, pluralistic effort of reading Milton historically and critically without having to bow to any current ideology. I hope also to have related past literary history to the most profound religious truths without turning literature or criticism into religious allegory. I hope to have nourished the discovery of new literary knowledge without pitting the secular against the religious sensibility or ignoring the possible tensions between them.

In his excellent study of Milton and the eighteenth century, Dustin Griffin concludes that one reason England, unlike France, suffered no revolutionary break with the past may have been the continuing availability of Milton's "powerful myth of paradise."[107] The language of blessing in Milton's paradise ramifies into the complex kind of pleasure that is the hallmark of Johnson's criticism. The fine balance between human art and created nature, denied by the eighteenth-century revolutionary mind, is one of Milton's legacies to Edmund Burke. As I shall explain in the next chapter, this balance is evident in Burke's treatment of "sympathy," which enables him to understand an alien, Asian civilization in ways that our current language of multiculturalism cannot reach.

107. Dustin Griffin, *Regaining Paradise: Milton and the Eighteenth Century* (Cambridge: Cambridge University Press, 1986), 133.

CHAPTER 4

From Babel to Pentecost

George Psalmanazar's "Formosa," Burke's India, and Multiculturalism

During the eighteenth century European civilization was distinguished by its massacres of native peoples from the East Indies to the West Indies. The British treatment of India may serve as a case in point of Britain's inability to see other peoples from any viewpoint other than its own interests. As it added imperial to commercial interests, the East India Company began a systematic plunder of India. Its rents and land revenues were obtained by coercion, and turned cultivated fields into deserts. It overwhelmed the native customs of Hindu and Islamic culture by imposing British law and ignoring the ancient civilizations it encountered. It smashed the traditional orders of a society that had achieved a moral level at least the equal of Britain. Its systematic pursuit of wealth produced a level of oppression that sank to Rome's treatment of its provinces in antiquity. Its inability to extend any sympathy toward the Indians as fellow human beings derived from its systematic pursuit of wealth. Britain's record calls into question the very notion of constitutional liberty that it claims to have given the world.

In many recent texts that emphasize multiculturalism, passages like this one are common, whether they indict the Europeans in the Americas, the British in India, or the Americans in Asia. Underlying such oppression, we are told, is an overall European practice of cultural superiority, or "hegemony." As described by Antonio Gramsci, "hegemony" describes the set of cultural practices that give intellectual legitimacy to a dominant group's control of others. Oppression is therefore not to be found primarily in the political acts of the British in India, for example, but in British culture itself. Nearly every aspect of European culture, from its literature to its history writing, from its mathematics to its ballet, illustrates the attempt to legitimate European oppression. The key task in the humanities today, as described in much multiculturalist theory, is not to discover new knowledge — not even new knowledge about different cultures — for the traditional methods of the humanities are part of the oppressive structure itself. Rather, the humanist's task is to reexamine European culture to expose its racist and imperialist foundations and to offer other, non-Eurocentric foundations for education. For this task, the humanistic disciplines must be largely replaced by the methods of ideological criticism, and especially its single-minded emphasis on discovering and denouncing oppression.

What is startling about my opening paragraph is that every charge comes from a man who loved the very idea of Europe and its culture. He was a man of the eighteenth century itself and is most often remembered for opposing radical revolution when it first appeared, in the French Revolution. His writings provide the foundations of modern conservatism. He was a member of the British Parliament and the Anglican Church, and he defended the landed and aristocratic orders of England against their egalitarian critics.

Edmund Burke is the last person that today's ideological multiculturalist would expect to find making the charges he does. In fact, Burke is held up as an "irony" in a 1989 book, in which the discipline of English literature is said to originate in "the imperial mission of educating colonial subjects" (in India) with the effect of "strengthen[ing] Western cultural hegemony":

> It is impossible not to be struck by the peculiar irony of a history in which England's initial involvement with the education of the natives derived less from a conviction of native immorality, as the later discourse might lead one to believe, than from the depravity of their own administrators and merchants. In Edmund Burke's words, steps

> had to be taken to "form a strong and solid security for the natives against the wrongs and oppressions of British subjects resident in Bengal."[1]

But there is really no "irony" in Burke's words or actions at all, unless one begins studying Burke — or British contact with India, or European culture generally — with a strong ideological bias. In fact, Burke's concern, which has to do with the Indian judicial system and not Indian education, comes from the high value he places on both local custom and universal "natural" law, and from his long-standing commitment to traditional (here, Hindu) rather than innovative legal establishments. Burke wants Britons to sympathize with persons of other cultures, and he knows how difficult that will be. Burke's intense interest in India and his criticisms of British imperial policy are of a piece with his entire life work. He was the most multicultural European of his era. To paraphrase Carlyle, close thy Gramsci, open thy Burke.

While the most influential theorists of multiculturalism have strong ideological foundations, not all multiculturalism presupposes a particular ideology. "Pluralistic multiculturalism" is the term Diane Ravitch has used for the nonideological approach.[2] It seeks to value the finest achievements of all cultures, without first insisting upon a particular, ideological critique of European culture. As it relates to America, this approach acknowledges that many different races, religions, and ethnicities have contributed to a common American culture, which is bound together by its political (not ethnic) values. While these values are historically associated with Anglo-Saxon culture, their contemporary application in every age has required interpretation by persons from a wide variety of cultures — from Frederick Douglass and Lincoln, from Justices Frankfurter and Harlan, from Martin Luther King

1. Gauri Viswanathan, *Masks of Conquest: Literary Study and British Rule in India* (New York: Columbia University Press, 1989), 2, 27. The quotation from Burke comes from the *Ninth Report of the Select Committee* (1783), in *The Writings and Speeches of Edmund Burke,* gen. ed. Paul Langford (Oxford: Clarendon, 1981-), 5:204. Subsequent references will use the abbreviation *WS.* Viswanathan found the quote in Eric Stokes, *The English Utilitarians and India* (Oxford: Oxford University Press, 1959).

2. Diane Ravitch, "Multiculturalism: E Pluribus Plures," *American Scholar* 59 (1990): 340.

Jr. and Hubert Humphrey. Our common language is English, but our language has been able to support a luxuriant growth of culture that reflects our diversity while remaining within a common American civilization. Pluralistic multiculturalism finds expression in inclusive anthologies, histories, and book lists. For instance, a book list produced by my city library (St. Paul, Minnesota) stresses stories told by black Americans, Asian Americans, and Mexican Americans, including the discrimination they endured and the acceptance they found here. My fifth-grade son used a history text with similar emphases. "Pluralistic multiculturalism," then, accepts the intellectual methodologies of the traditional humanities. It uses them to emphasize the contributions of different peoples to a common American culture, and to produce a heightened awareness of the obstacles faced by those outside the dominant ethnic groups.

Pluralistic multiculturalism is evident in some literature anthologies, such as *Kaleidoscope* (Oxford 1993), where college students may read fiction and nonfiction by American Indians, Jews, blacks, and immigrants, organized loosely around the theme of the book's subtitle, "stories of the American experience." These book lists and anthologies are produced for all readers, irrespective of race. They increase our knowledge and appreciation of all Americans, a goal that is embraced by conservatives and liberals, traditionalists and progressives. "The pluralists say, in effect, 'American culture belongs to us, all of us; the U.S. is us, and we remake it in every generation.'"[3] What Ravitch calls "pluralistic multiculturalism," then, assumes that this culture is available to any American with sufficient imagination and intellectual discipline to embrace it, given the opportunity.

On the other hand, "ideological multiculturalism," as I would name it, denies that a common culture is possible or desirable. It assumes that culture is determined by one's race or ethnic group, and therefore the "majority, white" culture of America can never be the culture of nonwhites. The European roots of American culture (especially as seen in colonialism and capitalism) are the source of hostility and degradation of all nonwhites. Therefore, in an effort to raise their self-esteem and establish their identity, children should study their own,

3. Ravitch, "Multiculturalism," 341.

race-based culture, whether it is African, Asian, Hispanic, Indian, European, or Pacific Islander. One of the embedded, unexamined assumptions of ideological multiculturalism is that one's ethnic upbringing initiates one into an understanding of the culture produced by one's own racial group. All white Americans are therefore presumed to have a particular cultural affinity for European authors because their skin is white. But that Greek Americans have greater affinity for Homer or Swedish Americans have greater affinity for *Beowulf* is a hypothesis that no American teacher of Homer or *Beowulf* seriously believes: racial identity and ethnic upbringing are different from education.

A second assumption follows from the first: ideological multiculturalism assumes that values not only originate in particular cultural or ethnic groups, but they are also relative to those groups. Values are not cross-cultural. For instance, a local educator in the Portland, Oregon, public schools, where this approach has been tried, says that "the 'truth' for one group does not necessarily have to be the 'truth' for another," but apparently "the truth" *is* to be found within the culture of Pacific Islanders, Asians, and so on.[4] The notion that values can be cross-cultural, a belief shared by Burke and the advocates of "pluralistic multiculturalism," is considered merely a European idea, as many attacks on "Eurocentrism" will attest.[5]

A third assumption of ideological multiculturalism is that the most significant — and in some ways the only — phenomenon worth our consideration is that of oppression, especially as evidenced in racism, colonialism, or imperialism. Gauri Viswanathan, for instance, concludes her book on the origin of English studies by linking the supposed "universality" of Western literature to European imperialism.[6] It transpires that every attempt to transcend race and national origin in the traditional academic arts and sciences has been essentially the work of the racist, European intellect, and must therefore be exposed

4. Robert K. Landers, "Conflict over Multicultural Education," *Editorial Research Reports,* 30 November 1990, 691-92.

5. Ravitch quotes Asante's advice to black students thus: "'Do not be captured by a sense of universality given to you by the Eurocentric viewpoint; such a viewpoint is contradictory to your own ultimate reality" (Ravitch, "Multiculturalism," 342).

6. Viswanathan, *Masks of Conquest,* 167.

and subjected to relentless criticism. Moreover, even attempts to "broaden the curriculum to include the literature of other cultures" may be used as an instrument of hegemonic control, according to Viswanathan, unless it is founded in a criticism of the dominant culture.[7] It follows that any historical figure or work of literature is suspect if the outcome suggests mutual accommodation between the races, or any understanding of reality other than the ideological framework of oppressor versus oppressed. Booker T. Washington, for instance, is held up for scorn by the influential multiculturalist James A. Banks as one "who helped Whites to conquer or oppress powerless people rather than [one] who challenged the existing social, economic, and political order."[8] The same criticism is made of *Sounder,* a moving, Newberry Award-winning book about a black sharecropper's son who searches for his unjustly punished father, jailed for a trivial offense. There is a single, correct understanding for the ideological multiculturalist of how blacks ought to regard all reality: the hostile, confrontational approach is correct; stories and persons that propose other values — education, self-development, sympathy among all persons — are incorrect. In broad terms, this is the debate between Washington and W. E. B. Dubois, carried down through the conflicting positions of Martin Luther King Jr. and Malcolm X. But how does one know which side is correct without looking at the content of the debate and its aftermath? And what happens if a teacher wants to prepare his or her students to make up their own minds, rather than indoctrinate them with a single view of the history, literature, and art they encounter?

In this chapter, I will look at the foundations of recent ideological multiculturalism to demonstrate how its manipulation of current prejudices, its willingness to overlook conflicting evidence, and its denunciation of opponents have a parallel in the eighteenth-century visit to England by the "Formosan," George Psalmanazar. An alternative approach to an alien culture is Edmund Burke's, which presupposes a common sympathy among humanity. While it embraces what it can

7. Viswanathan, *Masks of Conquest,* 167-69.

8. James A. Banks, "A Curriculum for Empowerment, Action, and Change," in *Empowerment through Multicultural Education,* ed. Christine E. Sleeter (Albany: State University of New York Press, 1991), 131.

of the other culture and criticizes what it must of its own, it does not see a love of British culture as requiring the domination of others. While it acknowledges that a system of oppression does exist, the removal of that oppression does not require the imposition of an alternative ideological system.

The theoretical basis for my own, pluralistic form of multiculturalism comes ultimately from the biblical accounts of the Tower of Babel and Pentecost. These stories offer an alternative to ideological notions of human unity and diversity. In the first story, human beings try to impose a purely secular, coercive unity on everyone, a unity that is outside the blessing of God. They are then scattered, not so much as a punishment for what they have done, but for what they may do in the future. In the story of Pentecost, the reuniting of mankind is prefigured, not by having everyone speak a single language, but by allowing everyone to listen obediently in his or her own language to the wonders of God.

In this chapter, my method is close to an "intertextual" reading of biblical, eighteenth-century, and recent texts. I am not claiming any direct historical connection between the biblical accounts and Burke, Psalmanazar, or recent writings on multiculturalism. Rather, I find common themes and concerns that are mutually illuminating. The difference between my method and that of other intertextual readings, however, is this: I do not regard the texts as having strictly parallel value; rather, the biblical accounts lead to a deeper, more rigorous teaching regarding linguistic (and cultural) diversity. In this chapter a biblical poetics involves the search for that teaching.

George Psalmanazar's "Formosa" and Parallels to Recent Multiculturalism

In 1703 a young man claiming to be an inhabitant of Formosa landed at Harwich at the invitation of Henry Compton, bishop of London. A soldier in the regiment of the duke of Mecklenburg, he had been discovered by the chaplain of some Scottish troops when both regiments were quartered in Holland. For five years George Psalmanazar enjoyed the life of a celebrity in England. He published his *Description of*

Formosa (1704) shortly after arriving, dividing the book roughly in half between his quarrels with the Jesuits and an account of the religion, agriculture, arts, social customs, and language of Formosa. He disputed successfully with doubters at the Royal Society, conversed amicably in Latin with bishops and the archbishop, won the patronage of the earl of Pembroke, and studied at Oxford at Compton's expense. To entertain Psalmanazar became a mark of social distinction. His tongue silenced all doubters with its wit and confidence. But without the help of his chaplain, Alexander Innes, who deserted Psalmanazar while he was at Oxford, he found it increasingly difficult to keep up his story, especially the patent falsehood that Formosa was a possession of Japan. As authentic accounts of Formosa uncovered his imposture, his patrons abandoned him and gradually Psalmanazar sank under derision, though not without a fight. In 1711 a mock advertisement appeared in the *Spectator* (no. 14), announcing an opera entitled *The Cruelty of Atreus*, in which "the scene wherein Thyestes eats his own children is to be performed by the famous Mr. Psalmanazar, lately arrived from Formosa." His degradation was complete.

Psalmanazar was originally from south France, where he had been educated by Jesuits, among others, and made a reputation for his quick wit. Unsuccessful in a teaching career, he began his impostures as an Irish pilgrim and later as a Japanese convert to Christianity. In a moment of inspiration, he reversed his religious status, and began to pose as an unconverted Japanese. In this guise, he enlisted with first one German regiment, then another. He delighted his Lutheran officers by his ability to defend his concocted "heathen religion" against Roman Catholics, then pleased the Calvinists in Holland by tweaking the Lutherans. When Innes discovered him in Sluys, he asked Psalmanazar to translate a passage from Cicero into Japanese. Upon finishing, Innes asked him to do it again. The differences between the two translations exposed Psalmanazar's fraud, but as Innes was the only witness, he resolved to present Psalmanazar in England as a Formosan and a convert to Anglicanism. After the fraud was exposed to the general public, Psalmanazar embarked on the toilsome life of a literary hack, turning out volume upon volume of Grub Street fare. He underwent a genuine repentance of his "youthful folly and vanity" and converted to a pietistic Anglicanism, whose hallmark was charity among different Christian sects.[9] Late in life, he became friends with Samuel Johnson, who sought out his company because of Psalmanazar's saintly life. He died in 1763.

In 1700, perhaps the closest English parallel to an ideology was the anti-Catholic and especially anti-Jesuit bias of much English thought. In 1679, Titus Oates had published *The Cabinet of the Jesuits Secrets,* a forgery which claimed to lay bare the Jesuit plan to reduce England to a state of subservience to the "seven sages of the Society of Jesus."[10] Oates's work was designed to whip up anti-Catholic feeling against King Charles II (who was suspected of being a Catholic) and prevent his brother, the future James II (who was indeed a Catholic), from succeeding to the throne. Everyone has reason to complain of the Jesuits, wrote Oates, for they oppress the poor, defraud widows, ruin noble families, and raise discords among Christian princes.[11] In short, the Jesuits were conspiring to raise their own organization at the expense of every nation of Europe, particularly England.

Although Oates's "Popish Plot" had been largely discredited by the time Psalmanazar arrived, the misrule of James II (1685-88) had allowed the purveyors of anti-Catholic sentiment to gain adherents. Psalmanazar plays on this sentiment in the prefatory matter of his *Description,* justifying the horrible persecution of the Jesuits in Japan and emphasizing their alleged wickedness. The book, which is purportedly concerned with Formosa, begins with a description of the deceptive Jesuits who first taught him to read, then tricked him into traveling to Goa and then to France. The first half of the book (an account of his travels and conversion), ends with long, rationalistic disproofs of Catholicism, Lutheranism, and Calvinism, arriving at last to the only true faith: Anglicanism. Having thoroughly engaged the prejudices of his readers, Psalmanazar moves to the descriptive portion of the book. The most spectacular element of Formosan religion is the annual sacrifice

9. George Psalmanazar, *Memoirs of **** Commonly known by the Name of George Psalmanazar a Reputed Native of Formosa* (London, 1764), 204, 34.

10. [Titus Oates], *The Cabinet of the Jesuits Secrets Opened In Which there are many things relating to the Church and Clergy of England. As also the ways by which they encrease the Number and Wealth of the Society, on the ruines of Kingdomes and Families* (London, 1679), 14.

11. [Oates], *The Cabinet,* 12.

of 18,000 boys: "After the Flesh is boyl'd, every one of the People takes a piece of the Flesh from the Priest and eats it, and what remains, the Priests keep for themselves."[12] The book concludes with yet more polemic against the Jesuits whose plan to insinuate themselves into the favor of the Japanese nobility has much in common with Oates's *Cabinet of Secrets.* Beyond this, the Jesuits had a genocidal plan to kill all the pagans of Japan which backfired, as Psalmanazar notes, just as the Catholic Gunpowder Plot had done in England.[13]

Now Psalmanazar's account is an outright fraud. In this respect it is unlike most multiculturalism, except for certain proponents of "Afrocentrism" who claim the Greeks "stole" their philosophy from African sources. This theory, pioneered by George G. M. James in *Stolen Legacy* (1954), has been revived and his book reissued by the prominent Afrocentrist Asa Hilliard. The book, which is less a narrative than a bizarre collection of notes from secondary sources, typically selects an extremely abstract idea (such as "the summum bonum") and points out "parallels" between Greek, Egyptian, and occasionally Christian thought on the subject. The ideas are so general — for instance, the teaching of the "summum bonum" that man achieves godlike status by "education and virtue" — that James is able to conflate the ideas of very different characters (in this case, Buddha, Jesus, Socrates, and the Egyptian god Horus) and find an Egyptian source for them all.[14] The Greeks allegedly stole these ideas during the campaigns of Alexander the Great, who "by an act of agression [*sic*] invaded Egypt in 333 B.C., and ransacked and looted the Royal Library at Alexandria and together with his companions carried off a booty of scientific, philosophic, and religious books," which he made available to Aristotle.[15] But since Alexander founded the eponymous Alexandria, he couldn't have ransacked it, and since the library wasn't founded until fifty years later, he

12. George Psalmanazar, *An Historical and Geographical Description of Formosa,* ed. N. M. Penzer, vol. 2 of *The Library of Imposters* (1704; reprint, London: Holden, 1926), 175.

13. Psalmanazar, *An Historical and Geographical Description of Formosa,* 268.

14. George G. M. James, *Stolen Legacy* (New York: Philosophical Library, 1954), 72-73.

15. James, *Stolen Legacy,* 153, 130.

couldn't have looted it. It's rather like saying George Washington ransacked Washington, D.C., in 1775, looted the Library of Congress (founded earlier by Pocahontas), and gave the books to Thomas Jefferson, who then stole the ideas for the Declaration of Independence.

Whether one is dealing with a passionate Afrocentrist or a passionate anti-Catholic, however, argument from evidence will never shake the committed ideologue. What is more significant is the ideologue's "plausibility structure," Peter Berger's term for the structure of ideas and practices that create the social conditions for making a belief plausible. The overall plausibility of Psalmanazar's story was due to his harsh anti-Catholicism, which found a ready audience in England. Multiculturalism's overall plausibility in today's climate is due primarily to the dominance of ideological approaches to education and to the grain of truth they contain — especially their desire to put cultural achievements into historical context and to acknowledge the existence of oppression. Ideology goes beyond the commonsensical acknowledgement of historical context and oppression, however, and maintains that *all* evil is caused by, and embodied in, an oppressive social system; that what passed for "knowledge" in the past can be shown to serve the historical interests (understood in terms of class, race, and gender) of a single "dominant class"; that all past historical accounts and all older literature embody this flawed, oppressive class perspective; that new ideological understanding of the past cannot be wrong and any doubters must be guilty of some moral shortcoming; and finally, that the evidence from other cultures confirms the truth of multiculturalist ideology. Psalmanazar's success is more interesting from this perspective, for its plausibility in the eighteenth century has parallels to the ideological plausibility of multiculturalism.

To begin with Psalmanazar's conclusion, he provided the Anglican bishops with "proof" from another culture that their English version of Christianity was the true one. If his account in the *Description* wasn't enough, Psalmanazar had also written a *Dialogue Between a Japanese and a Formosan* (1707) in which a skeptical, free-thinking Japanese is shown the validity of the reasonable, hierarchical religion of Formosa. In an astonishingly exact parallel to contemporary Anglican apologetics, the Formosan explains the miracles of his religion as being above reason without contradicting it. Psalmanazar's Anglican readers, however little interest they really had in Formosa, could be soothed by his confirmation of their primary religious convictions.

Similarly, in the more ideological forms of multiculturalism today, interest in other cultures is secondary to the empowerment of multiculturalism's ideological allies. This is evident in the title and content of an important theoretical book, *Empowerment through Multicultural Education.* Other peoples are used for outside confirmation of the oppressive structure of Western societies and the empowerment of a new, liberating force: whites are competitive and independent, blacks are cooperative; whites are task-oriented, blacks are people-oriented; whites like to read, blacks like to discuss.[16] In fact, if some nonwhite group seems to confirm certain Western values, the multiculturalist doesn't know what to do. For instance, in an essay entitled "Multiculturalism and Feminism," the Australian Jeannie Martin struggles for an ideologically acceptable way to understand why recent, nonwhite, female immigrants to Australia work so hard to reunite and better their families. After all, "the concrete family assumed as the locus of oppression in feminist accounts is the privatised bourgeois family of Western capitalism." Perhaps feminists should "support the struggles by migrant women for . . . family reunion," she admits, "and reserve judgment on the(ir) families *pro tem.*" Perhaps family reunion efforts can be understood, theoretically, as "resistance to Anglo domination" and the migrant families can be understood, theoretically, as a different category altogether from the bourgeois family-as-locus-of-oppression.[17] What is impossible for Martin to conceive is that the value that migrant women place on family might teach her something that conflicts with her feminist and multiculturalist ideology. Ideological criticism like Martin's lacks the flexibility of traditional academic inquiry because it must relate every phenomenon to a structure of oppression. She simply cannot

16. Carl Grant and Christine E. Sleeter, *Making Choices for Multicultural Education: Five Approaches to Race, Class, and Gender* (Columbus: Merrill, 1988), 16. Christine Sleeter also edited *Empowerment through Multicultural Education* (Albany: State University of New York Press, 1991).

17. Jeannie Martin, "Multiculturalism and Feminism," in *Intersexions: Gender/class/culture/ethnicity,* ed. Gill Bottomley, Marie de Lepervanche, and Jeannie Martin (North Sydney, Australia: Allen & Unwin, 1991), 127-28, 130.

conceive that real women may actually benefit by living in bourgeois families. As a consequence, she can teach us no more about migrant women than Psalmanazar could teach Britons about Formosans.

Today's multiculturalists parallel Psalmanazar as well when they treat European culture as a single unity, to be contrasted at all points with other cultures, which are also treated as a single unity. "I supposed [the Japanese] were so little known by the generality of the Europeans," writes Psalmanazar, "that they were to be looked upon, in the lump, to be Antipodes to them in almost every respect, as religion, manners, dress, &c."[18] At many places, then, Psalmanazar simply takes European manners and invents an "other": Formosans write from right to left (a skill he was at pains to master), their religion is cannibalistic, their temperate mode of life contrasts with English drinking habits, and so on.

Similarly, in much multicultural theory, a monolithic, white, male, European, upper-class culture is made to represent a dominant, oppressive position, which is then criticized from the position of the "other." It does no good to point out the tremendous variety within the many different European traditions: like Psalmanazar, the ideological multiculturalist needs a unitary European construct, which can then be criticized from an "other" construct. As we have seen in the example from Jeannie Martin, both constructs can seriously distort actual cultural artifacts. To take another example, Shakespeare's *Othello* is recommended by an essay on a "multicultural introduction to literature" in these words: "Permeated with sixteenth-century sexism, racism, and class bias, *Othello* is an excellent traditional text to use as a springboard toward transforming the curriculum."[19] This essay, in the section on multicultural theory, finds the excellence of *Othello* in how it represents a monolithic, oppressive, Eurocentric order, which the multiculturalist can then subject to withering ideological criticism. The author even anticipates the response that *Othello* is a complex tragedy and irreducible to political terms. "The terms 'epic' and 'tragedy,'" she writes,

18. Psalmanazar, *Memoirs,* 135.

19. Phillipa Kafka, "A Multicultural Introduction to Literature," in *Practicing Theory in Introductory College Literature Courses,* ed. James M. Calahan and David B. Downing (Urbana, Ill.: National Council of Teachers of English, 1991), 183.

"tend to be applied by traditionalists to those works which valorize and aggrandize pathetically petty and quibbling male pecking orders."[20] That this essay appeared in an anthology sponsored by the influential National Council of Teachers of English indicates how deeply the ideological approach has affected the mainstream.

The theorists go much further than Psalmanazar with their next step: the "other" becomes the source of liberation. The prolific multiculturalists Carl Grant and Christine Sleeter recommend that schooling should teach students how " 'the system' " of sexism, racism, and classism works, and "develop constructive responses" to its injustices.[21] Multiculturalism, they say, brings together all the issues of race, class, and gender, so that whether an educator advocates "emancipatory pedagogy, . . . multicultural education, . . . [or] socialist feminism . . . their basic goals and theoretical assumptions are very similar" (192, 177). They are all united in a common faith commitment that "the system" is the source of evil and the multicultural "other" is the source of liberation. Once the students have been persuaded of the truth of multiculturalist ideology, it is but a short step to involve them in "social action projects." Grant and Sleeter recommend a proposal (of James Banks) of " '[c]onducting a survey to determine the kinds of jobs which most minorities have in local hotels, restaurants, and firms, and if necessary, urging local businesses to hire more minorities in top level positions. Conducting boycotts of businesses that refuse to hire minorities in top level positions . . .' " is another recommended project (191). The authors suggest that the local school could serve as a base for all such projects (193). But what happens if a student concludes that affirmative action hiring increases racial tension and misunderstanding, creates a glass ceiling for affirmative action hires, lumps all minorities into false unity, and produces self-doubt in the minorities it supposedly benefits? What happens if the student questions the academic value of boycotts and school-based political action, and suggests that his radical teachers would learn more by actually starting a business than by criticizing those that exist? What happens, in short, if this exercise in cultural diversity produces true diversity of opinion regarding economic development? True diversity is really incon-

20. Phillipa Kafka, "A Multicultural Introduction to Literature," 185.

21. Grant and Sleeter, *Making Choices for Multicultural Education,* 189.

ceivable within the plausibility structure of ideological multiculturalism. Leading theoreticians like Banks, Sleeter, and Grant want the schools to teach that there is a single, identifiable system of oppression and that multiculturalism serves as the umbrella term for the liberating "other." Diversity requires uniformity.

A third multiculturalist parallel to Psalmanazar is the insistence upon the novelty of their approach. "I undertook the work and resolved myself to give such a description of [Formosa] as should be wholly new and surprizing," claimed Psalmanazar, "and should in most particulars clash with all the accounts other writers had given of it; particularly that it belonged to Japan."[22] Psalmanazar had to discredit all past knowledge of Formosa, a task he found easy at first because his most knowledgeable critics were Catholics and, even better, Jesuits, whom his primary English audience despised. Multiculturalist theoreticians also need to discredit alternative views of the past and present their own approach as new.

Little in ideological multiculturalism, however, is truly new. Take three issues: the inclusion of others, the West's need to acknowledge its own failures, and historical parallels to Afrocentrism. Reading lists and anthologies from the nineteenth century and the early part of the twentieth frequently include stories by and about American Indians, American blacks, Arabs, Africans, Chinese, Japanese, and persons from still other cultures.[23] Irving Howe has argued that one of the striking features of the Western tradition is its self-criticism and consciousness of its own shortcomings, especially in the novels of Dickens and Balzac, Melville and George Eliot.[24] Mary Lefkowitz has explained parallels to

22. Psalmanazar, *Memoirs,* 216-17.

23. One such anthology (a children's anthology, in this case) was arranged in 1912 by William Patten, the managing editor of the Harvard Classics. In the "Reading Guide," William Allen Neilson, a Harvard professor and later president of Smith College, defends the choice of multicultural, fictional tales against the prejudices of contemporary realism on the grounds that they are the best way to nurture the imagination: "In the field of morals, it needs imagination to create that sympathy, that power of putting one's self in the other man's place. . . . In the fields of science and industry, imaginative range . . . is the most precious of faculties" (*The Junior Classics* [1912; reprint, New York: P. F. Collier, 1918], 10:454).

24. Irving Howe, "The Value of the Canon," *New Republic,* 18 February 1991, 43.

the Afrocentric effort to locate the origins of culture in Africa in similarly flimsy, "custom-made ethnic histories" by the Jew Aristobulus, the Englishman Geoffrey of Monmouth, and an early Renaissance Italian monk with Etruscan prejudices — all of whom locate the origins of culture in their own religion, race, or locality.[25] But none of these three examples can convince an ideological multiculturalist. The past structure of knowledge is fatally compromised by oppression, he or she thinks, and the multiculturalist has little difficulty showing where it lies. "Most of us imbibed a Western, patriarchal curriculum in our graduate schools," writes Phillipa Kafka. "Western patriarchal hegemony comes with our territory."[26] Armed with a new, Gramscian critique of cultural domination, Kafka can reinterpret all literature anew, from *Othello* onward, so that it conforms to her ideological attack on white Western hegemony.

A final parallel between Psalmanazar and the multiculturalist is the confident assertion that his account cannot be wrong. "[W]hatever I had once affirmed in conversation, . . . tho' ever so improbable, or even absurd, should never be amended or contradicted in the narrative," he writes.[27] For instance, Psalmanazar quickly realized that an annual sacrifice of 18,000 boys would depopulate Formosa. Nevertheless, he stuck to his story, realizing that the entire structure would fall if but a chink came loose.

The ideological mode of assembling information is fundamentally different from true academic inquiry. When the deciphering of Linear B showed that the peoples who lived in Greece during the Homeric era did, in fact, speak Greek, it didn't overthrow all past work in classics. Nor were older scholars obliged to attack this discovery as a threat to their entire worldview. This fact required the discarding of some older scholarship regarding the Homeric epics, the revision of other parts, while leaving still other views unchanged. In multiculturalist theory, however, there is no alternative to the ideological view of the past. For instance, in describing a program for "staff development," the promi-

25. Mary Lefkowitz, "Ethnocentric History from Aristobulus to Bernal," *Academic Questions* 6, no. 2 (1993): 12-20.

26. Kafka, "A Multicultural Introduction to Literature," 182.

27. Psalmanazar, *Memoirs,* 218.

nent British multiculturalist James Lynch (who is relatively moderate) offers this reflection: "Teachers should also know about the interdependence of developed and developing countries and the ways in which the 'North' has developed a relationship with the 'South', which involves economic and environmental exploitation and cultural hegemony."[28] But what if a teacher rejects the statement's underlying economic theory, which maintains that economic hardship in "the South" is explained by its position of dependency on the "North"? What if he or she doubts the usefulness of lumping the world indiscriminately into "North and South," or the value of vague and tendentious terms like "exploitation" and "hegemony" for understanding global economics? What if he or she regards this statement, which Lynch considers obvious, not as knowledge but as a refutable opinion? There simply is no way for such a teacher to fit within the plausibility structure of current multiculturalism. He or she is an oppressor. To recall Kenneth Minogue's description of ideology, the dissenter cannot be reasoned with; he must be denounced.

The Foundations of Ideological Multiculturalism

Several times in this chapter, the term "hegemony" has occupied a strategic place in the multiculturalist critique of Western education. At this point, I must leave Psalmanazar, for his anti-Catholicism cannot come close to achieving the structural unity that this concept gives to ideological multiculturalism. In the work of the Italian communist Antonio Gramsci, hegemony refers to the cultural means by which a class controls the intellectual life of an entire society.[29] The root of this concept lies in Gramsci's thoroughgoing commitment to "historicism," which presupposes that every activity, whether practical

28. James Lynch, *Multicultural Education in a Global Society* (n.p.: Falmer, 1989), 164.

29. Leszek Kolakowski provides a full explanation of the contours of Gramsci's thought in the third volume of his magisterial study of Marxist thought, *Main Currents of Marxism,* to which this discussion is indebted. See *The Breakdown* (New York: Oxford University Press, 1978), 220-52.

or mental, scientific or artistic, can be understood only in relation to the historical process of which it is a part. Gramsci is not just making the commonsense observation that we can learn something about literature by examining the historical context in which it arose — although multiculturalists will often retreat to that position if pressed. He is committed to the assumption that the *only* valid mode of understanding is one that locates literature, science, economic development, and other cultural expressions within the "historical process," understood in Marxist terms. This is the mode of understanding emphasized in leading works of multiculturalist theory. There can be no universal truths given its presuppositions, for all cultural expressions merely describe their stage of historical development. Nor are the humanistic disciplines, as traditionally practiced, useful in themselves: they do not reveal knowledge that may transcend the particular culture in which it originated, but only the contemporary stage of that culture's historical development.

Gramsci's next step is also crucial for today's multiculturalists: before any class can secure a position of political dominance, it must subjugate its rivals by cultural means. This intellectual dominance is what Gramsci means by "hegemony." No aspect of culture therefore has any autonomous meaning. The meaning of literature, for instance, is discoverable only in relation to how literature has been used for the attaining and maintenance of hegemony. The American critic Richard Ohmann put it this way in a 1990 volume:

> Marx and Engels provided the fundamental explanation in their notion of a superstructure — laws, institutions, culture, beliefs, values, customs — that rises from the economic base, rationalizes it, and protects its relations. In this century, Antonio Gramsci elaborated this idea through his account of the hegemony of the dominant class: a whole way of life including culture and ideas, and supported by ideological institutions, which effectively enlists almost everyone in the "party" of the ruling class, sets limits to debate and consciousness, and in general serves as a means of rule. . . .
>
> The humanities, like the schools and universities within which they are practiced, have contributed through the hundred years of our profession's existence to this hegemonic process. English teachers have helped train the kind of work force capitalists need in a pro-

ductive system that relies less and less on purely manual labor. More, we have helped to inculcate the discipline — punctuality, good verbal manners, submission to authority, attention to problem-solving assignments set by somebody else, long hours spent in one place — that is necessary to perform the alienated labor that will be the lot of most.[30]

It is odd to read these paragraphs, published years after the atrophy of Marxist theory generally and a year after the fall of Marxist governments in Eastern Europe. Why does "historical contextualization," as it is called, seem to have so little to do with history? Ohmann's ideology is so detailed that he can relate even punctuality and good manners to the oppressive hegemony of the capitalistic system. But how much does it tell us about history or literature? Surely most people would find the theory more persuasive, for instance, if frequently taught British and American novels regularly promoted capitalism. But most of them, to the extent that they deal with economic issues at all, are quite critical of industrial capitalism. Moreover, Ohmann's casual observations on an education in the humanities could equally prove the opposite of his conclusions: that the humanities encourage a critical attitude toward culture, including one's own; that the "long hours" of individual, original thought make one peculiarly unfit to carry out tasks set by others; and that the "verbal manners" one learns in the humanistic disciplines incline one more for disputation than submission. All of this, of course, is irrelevant to the critic equipped with a faith commitment to the concept of "hegemony," for hegemony there must be and hegemony he will find.

Gramsci took a further step, which today's multiculturalists avoid discussing, but which is evident in many of their writings: to oppose the old cultural hegemony and overturn the political order, a new cultural hegemony must first gain supremacy. That new hegemony, Gramsci believed, would prepare the way for a communist revolution.

30. Richard Ohmann, "The Function of English at the Present Time," in *Left Politics and the Literary Profession,* ed. Lennard J. Davis and M. Bella Mirabella (New York: Columbia University Press, 1990), 42. At the risk of quibbling, Gramsci himself rejected "this idea" of a distinct "economic base" and "superstructure."

Multiculturalists prefer the word "transformation" to "revolution." The leading multiculturalist theoreticians clearly regard social transformation as the ultimate outcome of their project, and for it to succeed within their own Gramscian worldview, they must first gain cultural dominance. In an essay entitled "A Curriculum for Empowerment, Action, and Change," Banks writes, "Teachers must not only understand how the dominant paradigms and canon help keep victimized groups powerless but also be committed to social change and action if they are to become agents of liberation and empowerment."[31] Grant and Sleeter write that their version of multiculturalism "prepares future citizens to reconstruct society so that it better serves the interests of all groups of people and especially those who are of color, poor, female, and/or disabled."[32] It is no accident, then, that dissent from ideological multiculturalism is intolerable. If one holds a different view of how the interests of the poor and powerless are best served, one must be a servant of the oppressor. If one suggests that social change along their line would be change for the worse, one must be a representative of the old hegemonic order.

Nearly every academic skeptic of multiculturalist ideology can tell a story about its intolerance. Miami-Dade Community College, for example, has threatened that lack of cooperation in incorporating "diversity" into the curriculum will weigh heavily in promotion and tenure decisions and, for senior faculty, in merit pay increases.[33] Professors on hiring committees tell of jobs being closed, in reality if not in appearance, to candidates who are white or male. I have argued at a multiculturalism seminar that the "structure of racism" does not explain family poverty nearly so well as the structure of the family: the evidence shows that the median income of black families with related children in 1989, for instance, was ten percent higher than white families headed by men and nearly twice as high as white families headed by women. The seminar leader said he "had a problem" with my statistics because they came from the Census Bureau, an agency of the United States

31. Banks, "A Curriculum for Empowerment, Action, and Change," 141.

32. Grant and Sleeter, *Making Choices for Multicultural Education,* 176.

33. Glenn M. Ricketts, "Multiculturalism Mobilizes," *Academic Questions* 3, no. 3 (1990): 59.

government.[34] As Kenneth Minogue writes, ideological explanations "will generally be found in bold and interesting formulations which splendidly defy most of the evidence we have, indeed even common sense itself; then, when pushed into tight intellectual corners, [the ideologues] retreat, flinging as they go defiant remarks expressing contempt for rigid, mechanical, and undialectical understandings of the theory, [and] relatively banal assertions about the significance of the material, sexual, racial, or other factors in human life."[35] The lack of true diversity within a movement whose slogan is "cultural diversity" is entirely comprehensible within its Gramscian framework: a new hegemony must replace the old one.

Gramsci's criticism of the oppressive hegemony of the past also helps one understand why ideological multiculturalism must be an essentially negative undertaking, committed to portraying the past in an extremely unfavorable light. "The cultural aspect, above all, will be negative," writes Gramsci,

> directed towards criticism of the past, obliterating it from memory and destroying it; the lines of construction will as yet be outlines only, rough sketches that can and must be revised at any moment to conform to the new structure that is being built.[36]

In their presentation to the general public, multiculturalists often say they merely wish to introduce students to previously neglected works or approaches to history. Most traditional humanists, like Arthur Schlesinger and Diane Ravitch, applaud such efforts and wish to be made aware of nationalist, religious, racial, or class-laden assumptions that often excluded this learning from the traditional curriculum. But it is one thing to point out these assumptions in past scholarship and view them as shortcomings. It is quite another to maintain, first, that to understand a past work is to understand its role in the construction of an oppressive, hegemonic structure; and, second, that we should

34. The figures are from table 732 of the 1991 *Statistical Abstract of the United States.*

35. Kenneth Minogue, *Alien Powers: The Pure Theory of Ideology* (New York: St. Martin's Press, 1985), 70.

36. Quoted in Kolakowksi, *The Breakdown,* 244.

substitute an alternative hegemony that will replace the first one. Ideological multiculturalism is marked by the latter gestures. Kafka recommends *Othello* as a good traditional text because it illustrates everything evil in the tradition. Shakespeare and Milton can continue to be taught, writes Viswanathan, as long as their alleged role in Britain's hegemonic control of India is intrinsic to the presentation.[37] "The canon" of secular literature, as I tried to show in the second chapter, is to be re-read not for pleasure or insight into universal human nature, but to uncover traces of how the dominant class controlled everyone else. All of these conclusions about literature flow directly from the critic's ideological assumptions.

Ideological multiculturalism is not much interested in other cultures except as they illustrate the oppressive system of the present. It demonstrates "historical contextualization" through relatively trivial examples (like punctuality) and overlooks large historical events (like the fall of communism). It cannot recognize other systemic analyses of social ills, such as the breakdown of family structure, when they fall outside its plausibility structure. It translates the discipline of literary study into a vague yet predictable exercise in the criticism of hegemony.

Perhaps the fundamental objection to ideological multiculturalism, however, relates to the thoroughgoing historicism on which it is based: it denies that cultural artifacts can aspire to a measure of truth or beauty whose standards transcend the time and place in which the artifact was created. Rather, the validity of a painting or poem or university curriculum lies in its use by a class that seeks to gain or extend hegemony over society. Cultural standards can always be shown to arise in a historical context which implicates them, in a favorite phrase of current criticism, in a hegemonic system. But to turn the tables on the multiculturalists, why should *their* hegemony prevail? Having cut the supports from beneath any normative measures of cultural value, they have no basis for preferring — or privileging, as they would say — their own point of view. They would have to acknowledge that their criticisms of the past serve their own class interests; that the journals, anthologies, and conferences which promote multiculturalism serve their present interest; that their success in acquiring

37. Viswanathan, *Masks of Conquest,* 169.

monies from foundations, legislative support for their curricula, and enforcement mechanisms in the hiring and promotion of teachers serve their future interest in imposing their own hegemonic control over culture. If one applied their terms to their own activities, one would come to regard multiculturalism as fundamentally unjustifiable because it promotes their interests of a multiculturalist hegemony.

Like feminism and the criticism of the canon, the ideology of multiculturalism tells us relatively little about the subject at hand — in this case, other cultures — but a lot about the ideologue. The criticism of the hegemony of the past tells us little about the past, but it serves as a warning of what the future, under such a view of education, will hold.

Multiculturalist Ideology and the Orient

The eighteenth century in England saw the explosion of contact between British and non-European peoples. Travel literature recorded British impressions of Africans, Asians, Pacific Islanders, and American Indians — along with prejudices favoring and criticisms condemning British society. The beginnings of the British empire and the rise in world trade — including the slave trade — forced Britons to deal with other cultures at least on a practical level, if not with understanding or empathy. On the more academic side, the Royal Society was eager to gain what we would call "ethnographic" knowledge of other peoples, advising Captain Cook to use " 'the utmost patience and forbearance with respect to the natives' " whom he met in the Pacific and " 'to observe [their] genius, temper, disposition and number. . . .' "[38] The artists on his voyages inaugurated profound changes in European art by their efforts to represent their experiences in non-European modes. In the late eighteenth century, scholars laid the groundwork for Oriental studies in Britain by their pioneering work in the Arabic, Persian, and Sanskrit languages and literatures, and their translations of the Qur'an, the *Bhagavad Gita,* and the Hindu law code.

38. Glyndwr Williams and Peter Marshall, *The Great Map of Mankind* (Cambridge: Harvard University Press, 1982), 269.

To the committed ideologue, it is not difficult to explain all of these contacts, even the ones that seem motivated by the desire to advance knowledge or a willingness to conceive new modes of perception, in the terms of European oppression or control. The most influential ideological description of the nineteenth-century European study of the Orient is Edward Said's *Orientalism.* While Orientalism can simply refer to all academic study of the Orient (as "Classics" refers to the study of Greek and Latin culture generally), Said is most interested in it as "a Western style for dominating, restructuring, and having authority over the Orient."[39] Gramsci's concept of hegemony provides Said with his framework for understanding the Western knowledge of the Orient:

> It is hegemony, or rather the result of cultural hegemony at work, that gives Orientalism the durability and the strength I have been speaking about. Orientalism is never far from what Denys Hay has called the idea of Europe, a collective notion identifying "us" Europeans as against all "those" non-Europeans, and indeed it can be argued that the major component in European culture is precisely what made the culture hegemonic both in and outside Europe: the idea of European identity as a superior one in comparison with all the non European peoples and cultures.[40]

Like all ideologues, Said goes far beyond the commonsense observation that knowledge about India or Egypt will be colored by the economic interests that scholars may have in those countries, the degree to which they identify with (or dissent from) the contemporary national interest of their country, and the degree to which they are able to bring a self-critical eye to their research. Now Said does not maintain that Orientalism produced myths and lies about the East, nor that it was conspiratorially involved with imperialism. Said, like Gramsci, is far more nuanced than that. Rather, he maintains that the Western orientalist "is never concerned with the Orient except as the first cause of what he [the westerner] says."[41] The orientalist's statements are interesting not because they tell us the "'truth'" about the Orient, but because they reveal the "formidable

39. Edward W. Said, *Orientalism* (New York: Pantheon, 1978), 3.
40. Said, *Orientalism,* 7.
41. Said, *Orientalism,* 21.

structure of cultural domination" that enabled the West to control the Orient through imperialism, colonialism, and other political and economic means.[42] "[A]ll academic knowledge about India and Egypt is somehow tinged and impressed with, violated by, the gross political fact — . . . *that is what I am saying* in this study of Orientalism."[43]

Said's learned and clever book rests on the ideological faith in historicism, and in the faith that all past descriptions are violated by the cultural hegemony in which they are implicated. It rests upon the faith that his ideology can demystify the scholarly illusion of free research and expose the structure "whose internal constraints upon writers and thinkers were *productive*" of cultural hegemony and its "patriarchal authorities, canonical texts, doxological ideas . . . and new authorities."[44]

In response, one could locate Said's own book in its own historical context. One could argue that his text is "violated by" his commitment to the Palestinian cause. His "patriarchal authorities" are Gramsci, Foucault, and Marx. His "doxological ideas" are hegemony, discourse, and representation. In sum, one could argue that his book tells us as little about the history of Oriental studies as (in his view) Oriental studies tell us about the Orient.

Since Said's book contains a great deal of valuable information, however, he deserves much more substantive questions: how can Said overlook the "historical origin" of the idea of Europe, which saw its deepest threat not in Asia or Africa but in its own European barbarians?[45] How can he ignore the declining confidence in European cultural superiority in the eighteenth century, evident in Burke's writings and due in part to the very Oriental studies he accuses of establishing cultural superiority? Or further, if Europe's identity is essentially one of superiority "in comparison with all the non-European peoples and cultures," how was the eighteenth-century orientalist William Jones able to conceive a *common,* Indo-European root for Sanskrit and most of the European languages? If Europeans like Jones thought of India

42. Said, *Orientalism,* 21, 25.

43. Said, *Orientalism,* 11, Said's emphasis.

44. Said, *Orientalism,* 14, 22.

45. Denis Hay, *Europe: The Emergence of an Idea,* rev. ed. (Edinburgh: Edinburgh University Press, 1968), 1.

only as an "other," shouldn't the "internal constraints" on his mind have prevented his discovery of a common Indo-European language?

Unlike other academic inquiry, however, ideology can never be falsified. Of Jones's discovery, Said remarks that it shows that the "principal goal [of Orientalism was] the grounding of the European languages in a distant, and harmless, Oriental source."[46] If one doesn't already believe in Said's ideology, one is apt to respond to Jones's discovery of Indo-European very differently — as a genuine advance of knowledge by an imaginative intelligence.

We move a step closer to Burke by looking at a more narrow treatment of English studies in India, written by Gauri Viswanathan (under Saids' inspiration), whose misunderstanding of Burke was noted early in this chapter. Since English literature became a "subject" in colonial India — before it entered the curriculum in England — its provenance implicates it in "Western cultural hegemony."[47] Announcing her Gramscian framework on the first page, Viswanathan proposes to examine the way that the content of English literature was used for social and political control.[48] She concludes her book by hoping it will serve the cause of multiculturalism by "forc[ing] its opponents to reconsider the premises of the traditional Eurocentric curriculum."[49] The premises of traditional literary study, in her view, are the ones we have seen throughout this chapter: past literary study has attempted to achieve, maintain, and extend control over subjugated peoples.

All efforts of disciplined ethical thinking, all promotion of personal virtues, and all Christian evangelization are bundled together under the abstraction Viswanathan labels "control." For instance, she believes that the British government was initially persuaded by evangelicals to adopt a religiously based curriculum because Christianity's political effects would serve to control the natives. "[H]istorically Christianity had never been associated with bringing down governments, for its concern was with the internal rather than the external condition of man."[50]

46. Said, *Orientalism,* 78.
47. Viswanathan, *Masks of Conquest,* 2.
48. Viswanathan, *Masks of Conquest,* 3.
49. Viswanathan, *Masks of Conquest,* 166.
50. Viswanathan, *Masks of Conquest,* 76.

Given such a high level of abstraction and such a willingness to ignore history — for historically, Christianity has been associated with the fall of many governments — it would seem possible to locate anything one likes within the structure of control. And yet in the entire book, there is not a single analysis of a poem or novel used for the purpose of control. In fact, the book records the utter failure of literary education to control Indian students. Instead, imperial agents observed that educated Indians became discontent with their status.[51] Even if one granted Viswanathan's dubious position that the purpose of teaching Milton was to control Indians by instilling religious values, the schoolmasters found that English literature did as little for spreading Christianity in India as Greek classics did for spreading paganism in Britain.[52] No doubt some British agents did believe they could control their subjects, in the commonsense meaning of that phrase, through education.[53] But without Viswanathan's ideological framework, most of her evidence could support an equally persuasive argument that religious and literary education had the function of decolonizing India. For instance, Sir Charles Wood, whose 1854 "Despatch" is a capitalist smoking gun in Viswanathan's book, presented his educational proposals for India to the House of Commons in these terms:

> [E]ven if the result should be the loss of that empire — it seems to me that this country will occupy a far better and prouder position in the history of the world, if by our agency a civilized and Christian empire should be established in India, than if we continued to rule over people debased by ignorance and degraded by superstition.[54]

Wood is willing to lose vast material benefits and political power, which

51. Viswanathan, *Masks of Conquest,* 156-57.

52. Viswanathan, *Masks of Conquest,* 84-85.

53. She quotes a minute from the Bombay Presidency which reads, " 'The Natives must either be kept down by a sense of our power, or they must willingly submit from a conviction that we are more wise, more just, more humane, and more anxious to improve their conditions than any other rulers they could possibly have' " (*Masks of Conquest,* 2). But even this sample is exceptional among the evidence she produces, and the book moreover records the general unwillingness of educated Indians to "submit."

54. Quoted in Stephen Neill, *Christian Missions,* vol. 6 of *The Pelican History of the Church,* gen. ed. Owen Chadwick (Harmondsworth: Penguin, 1964), 357.

the ideologue considers the motivation for most human actions, for the sake of what he considers civilization and Christianity. But if Wood is to be understood in Gramscian terms by his role in the maintenance of hegemonic control over India through education, how could he consciously propose an educational system that could undermine the empire? How could he speak so insouciantly of its loss? The answer is that he cannot, and Viswanathan omits this passage from her extensive treatment of Wood.

Viswanathan's use of other historical characters raises similar questions. For instance, she implicates the Clapham Evangelicals (and by extension the Sunday school promoter Hannah More and the missionary William Carey) as agents of social control because of their promotion of missionary activity and personal morality. But shouldn't she explain how William Wilberforce and Zachary Macaulay, the Clapham members best known for their abolition of the slave trade, were guilty of controlling other human beings? Does it really increase our understanding to make no distinction between the structures of the imperial enterprise and the Sunday school? When questions like these are raised, the multiculturalist ideologue can always withdraw to the position, disputed by no one, that culture is produced in a social context that influences its producers unconsciously as well as consciously. But the main thrust of the book is that "the Gramscian notion [of hegemony] is not merely a theoretical construct, but an uncannily accurate description of historical process."[55] To a nonbeliever who is skeptical of her selective presentation of data and structures, however, her description of literary study in India is neither uncanny nor accurate. Like Said's *Orientalism,* the valuable information in her book must often be separated from the surrounding ideology to be useful. It contributes to our understanding of imperial India in spite of its ideology, not because of it.

Viswanathan concludes her book by stopping just short of recommending an end to English literary study:

> I am not advocating that today's students must close their English books without further ado because those works were instrumental in holding others in subjugation or, if that is too extreme, that at

55. Viswanathan, *Masks of Conquest,* 2.

> least Shakespeare and Milton must be dropped . . . because their texts were used at one time to supply religious values that could be introduced into the British control of India in no other way. What I am suggesting, however, is that we can no longer afford to regard the uses to which literary works were put in the service of British imperialism as extraneous to the way these texts are to be read.[56]

Shakespeare and Milton can remain in the syllabus, on suffrance, as long as we teach them in a correct manner. Her book never deals with a single passage by these authors to illustrate her point, but we all know what she means.

Burke's India and the Political Rhetoric of "Sympathy"

Edmund Burke wrote thousands of pages on Britain's involvement in India. In sheer magnitude, the Indian writings make up about as much of his total works as his writings on the French Revolution — quite possibly more. Burke presents this alien, Indian people to his audience through the literary and moral category of "sympathy," which he developed early in his career. Burke's "sympathetic" approach has its limits, but it leads to a deeper understanding of other peoples than ideological multiculturalism does. Trying to understand Burke's sympathetic approach from within the discipline of literary study shows why the traditional humanities offer more insight than ideological multiculturalism. In this case, a literary analysis of structure (here, the structure of "sympathy") and of allusion (here, classical allusion) can illuminate Burke's achievement. This method of reading Burke is incompatible with ideological criticism, but quite compatible with a biblical poetics. First, however, some background is necessary.

During Burke's career, the East India Company completed its transformation from a commercial, trading company to an imperial power, with vast holdings of lands and ambitions for more. When he began his systematic study of India in the 1780s, Burke dated Britain's oppression of India from twenty years before, when it began to acquire large territorial revenues. He soon became convinced that the Com-

56. Viswanathan, *Masks of Conquest,* 169.

pany's administration of India was not just faulty in this or that particular, but that it was based on a system of extortion and bribery. Even more profound, he was becoming convinced that Britain had destroyed the Indian social order and had deepened its offense by attempting to establish English legal forms there.

Despite the failure of "Fox's East India Bill" (1783) and with very little hope of success in a Commons securely under Tory domination, Burke gave notice in 1785 that he would attempt to impeach the East India Company's governor-general, Warren Hastings. Burke had increasingly located the source of Indian oppression in Hastings himself, and he began framing lengthy charges that seemed designed less for actual conviction than for the exposure of British misrule in general. The first charge was turned down, but on the second, Pitt himself dramatically joined with the Whig side of the debate. Commons voted to impeach Hastings, and it soon became clear that Hastings would stand trial in the House of Lords. Burke was named chairman of the Committee of Managers for the impeachment and opened the case in February 1788 with a speech that lasted over the course of four days.

Burke was now at the height of his political influence, but within a short time his fortunes reversed again. Lord Chancellor Thurlow, who presided over the trial, was a schoolboy friend of Hastings, and his narrow rulings on the evidence hamstrung the prosecution, slowed the trial, and virtually guaranteed an acquittal. Then a weightier blow fell: intense disagreement over the French Revolution strained relations with his own Whig leaders to the point where Burke exiled himself from his party in May 1791. Hastings was acquitted in 1795, and this, coupled with his inability to rouse British opinion against the French Revolution, persuaded Burke that his life had ended in isolation and failure. Despite Burke's self-doubts, however, Hastings himself at least gave lip service (and possibly more) to Burke's principle that the welfare of the Indian people should come before the interests of the Company. At the very least, the trial established that British imperial rulers were answerable to Parliament for their treatment of native peoples. But perhaps more important in political terms, Burke's work on India argues comprehensively that the intervention of one nation in the lives of other peoples is justifiable only if it benefits those peoples and respects their native cultures, and that the performance of the dominant nation can be judged on international, non-racial principles of law. Many of those principles have been honored only in the breach, but it is to Burke's credit that he helped a dominant nation begin to cast a critical eye on its treatment of other peoples.

* * * * *

How should one read Burke's Indian writings? They may usefully be read within the context of political conservatism. The alarm he takes when a people exert their unchained will without regard to moral law; his distress over the rise of a new class of outsiders who confiscate the property of established landholders; the favor with which he regards traditional forms of religion, law, and social structure — all of these are genuine parallels between Burke's Indian writings and the foundations of conservatism. Burke's India may also be read psychoanalytically, seeing his fury at the Protestant ascendancy in his native Ireland displaced in the attacks on Anglo-Indian rule. Both approaches may be useful as long as one does not fit Burke into an overarching theory that forces one to ignore crucial parts of his work and to distort others.

If one wishes to place the discipline of literary study at the center of one's reading, however, it is more useful to see the works of an author whole, relating one part to the others *in the author's own terms,* to the degree that is possible. In the second chapter, I tried to read Johnson's *Lives* in the context of his other criticism, sermons, essays, prayers, and meditations. True literary study is laborious, but it prevents one from distorting an author so that he or she can be illegitimately used for the canon wars. David Bromwich calls this procedure "triangulation," in which a mere sample of a major author is read in light of recent literary conflicts, followed by the reader's own position.

Burke too may be "triangulated." But he may also be read. Perhaps his other writings provide a context for understanding his India in a way that has been little noticed. Perhaps the connections between his rhetorical achievement, history, and politics can be understood better without borrowing concepts from Gramsci.

Burke realized that his main difficulty in the India speeches was to create sympathy in his audience for a different culture. In this respect, his task was similar to that of virtually every teacher of the humanities whose subject is another people or another time. "[D]istance of place . . . operates as remoteness of time," comments Burke on the difficulty of understanding any subject outside one's immediate experience.[57] But how does one get one's listeners to sympathize with the terrible experiences endured by the remote characters of history or literature?

According to Burke's early *Philosophical Enquiry into . . . the Sublime and Beautiful*, sympathy arises (oddly enough) from the undeniable pleasure one has in contemplating the calamities of others. The vicarious experience of real terror and pity is similar to that of dramatic tragedy. But Burke recognized that the great speaker, in describing such calamities, doesn't want his audience simply to enjoy the spectacle of pain. The moral responsibilities of the speaker in Burke's *Enquiry* are then in conflict with the natural reactions of his audience. Burke found a solution to this conflict in the nature of the pleasure of contemplating others' misfortunes: it is mixed with pain.

Burke believed that God had created mankind so that "we should be united by the bond of sympathy, [and] he has strengthened that bond by a proportionable delight; and there most where our sympathy is most wanted, — in the distresses of others." Sympathy, or social affection, should naturally produce pity for the suffering of others, whether they are English or not. The sympathetic pain one feels in "real calamities," he says, "prompts us to relieve ourselves in relieving those who suffer." In the "imitated distresses" of a tragedy, pleasure comes from the same source, namely sympathy with the pains endured by the characters, combined with the added pleasure "resulting from the effects of imitation." Burke wrote these words in the first edition of his *Philosophical Enquiry into . . . the Sublime and Beautiful*, in 1757.[58] Two years later, in the second edition, Burke expanded the work by showing how words, especially the words of poetry and "eloquence," can raise sympathy.

57. Edmund Burke, *The Correspondence of Edmund Burke,* ed. Thomas W. Copeland (Chicago: University of Chicago Press, 1959-78), 2:513. Subsequent references will use the abbreviation *C*.

58. Edmund Burke, *A Philosophical Enquiry into the Origin of Our Ideas of the Sublime and Beautiful,* ed. J. T. Boulton (Notre Dame: University of Notre Dame Press, 1968), I.xi-xv. Subsequent references in the text will identify part and section numbers.

Many recent treatments of Burke have noted how the aesthetic concepts of "sublime and beautiful" make their way into his political writings on the French Revolution. But while Burke's India speeches have often been compared to theater and described (usually antagonistically) as "histrionic," few have taken seriously the moral and rhetorical significance of "sympathy" in Burke's *Enquiry* and his Indian writings. The word occurs frequently in the India speeches, particularly where Burke's rhetoric is most urgent. Sympathy provides something like a structural principle for Burke's own approach to an alien people. Sympathy has no connotation of condescension in Burke. It is a technical term that connects his religious, moral, political, and aesthetic sensibilities at their deepest levels. These connections refute the suggestion often made by ideological critics that their approach uniquely takes into account the historical or political context of literature. I hope to suggest that Burkean sympathy is a more valuable tool for approaching an alien culture than that of ideological multiculturalism.

The last two sections of Burke's 1759 *Enquiry* argue that poetry and eloquence, which would include parliamentary eloquence, affect their hearers less by verbal representations of the objects they describe than by representing the passionate impressions those objects make on a perceiver. When a literary character or speaker expresses the passions that an experience raises in him, "we are easily affected and brought into sympathy" with him (V.vii). At the risk of oversimplification, Burke's theory is "expressive," while Johnson's, as we saw in the second chapter, is "imitative," or mimetic. Burke would alter the Horatian formula to read *ut pictura non poesis:* a poem should *not* be like a picture. Rather than representing its objects, a poem should express the passions and powers of its objects. This helps to explain why the portraits of heroes and villains in Burke's India lack much individual character, and why the descriptions of flourishing Indian landscapes start to run together. Burke is not trying to describe the objects themselves, but rather the effect of them on an imagined observer. Occasionally Burke's passions were engaged by less than trustworthy informants, a risk that everyone studying another culture must face. But in general, Burke's sympathy was not misplaced, and it gave him a powerful rhetoric for conveying the significance of an alien culture he knew in the way most of us know other cultures — secondhand.[59]

Exactitude Burke could not hope to achieve, but he had never believed that the most powerful rhetorical descriptions were those that attempted to render an exact picture:

> [P]oetry and rhetoric do not succeed in exact description so well as painting does; their business is, to affect rather by sympathy than imitation; to display rather the effect of things on the mind of the speaker, or of others, than to present a clear idea of the things themselves. (V.v)

Exact descriptions, Burke concludes, convey a "poor and insufficient idea of the thing." But "[w]e yield to sympathy what we refuse to description." When a speech is marked by the "strong and lively feeling" in the speaker, then "by the contagion of our passions, we catch a fire already kindled in another . . ." (V.vii). It is highly significant, and rarely noted at present, that Burke here joins the work of speakers — presumably including orators — with poets, and unites the appeal of rhetoric with tragedy.

From the *Enquiry* through the Indian and anti-revolutionary writings, Burke treats sympathy as simultaneously natural and conventional in a manner characteristically his own. He believed that God had created man for the exercise of sympathy, but that the artificial works of human art were often needed to elicit it. In this sense Burke's thought is diametrically opposed to the popular, radical sentimentalism of Rousseau of his own day, whose *Emile* describes pity (or "compassion") as a natural faculty ruined by the very type of literary art that Burke recommends. It is opposed as well to much modern literary theory that equates the conventional with "arbitrary" and "unnatural."

59. Occasionally Burke relied on witnesses and reports whose credibility could be too easily undermined. The most notorious example was the inclusion in his speech on the opening of the impeachment (18 February 1788) of a report of atrocities in Rangpur. The report had reached him after the charges were voted, so that they were legally irrelevant to the case. More important, Hastings could not be shown to have direct responsibility for them and, to top it off, their allegations often went unsubstantiated. The theatrical spectacle of the melodramatic fit of Mrs. Sheridan during this portion of the speech gave rise to charges of histrionic excess, especially as the trial dragged on.

Human nature and the artifice of tragedy are brought together in Burke's speech on the "third day of reply" of the Hastings trial, June 3, 1794:

> It is wisely provided in the constitution of our heart that we should interest ourselves in the fate of great personages. They are, therefore, made everywhere the objects of tragedy, which addresses itself directly to our passions and feelings.[60]

In this speech, Burke describes the story of Chait Singh, raja of Benares, whose treatment by Hastings is regarded as unjust even by those prone to take Hastings's side.[61] Chait Singh was the zemindar for Benares, which means that he nominally held the land (subject to the sovereignty of the Company) and collected its rents and revenues on the Company's behalf. In 1778, the Company needed funds for its war with the Marathas confederacy in west India. It could not count on revenues from the other zemindaries in and around Bengal, but Benares was still solvent. In that year, and through 1780, the Company demanded additional tribute to finance its wars, and when Chait Singh finally balked, in 1781, Hastings himself came to Benares to arrest him, demanding a fine worth between £400,000 and £500,000 (*WS* 5:413-16). An armed rebellion ensued in which the raja was deposed and exiled.

Burke had already recounted Chait Singh's story in the 1783 *Speech on Fox's India Bill.* The Benares episode was the substance of the first charge of impeachment to pass the House of Commons (1786). Of all the charges, this one would likely get a sympathetic hearing, even at the close of the trial in 1794.

In the *Speech on Fox's India Bill,* Burke had remarked on the difficulty of getting Englishmen to sympathize with Indians like Chait Singh:

60. Edmund Burke, *The Works of the Right Honourable Edmund Burke* (London: Bohn, 1854-60), 8:59. Quotations from this source will hereafter be cited in the text with the abbreviation *W.*

61. An excellent description of this episode, to which I am indebted, is found in Regina Janes, "Edmund Burke's Flying Leap from India to France," *History of European Ideas* 7 (1986): 509-27.

> [W]e are in general, Sir, so little acquainted with Indian details; the instruments of oppression under which the people suffer are so hard to be understood; and even the names of the sufferers are so uncouth and strange to our ears, that it is very difficult for our *sympathy* to fix upon these objects. (*WS* 5:403-4, emphasis added)

Burke's sympathetic understanding of India was the result of massive research received by a mind like that described in the *Enquiry.* Burke did not believe in the naive objectivity that current multiculturalists often present as the only alternative to their ideological mode of understanding. He agreed that the mind perceived reality through certain categories which he had described three decades earlier in the *Enquiry.*

Burke's knowledge of India was greater than that of any Englishman who had not actually been to India. The distinguished historian P. J. Marshall concludes that "Burke's study of India was probably more intensive and more prolonged than any study of a non-European people undertaken by any of his great contemporaries, Voltaire and Diderot included."[62] In addition to the scores of reports and witnesses he examined as a member of the Select Committee of the House of Commons, Burke had read the Qur'an and the *History of Genghizcan.* He had studied the legal forms of Hindu society in the recently translated *Code of the Gentoo Laws* (1776) and those of Islamic society in the *Institutes* of Tamerlane. He had read the voyages of the philosophical *Travels* of Sir John Chardin with a critical eye, accepting some of his judgments, such as the customary nature of Islamic society, while rejecting others, such as its alleged "lethargy" due to its climate.[63] While he generally mentions Montesquieu's political works with respect, Burke had nothing but contempt for his popular cliché that Asian governments were despotic (*W* 7:488). "To name a Mahometan Government," says Burke in the opening of the impeachment, "is to name a Govern-

62. P. J. Marshall, introduction to *India: The Launching of the Hastings Impeachment,* in Burke, *WS,* 6:20.

63. Percy G. Adams's *Travelers and Travel Liars, 1660-1800* (Berkeley: University of California Press, 1962) remains a good general introduction to the eighteenth-century travel book. It recounts the efforts of authentic reportage as well as outright fraud in the genre.

ment by law." He dared Hastings's supporters to show him a syllable in the Qur'an that could justify despotism based upon Islamic principles (*WS* 6:353).

Burke came by his knowledge through sympathy, sympathy on the basis of a common creation by God and the natural law that bound him and all mankind together on the basis of their moral duties:

> There is but one law for all, namely, that law which governs all law, the law of our Creatour, the law of humanity, justice, equity: — the law of nature and of nations. So far as any laws fortify this primeval law, and give it more precision, more energy, more effect by their declarations, such laws enter into the sanctuary, and participate in the sacredness of its character. (*W* 7:504)

Like sympathy, "law" is both natural and conventional: positive, prescriptive laws fortify natural law and make it more precise, particularly by a prudential engagement with the customs of a people. Fox's India bills, he argued, would have that effect.

In the *Speech on Fox's India Bill,* Burke attempted to stimulate the sympathies of his audience in a number of ways. He portrayed the bills as "the Magna Charta of Hindostan." By restraining power and destroying monopoly, Magna Charta is "dear to the heart of every Englishman." The comparison was intended less as an exercise in comparative politics than an attempt to move the hearts of his hearers on behalf of Indian reform. To lessen his audience's distance from such places as Oudh, Benares, Tanjore, and the Carnatic, Burke compared them to Prussia, Hesse, Bavaria, and Saxony. Their nabobs and rajas he compared to German princes and electors of the Holy Roman Empire. His purpose was not to make "an exact resemblance, but . . . to awaken something of sympathy for the unfortunate natives, of which I am afraid we are not perfectly susceptible" (*WS* 5:386, 384, 390).

Of Benares, the dominion of Chait Singh, Burke uses terms that record the way that city was perceived by those who reverenced it. The italicized words and phrases below represent Burke's efforts to transfer the passions of the raja's followers to the members of the House of Commons:

> Benares is the capital city of the Indian religion. It is *regarded as holy* by a particular and distinguished sanctity; and the Gentûs in general

> think themselves *as much obliged* to visit it once in their lives as the Mahometans to perform their pilgrimage to Mecca. By this means that city grew great in commerce and opulence; and so effectually it was secured by *the pious veneration* of that people, that in all wars and in all violences of power there was so sure an asylum, both for poverty and wealth . . . that the wisest laws and best assured free constitution could not better provide for the relief of the one, or the safety of the other. (*WS* 5:412, my italics)

Those who listened to the speech or read it later had no idea what Benares looked like. Burke's rhetoric is expressive, not mimetic. It tries to create sympathy in the English audience by conveying the passions that Benares raised in a Hindu: holiness, obligation, veneration.

Earlier in this chapter, I mentioned a second element of literary study, allusion, which is related (in the East India speech) to the first, the study of structure. Although I will reserve a full discussion of allusion for the next chapter, some passages from Burke's speech deserve mention. He proceeds to describe the raja's expulsion and the insolent treatment he received from Hastings: "Nothing aggravates tyranny so much as contumely. *Quicquid superbia in contumeliis* was charged by a great man of antiquity, as a principal head of offence against the governor general of that day" (*WS* 5:416). The allusion is to Cicero's prosecution of Verres, the provincial governor of the first century B.C. who plundered Cilicia and extorted wealth in Sicily. Nothing could make a deeper impression of their political and moral responsibilities than for the House of Commons to regard their proceedings in the light of Roman history, and particularly during the climactic change from republic to empire. Cicero "became a kind of Whig hero of the Roman Republic," writes Geoffrey Carnall, "its heroic defender and, in the end, a martyr to liberty."[64] Burke's use of classical allusion, here and elsewhere, has the purpose of eliciting the powerful passions with which his audience regarded classical history, and especially the low opinion in which the Roman empire (as opposed to the republic) was held. In 1788, he alludes to Roman history again, warning his audience that Roman law considered the combination of commercial and

64. Geoffrey Carnall, "Burke as Modern Cicero," in *The Impeachment of Warren Hastings*, ed. Colin Nicholson and Geoffrey Carnall (Edinburgh: Edinburgh University Press, 1989), 78.

imperial power "unsuitable" and strongly implying that Britain would follow the decline of that civilization (*WS* 6:283).

Later in the speech on Fox's bills, Burke loses his audience temporarily when some "young gentlemen" laugh at the mistreatment of the raja's mother. "I see no cause for mirth," Burke retorts. "A good author of antiquity reckons among the calamities of his time, *Nobilissimarum faeminarum exilia et fugas*" (*WS* 5:419). "The flight and exile of most honorable women" was a calamity to Tacitus. Being an "ancient" in the tradition of Swift, Burke finds the mistreatment of high-born women a calamity as well. A decade later, when Philip Francis referred to his portrait (in a draft of the *Reflections*) of Marie Antoinette as "pure foppery," Burke responded that his moral sympathies had been formed by *Hamlet:* "The minds of those who do not feel thus [for the sufferings of queens] are not even Dramatically right. 'Whats Hecuba to him or he to Hecuba that he should weep for her?' Why because she was Hecuba, the Queen of Troy, the Wife of Priam, and sufferd in the close of Life a thousand Calamities" (*C* 6:90). It is natural to feel such sympathy for noble women, whether they are Roman matrons, French queens, or Indian begams, whether fictional or historical. That sympathy has to be awakened by the conventions of a literary education. Burke's allusions, in short, are part of his moral and political fiber; through sympathy, literary study is integrated into Burke's very identity.

Burke's use of classical allusion, which could be multiplied many times over, illustrates the fact that ancient literature — the very center of the "hegemonic, Eurocentric" tradition — is a key resource on which Burke draws to arouse his audience's horror at the structure of British imperial oppression. In other words, when we see someone actually using the tradition, we find him using it in precisely the opposite way the ideologue has led us to expect. Rather than helping to establish a structure of Eurocentric domination, the classical literary tradition gives Burke sympathy with contemporary victims of British domination. His encounters with Cicero's *Verrine Orations* heightened his capacity to feel for others outside his own ethnic and political group.

Burke felt that his 1783 speech on the East India Bill had failed to create much sympathy for India in general, or Hindu culture in particular. A year later, he wrote that the "destruction of the species made in the East Indies does by no means touch the humanity of our countrymen, who, if the whole Gentoo [Hindu] race had but one neck, would see it cut with the most perfect indifference" (*C* 5:151). Nor could his distant relative, Will, who had spent a great deal of time in India, understand "for the soul of me" how Edmund felt as he did about "the black primates."[65] Burke's respect for the moral level of Hindu society also contrasts with the low estimate in which most of his contemporaries held it, including contemporary radicals like Joseph Priestley, who opposed Burke on the French Revolution.[66] In the summer of 1781 Burke entertained the Brahmin agents of the Maratha's chief minister at his home and went so far as to let them take over his greenhouse so they could follow their dietary laws. Fox once said that Burke had an "awe bordering on devotion" for Hinduism (*WS* 5:13).

Burke's sympathetic admiration for other cultures and races was intense, but it had nothing of relativism in it. He hoped that every British subject would prefer his own "liberties, rights, and institutions . . . to [those of] every other country in the world" (*W* 7:490). He thought the legacy of "chivalry" distinguished European civilization "to its advantage" from Asian and classical civilizations (*WS* 8:127). But contrary to much recent theory, neither Burke nor many of his contemporaries considered European society the *only* advanced one. In large part, he measured civilizations according to their apprehension and prudent adaption of natural law. Hindu and Islamic society in India were particularly distinguished in this regard. In his speech on the opening of impeachment (1788), Burke affirms the religious origins and universal applicability of this "law" in unequivocal terms:

> We are all born in subjection, all born equally, high and low, governors and governed, in subjection to one great, immutable, preexistent law . . . by which we are knit and connected in the eternal frame of the universe, out of which we cannot stir.
>
> This great law does not arise from our conventions or compacts. On the contrary, it gives to our conventions and compacts all the force and sanction they can have. It does not arise from our vain institutions. Every good gift is of God; all power is of God. . . . (*WS* 6:350)

65. Quoted by Conor Cruise O'Brien in *The Great Melody* (Chicago: University of Chicago Press, 1992), 307n.1.

66. See Williams and Marshall, *The Great Map of Mankind*, 117.

Burke then goes on to quote at length from the Islamic *Institutes* of Tamerlane in order to "assert that their morality is equal to ours as regards the morality of Governors, fathers, superiors; and I challenge the world to shew, in any modern European book, more true morality than is to be found in the writings of Asiatic men in high trusts . . ." (*WS* 6:361). Burke wanted to prevent Hastings from arguing that British law was irrelevant to Indian circumstances. But beyond that, he wanted to make his audience regard the Hindu and Islamic legal traditions sympathetically by viewing them in the same framework as British Common law: all of them depend upon divine law, and all of them proscribe the activities of which Hastings stood accused. Burke was searching for "the grounds of social and moral community," as Gerald Chapman writes.[67]

Putting Burke's writings in historical context does not mean putting them into an ideological structure. The more one reads of Burke, the less applicable are the theories of Orientalism or cultural hegemony or any other ideology. I have no doubt that someone can retreat to so high a level of abstraction that Burke's attack on oppression can somehow be interpreted as a subtle justification of it. But what's the point? What will we learn about Burke, or English letters, or India?

* * * * *

Burke himself provides more worthwhile insights into multiculturalism than the practice of ideological criticism can. Burke was a man of practical affairs rather than theory. He actually undertook to relieve oppression in the arena of public justice rather than maintain that a new curriculum he devised was a bold stroke for equity. He opened his house to some lonely Brahmins and his mind to their culture, rather than patronize an alien culture by relativism or prejudge its significance by ideology.

Burke exposes the pretensions of theorists who think they have just discovered the connections between moral, literary, political, and historical writing. Many current readers will not share his theory of art

67. Gerald W. Chapman, *Edmund Burke: The Practical Imagination* (Cambridge: Harvard University Press, 1967), 249.

or his exposition of universal, natural law, but these provided him with a foundation for the most profound understanding of an alien people among eighteenth-century Europeans. They enabled him to assimilate thousands of pages of writing on India and the testimony of hundreds of witnesses without prejudging their significance. The ideological foundations of much recent multiculturalism, by contrast, provide so rigid a theoretical structure that a detailed inquiry into other cultures is hardly necessary and may even prove to be a hindrance.

Burke's India speeches expose as well the shallow understanding that multiculturalists have of the European tradition. He appeals to that very tradition to criticize the hegemony, if one wishes to use that term, of British relations with India. His hopes of reform rest on the tradition itself, on a renewed understanding of historical and literary education, broadly understood. Burke shows that the traditions of learning, which were changing rapidly at the time, were capable of receiving sympathetically the finest contributions of Hindu and Islamic culture. He used the classical and European traditions to overcome the clichés that described Asian societies as despotic and morally corrupt.

Burke's sympathetic understanding of India was no doubt inadequate. His begams are too much like European princesses and his flourishing landscapes too much like literary pastoral scenes. But all real attempts to understand other peoples are only approximate. To try to consider them sympathetically, as Burke did, risks translating their irreducible particulars into one's own culture. But will we have a better foundation for understanding India or any other culture or event of past history if we adopt an ideological multiculturalism? If we begin by assuming that all knowledge serves someone's political and economic interests, as theorist James Banks does, what's to prevent us from regarding every statement about or from another culture as, finally, a statement of self-interest, including Banks's own words?[68] Current multiculturalism speaks a great deal about empowering other peoples, although in the end intellectuals do all the talking for them. But at the risk of promoting the male pecking order that so disgusts multiculturalist Phillipa Kafka, aren't a great many tragedies about persons who become empowered without an acknowledgement of their superior,

68. Banks, "A Curriculum for Empowerment, Action, and Change," 126-27.

moral duty? From *Agamemnon* to *Coriolanus,* from Plato through Acton, from writers as different as Charlotte Brontë, Robert Penn Warren, and Mario Vargas Llosa, the willful use of power has been a major preoccupation of Western literature. If our students learn to read this literature in Professor Kafka's way, will they be capable of learning anything from Aeschylus or Shakespeare — or Burke — about the moral temptations of power?

Some would be content to end a discussion of multiculturalism by surveying its claims and comparing them to traditional literary study, as I have done with Burke. For a Christian, however, the value of the literary tradition is relative to even more important beliefs. In this respect Christianity is undeniably parallel to ideological criticism, for neither system accepts an absolute separation between the world of letters and the rest of the world. But where ideologies often seem to demand a kind of faith from their practitioners and to govern the outcome of their criticism rather rigidly, a biblical poetics can accommodate a great deal of autonomy for the academic disciplines. Faith commitments affect literary study, as I hope to show, but they do not determine its outcomes as ideology does. I wish to turn now to some biblical treatments of diversity and suggest how they might guide one's thinking about different cultures.

The Unity and Diversity of Peoples at Babel and Pentecost

Burke located the foundation for his sympathy with other peoples in his and their common creation in God's image. Two years before the impeachment proceedings began, Burke explained to a niece of Sir Joshua Reynolds his seemingly unaccountable behavior thus: "I have no party in this Business, my dear Miss Palmer, but among a set of people who have none of your Lillies and Roses in their faces; but who are the images of the great Pattern as well as you and I. I know what I am doing; whether the white people like it or not" (*C* 5:255). Burke apparently takes the significance of a common creation for granted, however, and provides no details of his theological thinking. The Bible speaks often about the different "peoples" of the earth, and a full treatment of this theme could fill an entire book. But there are two accounts that give particular attention to the linguistic unity and diversity of mankind: the Tower of Babel and the story of Pentecost. These accounts do not provide an ideology for approaching Burke or India or the academic study of other cultures. They do, however, provide a starting point that is more profound and yet less intrusive than ideology for approaching some of the issues raised by multiculturalism.

Many have noted the parallels between the two stories, where the confusion of tongues at Babel is answered by their intelligibility at Pentecost. In *Towards a Christian Poetics,* Michael Edwards sees these stories as part of the general "ternary" process of the Bible: creation, fall, and re-creation. The language of Adam is perfect at creation. But its fall comes quickly, and the Babel account displays the linguistic consequences of the fall. Pentecost, then, becomes "the third term in the biblical dialectic of language. . . . For if the Spirit comes at Pentecost as a beginning and pledge of the future transformation of the world, his sign is the miraculous transformation, very pointedly, of the apostles' speech."[69]

The Bible relates the account of the Tower as follows:

> 1 Now the whole earth used the same language and the same words.
> 2 And it came about as they journeyed east, that they found a plain in the land of Shinar and settled there.
> 3 And they said to one another, "Come, let us make bricks and burn *them* thoroughly." And they used brick for stone, and they used tar for mortar.
> 4 And they said, "Come, let us build for ourselves a city, and a tower whose top *will reach* into heaven, and let us make for ourselves a name; lest we be scattered abroad over the face of the whole earth."
> 5 And the LORD came down to see the city and the tower which the sons of men had built.

69. Michael Edwards, *Towards a Christian Poetics* (Grand Rapids, Mich.: Wm. B. Eerdmans, 1984), 12. My treatment of the two biblical accounts has been influenced by Claus Westermann, John Sailhamer, Walter Brueggemann, and I. Howard Marshall.

6 And the LORD said, "Behold, they are one people, and they all have the same language. And this is what they began to do, and now nothing which they purpose to do will be impossible for them.
7 Come, let Us go down and there confuse their language, that they may not understand one another's speech."
8 So the LORD scattered them abroad from there over the face of the whole earth; and they stopped building the city.
9 Therefore its name was called Babel, because there the LORD confused the language of the whole earth; and from there the LORD scattered them abroad over the face of the whole earth. (Gen. 11:1-9, NASB)

To avoid the misconstructions we have seen in ideological readings, we should place this story in its context, first in Genesis and then in the Pentateuch as a whole. It serves as a transition between the "primeval history" that treats all mankind in the first eleven chapters and the accounts of particular patriarchs and tribes in the following thirty-nine chapters. Moreover, it occurs between one genealogy of Shem (Hebrew: "name") which produces no descendants of historical significance and another which produces Abram. In the chapter that follows the Tower account, God makes his covenant with Abram, promising to give him a new land, to make of him a great nation and a great name, to bless him, and through him to bless all the families of the earth.

As we have seen in the previous chapter, in contrast with many contemporary Mesopotamian stories, Genesis locates human culture outside the creative activities of God himself — and instead, under God's blessing. The fall occurs when Adam and Eve ignore the blessing and try to grasp the good on their own. They are punished by being forced to travel east, out of Eden, but many aspects of the blessing continue to benefit all mankind, such as marriage, family relations, and the growth of culture.

The story of Babel has strong connections with what comes before and after. By traveling eastward (vs. 2), the direction of Adam and Eve's exile, the builders of the Tower are already involved in the pattern of leaving God's blessing, willfully in this case. God is not disturbed by the builders' linguistic unity in verse 1, but that unity contains many latent dangers. In verses 3 and 4, the people undertake a project that utilizes human art (brick manufacture) in erecting a structure that literally embodies their unity. In verse 3, their technological advance — brick making — is announced. Still, their common language does not guarantee full and open communication. The purpose of their brick making is concealed. Perhaps their project of building the city and tower does not occur to them until verse 4. It is just as likely, however, that verse 3 conceals some less-than-innocent objective that the laconic Hebrew narrative keeps hidden, some purpose that helps to explain why they left their home and traveled east.

True human unity, as the Pentateuch later reveals, and as we shall see in the Pentecost narrative, results from identifying oneself with God's name and listening to his voice. The builders' project, by contrast, ignores God's name altogether. The "whole earth" seems to be united by its common language, and three times the phrase "let us" introduces a common plan (vss. 3-4), but can we be sure this unity is real? As Walter Brueggemann notes, there are two kinds of unity, one based on loyalty to God's will and the other based on fear, coercion, and conformity.[70] The spare lines of the story coupled with the outcome suggest the possibility of a gap, this time between the appearance of unity and the actual situation among the builders. If there were a dissenter at Babel, would their common language contain the vocabulary even to allow him or her to pose a question about the purpose of their labor?

In verse 4, the builders propose the tower, which will apparently make their name by its height and structural unity. Having a great name is viewed as a good thing in the Pentateuch. But placed between the two genealogies of Shem ("name"), and contrasted with God's promise that *he* would make Abram's name great (Gen. 12:2), the builders' project of making their *own* name great is more than suspect. It puts them outside the blessing. They behave as though their achievements can ignore God entirely, for they omit the basic responses to blessing, reverence (in Calvin's view), and gratitude (as Paul says in Romans 1:21). They repeat the pattern of the first eleven chapters of Genesis by trying to grasp the good on their own, and they view with

70. Walter Brueggemann, *Genesis,* in *Interpretation: A Bible Commentary for Teaching and Preaching,* ed. James Luther Mays (Atlanta: John Knox, 1982), 99-100.

alarm any interruption of their endeavors.[71] And yet, God does not respond so much because of what the builders have done, but because of what they may "purpose to do." God's concerns are similar to those he has after the fall of Adam and Eve, when he removes them from the garden lest they eat of the tree of life (Gen. 3:22).[72] Like the story of the fall, the most destructive effects of sin lie in the future, but their model project has already exceeded the limits of blessing. While the destructive effects of uniformity lie in the future, the structure of control is already present in their language and model project.

God's scattering of the people appears to the builders as a punishment, but within the Pentateuch, the Old Testament, and the Bible as a whole, it is consistent with God's blessing. The division of mankind into separate peoples and language groups is viewed positively in the previous chapters of Genesis, as a consequence of God's having saved mankind from the flood (9:1; 10:5, 20, 31).[73] God's blessing is meant to extend to the whole earth in Genesis 1:28, and the Tower is an attempt to frustrate it under the color of human unity. But God's purposes shall be accomplished, and the Abrahamic covenant in chapter 12 begins again the long biblical process of extending the blessing through a particular tribe, then through the Sinaitic covenant with a chosen people, and then to the entire earth.

* * * * *

At Pentecost, Christ's followers are all together when suddenly a noise like a violent, rushing wind fills the house:

> 3 And there appeared to them tongues as of fire distributing themselves, and they rested on each one of them.
> 4 And they were all filled with the Holy Spirit and began to

71. See John Sailhamer, "Genesis," in *Genesis–Numbers,* vol. 2 of *The Expositor's Bible Commentary,* ed. Frank E. Gaebelein (Grand Rapids, Mich.: Zondervan, 1984), 105.

72. See Westermann, *Genesis 1-11: A Commentary,* trans. John J. Scullion, S.J. (Minneapolis: Augsburg, 1984), 551-52.

73. See Westermann, *Genesis,* 552.

speak with other tongues, as the Spirit was giving them utterance. (Acts 2:3-4, NASB)

It is unlikely that the Babel account serves as a literary source for the story of Pentecost, but Pentecost does have an Old Testament connection. The festival of Pentecost was traditionally associated with the giving of the law at Sinai, and Luke may have known the rabbinic tradition that God gave the law in the languages of the seventy nations of the known world. In any case, both the New Testament writer and the rabbinic tradition saw that the constituting event of God's chosen people, whether the Jews at Sinai or the church at Pentecost, had to embrace all the cultures of the world. God himself takes the initiative to overcome the linguistic barriers in both stories.

The contrasts between the Pentecost and Babel stories are quite sharp. The "constituting event" of the church is not a human project in conception or execution, although it relies upon obedient human followers. At Pentecost, God does not provide the hearers with the ability to understand a single, uniform tongue, nor do the followers of Christ speak one tongue. Instead, God accommodates the message of Christ to diverse listeners through diverse languages.

At Pentecost, as Brueggemann notes, Luke emphasizes the "hearing" of the listeners more than the "speaking" of the inspired apostles. That provides a significant contrast to the Babel account, where God's purpose "that they may not *understand* one another's speech" may be rendered "that they may not *listen* to one another." Some of the grossest violations of the Old Testament covenants are due to "not listening."[74] Luke's interest in obedient hearing provides a dramatic counterpoint to the Tower narrative.

Another contrast between Babel and Pentecost is found in the significance of the "name" that identifies the members of the new community and the blessing they enjoy. "What shall we do?" say Peter's hearers at the conclusion of his sermon (Acts 2:37). Peter replies:

38 "Repent, and let each of you be baptized in the name of Jesus Christ for the forgiveness of your sins; and you shall receive the gift of the Holy Spirit.

74. Brueggemann, *Genesis,* 103-4.

> 39 For the promise is for you and your children, and for all who are far off, as many as the Lord our god shall call to Himself." (Acts 2:38-39, NASB)

The name of God's son will provide your new identity, he says. This contrasts sharply with the self-made name of Babel. The new community among peoples is not identified with any name other than that of Jesus Christ himself. That identity, given by God, restores the blessing lost at the fall and unsuccessfully pursued at Babel, through forgiveness, the gift of the Holy Spirit, and the call of God to "all who are far off.'

A final relationship between the two stories concerns the matter of "scattering." Even after the coming of the Spirit, the apostles fail to understand God's purposes. Acts 2 concerns the preaching of the gospel to linguistically different Jews, but the structure of the book suggests the universality of the gospel by turning to the Gentile mission in chapter 13 and by ending with the entry of the gospel into the capital of the empire, Rome. To begin accomplishing this mission, the apostles had to be scattered. There are hints of God's purpose in Acts 8:1 and 8:4, when persecution scatters the church, "and those who had been scattered went about preaching the word." But the apostles remain in Jerusalem, largely unaware of God's purpose of including the Gentiles in the gospel. Shortly thereafter, Peter is specifically told by God to bring the message of Christ to a Gentile family and offer them baptism (Acts 10). In his comment on the church's reaction to Peter's experiences with the Gentiles, Luke brings the themes of scattering and obedient hearing together:

> 18 And when they heard this [account of the baptism of Gentiles], they quieted down, and glorified God, saying, "Well then, God has granted to the Gentiles also the repentance *that leads to* life."
> 19 So then those who were scattered because of the persecution that arose in connection with Stephen made their way to Phoenicia and Cyprus and Antioch, speaking the word to no one except to Jews alone.
> 20 But there were some of them, men of Cyprus and Cyrene, who came to Antioch and *began* speaking to the Greeks also, preaching the Lord Jesus. (Acts 11:18-20, NASB)

Unlike the Babel account, Acts makes immediately clear the beneficial effects of God's scattering: Christ's followers begin to spread the gospel to other cultures — here, the Greeks (vs. 20). These verses record the first widespread inclusion of non-Jews in the gospel message and begin Luke's transition to the second half of Acts, which shortly turns to Paul's mission to the Gentiles.

* * * * *

The stories of Babel and Pentecost suggest that the only, ultimate foundation for multicultural unity lies in subordinating our human ambitions to the purposes of God and in seeing human culture in the context of God's blessing. Cultural pursuits are human activities conducted in obedient response to God. They derive from God, as all good gifts do, but a biblical poetics cannot identify human, cultural activities with God. They are not part of God's work of deliverance, and attempts to treat them as the source of liberation or transformation produce a parody of salvation. Moreover, such attempts have a disturbing parallel to the Tower account. In both instances, culture is placed within a structure of control in which true diversity is seen as a threat.

We will not achieve understanding among the diverse peoples of the world by treating education as the sacred task of overcoming social oppression. Human beings are apparently incapable of understanding, let alone overcoming, oppression on their own. Even the apostles had to be shown that the gospel had a purpose larger than anything their own religious understanding could grasp. And biblical notions of oppression — or more broadly, sin — are far more comprehensive than the most cunning ideological critique.

The writer of the Tower account indulges in a bit of polemical etymology in his concluding verse, joining the name "Babel" to the Hebrew word for "confuse." The human project to build a unified structure of thought and practice outside the blessing of God, the conclusion suggests, deteriorates into confusion. The common language of Babel is a parody of the unity among God's people that one finds later in the Pentateuch and at Pentecost. Once the deceptive linguistic unity of Babel is broken, no one listens to anyone else.

More in keeping with Scripture is the kind of multiculturalism that slowly becomes apparent to the apostles after Pentecost. Its unity is founded in the gospel, which does not presuppose either the erasure of different cultures or political conformity. We see that, like Christians of every era, from the early church through the British eighteenth century and beyond, believers often mistake God's way of defeating sin: even the apostles do not fully understand that their identity comes not from their culture, but from the "name" of Jesus, in which they perform baptism (Acts 2:38). It takes much time for them to learn that this name transcends its contemporary cultural setting.

A structure that explains all social life with reference to an ideology removes the need to listen to dissenters, or to God, or even to inquire very deeply into another culture. It is no accident that current multiculturalist theory speaks very rarely about the most multicultural of all educational activities: learning another language. The ideological project may be religious or secular, right-wing or left-wing, racist or Marxist, nationalist or internationalist. The writer of the Tower account is not saying that all human projects have a structure that may be exposed as suspect, but he is warning against the unspecified evils of pretending to embrace all human endeavor under a single structure of human devising. Such a structure makes a show of diversity that masks a coercive uniformity. Its pretense of attentiveness masks a refusal to listen to authentic diversity.

The guidance that Scripture provides on this issue is different in kind from that of ideology: biblical faith is not an ideology. You can agree or disagree with my literary analysis of Burke without regard to any religious faith you may or may not have. A biblical poetics that uses the language of blessing for its cultural analysis, rather than making every issue a topic of faith or salvation, has room for a true, if limited, autonomy for literary study. Your status as a good ideological multiculturalist, by contrast, will be determined by how your readings tally with the movement's faith in its particular mode of salvation, namely its program of cultural transformation.

Ideological multiculturalism lacks the inner resources to restrain its own cultural power and criticize its own excesses, for it cuts off the tradition of self-criticism, founded on the presupposition of moral and religious duty, that Western literature often displays. This tradition is nowhere better exhibited than in Edmund Burke's attempt to relieve oppression in India. But his performance, misread at second hand by an ideological critic of "Orientalism," can only be understood as "ironic." In fact, however, Burke's speeches suggest a pluralistic multi-culturalism, based on sympathy and critical engagement with a wide tradition. With the warnings of Babel in mind, one can turn to the account of Pentecost and base one's approach on the firm foundation of an obedient, godly listening that spans, without obliterating, cultural differences.

CHAPTER 5

The End of the Blessing and Its Renewal

The Apocalypse, Pope's Dunciad, *and Deconstruction*

THE Genesis accounts of creation, blessing, fall, judgment, catastrophe, and renewal find their fulfillment in the book of Revelation, or the Apocalypse. Generally in biblical "apocalyptic," as this mode of writing is called, God allows the forces of evil to reissue from the abyss and gain complete cultural and political control over his people, seducing many of them away from true faith and martyring others, at which point he intervenes to bring an end to history. God issues final judgment upon the forces of wickedness and inaugurates a new epoch for his people, who will enjoy fully the universal blessing, which he had intended from the beginning, in a new heaven and earth. "Apocalypse" literally means the uncovering of something hidden, and the apocalyptist reports his prophecies as visions that have been revealed to him by God, as John does in the opening verse of Revelation. Apocalyptic is the most emphatically "literal" of the biblical modes and genres in that it originates in the writing down of visions, rather than in prophetic or evangelical preaching. The book of Revelation reflects this emphasis on writing in the first of its seven blessings: "Blessed is he that readeth and heareth the wordes of this prophecie: and keepeth those thinges which be written in it for the time is nigh" (1:3).[1]

Alexander Pope's *Dunciad* is a mock-epic, not an apocalypse. Its name obviously alludes to the *Iliad,* the *Aeneid,* and other epics. The allusion to the *Aeneid* in its plot is indicated by the words of Pope's fictional commentator, "Martinus Scriblerus": "the Action of the Dunciad is the Removal of the Imperial seat of dulness from the City to the polite world; as that of the Æneid is the Removal of the empire of Troy to Latium."[2]

Scriblerus's note appears in the second of five major versions of the poem. Originally published in three books without notes in 1728, Pope brought out *The Dunciad Variorum* in 1729, including the observations of Scriblerus. In 1742, a fourth book, *The New Dunciad,* appeared, with notes by Pope and his literary collaborator William Warburton. In late 1743, seven months before Pope's death, a revised version of the entire four-book poem was published, *The Dunciad, In Four Books,* with Colley Cibber dethroning Lewis Theobald as King of the Dunces. Even after Pope's death in 1744, however, the story doesn't end, for Warburton added some new notes to *The Dunciad* in his edition of Pope's *Works* (1751).[3]

The first book of *The Dunciad* concerns the anointing of Cibber as poet laureate by the Goddess of Dulness, the parodic deity of the poem. In the second book, Cibber's enthronement is celebrated with

1. Although Rev. 1:3 refers to reading a written text, it assumes that the text is read aloud (not silently), as was typical in antiquity. All quotations are from the Rheims-Douai Bible unless noted. I have used the first printing of the Rheims New Testament (1582) and the Douai Old Testament (1609-10). The editors of the Twickenham edition of Pope's poetry comment on his familiarity with this Catholic translation of the Bible in their note to his imitation of Psalm 91. See Alexander Pope, *The Twickenham Edition of the Poems of Alexander Pope,* ed. John Butt et al. (New Haven: Yale University Press, 1938-68), 6:70. The title is abbreviated as *TE.*

2. Pope, *TE,* 5:51.

3. This chapter will refer to the 1743 version of the poem (as printed in the Twickenham edition of Pope's poetry), unless noted. I have indicated my use of one note from the 1751 *Works* that has only Warburton's authority. See *TE* 5:249-50 for a fuller discussion of the later editions of *The Dunciad* and the notes by Warburton.

epic games, and in the third, he is conducted to the underworld. In the fourth book, the empire of Dulness is restored to Britain, and all the arts and sciences are banished as the Goddess's "uncreating word" buries all in darkness.

Scriblerus's description of the action of the poem indicates that the main allusive thread in the poem is that which connects it to the story of Aeneas. The language and action of the poem allude closely to *Paradise Lost* as well. At many crucial points, however, the poem goes beyond the epic texts it evokes, and even the critic most concerned to locate *The Dunciad* within eighteenth-century mock-epic literature acknowledges that "in the third and especially the fourth book of the final version, the epic structure is for the most part replaced by another."[4]

There are actually several other structures in the final two books of the *Dunciad:* the dream vision, the "sessions of the poets" genre, and the progress poem. More significant than these, however, are the apocalyptic elements of the verse, some of which have been recognized but never fully studied: the images of the ten-horned beasts and harlotry allude to biblical prophecy, especially in its apocalyptic mode. Pope seems to invert the apocalyptist's report that he "saw a great white throne" (Rev. 20:11) when he commands the reader to "behold" the Goddess on her "sable throne" (4:629-52); earlier in the poem, the characters of the Goddess of Dulness and her son, the "Antichrist of Wit," begin building an allusive, apocalyptic structure by referring to the blasphemous deity and the Antichrist in Revelation, and especially to the sections (such as Rev. 13:6-8 and Rev. 14–16) where the faithful are either overcome or, more ominously, tempted to apostatize (such as Rev. 12:15 and chapters 17–18). Finally, the plot of *The Dunciad,* with its pessimistic view of history and the seriousness with which it recounts the defeat of true wit, is parallel to the events typical of apocalyptic, especially its account of the inexplicable woes that will come to the faithful.

So large a collection of relatively clear allusions suggests that perhaps other elements of the poem gain resonance from their apoc-

4. Ulrich Broich, *The Eighteenth-Century Mock-Heroic Poem* (New York: Cambridge University Press, 1990), 154.

alyptic parallels as well: the presence of a faithful remnant (the wits of *The Dunciad*) whose identity is secure compared to the wicked (the dunces), whose identity will perish; the confusing nature of the threat of evil; the imagery of darkness and the abyss; the war in heaven; astronomical signs; and the use of trumpets and horns. At the end of his influential study of the poem, Aubrey Williams maintains that the "theological metaphor" undergirding the poem — "the anti-Logos of Dulness" — provides a set of "inversions of Christian themes" that modify the entire work.[5] To date, however, no full-scale study has attempted to estimate the significance of biblical apocalyptic for *The Dunciad.* I will argue that apocalyptic functions for Pope in a way similar to epic: as a mock apocalypse or an anti-apocalypse, *The Dunciad* approximates and distances itself from straight apocalyptic in order to achieve both the seriousness and the irony Pope wants. It simultaneously measures the dunces' serious threat to culture with apocalyptic imagery, and treats their threat comically through the pleasurable knowledge that the author is using apocalypse as an ironic figure.

Quite apart from the biblical issues, more recent readers have noted that the questions raised by *The Dunciad* have many parallels to those raised by the greatest philosophical challenge to traditional literary study in modern times: deconstruction. In his study of the poem's genre, Ulrich Broich writes, "this polyphonic work with all its mutually deconstructive discourses and allusions would lend itself" readily to deconstructive criticism.[6] In his deconstructive reading of Pope, G. Douglas Atkins notes that deconstruction "seems importantly to resemble duncery as Pope represents it," and pauses momentarily to worry that Pope's ridicule of Dulness might be read as a "prescient treatment" of the current battle between older "humanistic critics and 'hermeneutical' ones, most notably perhaps deconstructionists."[7] Maynard Mack refers to the tendency among critics, especially strong among poststructural-

5. Aubrey Williams, *Pope's "Dunciad": A Study of Its Meaning* (Baton Rouge: Louisiana University Press, 1955), 154.

6. Broich, *The Eighteenth-Century Mock-Heroic Poem,* 23.

7. G. Douglas Atkins, *Quests of Difference* (Lexington: University of Kentucky Press, 1986), 148-49.

ists, to consider their art or genius superior to that of poets, an attitude held by Pope's duncical philologist Richard Bentley.[8] But here as well, no full-scale study (including Atkins's) has examined the relationships between Pope's *Dunciad* and deconstruction.

As in my earlier chapters, I will argue that a biblical poetics provides a better basis for understanding literature than the current ideological schools of criticism. In the chapter on Milton, I examined the biblical concept of "blessing" as an alternative to ideological feminism, and in the chapter on Burke I looked at biblical narratives that offered an alternative to ideological multiculturalism. In this chapter, I will examine a biblical mode of writing — apocalyptic — to argue first, that an understanding of Pope's apocalyptic allusions can provide a deeper appreciation than we now have of the poem's cultural critique; and second, that the *Dunciad* and biblical apocalyptic provide a deeper understanding of the issues raised by deconstruction than deconstructive theory itself.

There are limits to the kind of allusive reading that I will attempt here: not every image or structure common to the *Dunciad* and apocalyptic is an allusion. For instance, the sibyl of book 3 alludes to the Cumaean sibyl of the *Aeneid* but seems unrelated to the large collection of apocalyptic Sibylline Oracles. Nor can *The Dunciad* be forced to accommodate the full parody of the Trinity that one finds in the Apocalypse (Rev. 13). Since Cibber and the Goddess of Dulness are obvious parodies of the Son and Father, it is possible that Elkanah Settle alludes to the "false prophet" or the "beast from the earth." But I believe the poem won't support that reading. Settle's allusive function in the poem seems limited to recalling the prophecies of Anchises in the *Aeneid.* He alludes to Aeneas's human father, but there seem to be no echoes of a comparable figure from the Apocalypse.

The study of allusion in traditional literary discipline is different from the current practice of "intertextuality," which sets correspondences in various texts side by side.[9] The results are sometimes intrigu-

8. Maynard Mack, *Alexander Pope: A Life* (New York: W. W. Norton, 1985), 483.

9. My study of Burke's Indian speeches and the accounts of Tower of Babel and Pentecost is closer to intertextual analysis with the exception that I consider the biblical texts as containing a kind of teaching about language. I do not consider the

ing, as Robert Alter says, but allusion is different: it "implies a writer's active, purposeful use of antecedent texts":

> Allusion occurs when a writer, recognizing the general necessity of making a literary work by building on the foundations of antecedent literature, deliberately exploits this predicament in explicitly activating an earlier text as part of the new system of meaning and aesthetic value of his own text.[10]

Alter discusses three variables that need examination in any allusive reading. First is the "marker" or indicator that signals the activation of an older text in the newer one.[11] Second comes the function of that marker in the alluding text. Is its significance broadly applicable to the entire text, as Virgil's *Aeneid* is to Pope's *Dunciad*, or does it have only local significance? Third is the difficult task of establishing the relations between the alluding text and the evoked text, which depends, according to Alter, "not on some arcane 'technique' of decoding but on common sense."[12]

I will attempt to show that Pope's structure of allusion to biblical apocalyptic has broad significance for the meaning of *The Dunciad*, similar in scope to the significance of his allusions to the *Aeneid*. The victory of the Lamb in Revelation is parodied by the apocalyptic victory of Dulness at the end of the poem. The final triumph of God is parodied by the triumph of Dulness. God's ultimate rule signals the restoration of universal blessing; the rule of Dulness signals the elimination of cultural blessings, whose proper enjoyment is one of the major, yet neglected, preoccupations of Pope's poetry.[13]

---

biblical texts and Burke's speeches as parallel in any theoretical sense. The biblical accounts rather serve as models from which I proceed to raise questions about Burke and current texts on multiculturalism. For a good example of a more intertextual approach (in this case, to biblical prophecy and literary satire), see Thomas Jemielity, *Satire and the Hebrew Prophets* (Louisville: Westminster/John Knox, 1992).

10. Robert Alter, *The Pleasures of Reading in an Ideological Age* (New York: Simon & Schuster, 1989), 112, 116.

11. Alter, *The Pleasures of Reading in an Ideological Age*, 120.

12. Alter, *The Pleasures of Reading in an Ideological Age*, 129.

13. A mere word count doesn't necessarily indicate importance, particularly when Pope's translations are included, but Bedford's *Concordance* to Pope's poetry lists "blest" and related words 372 times. Its frequency is similar to that of words that have

Characteristics of Biblical Apocalyptic and *The Dunciad*

Apocalyptic flourished between 200 B.C. and A.D. 100 and then declined, perhaps because the militant imagery of war against the forces of evil was no longer credible after the destruction of the temple in A.D. 70.[14] The book of Revelation announces itself as an apocalypse, and there are also apocalyptic elements in Daniel, Joel, Zechariah 9–14, Ezekiel 38–39, Isaiah 24–27, and Mark 13, among other places. Outside the Bible, apocalyptic is found in the fourth book of Ezra (traditionally included in the English Apocrypha), and in a wide variety of other Jewish and Christian books, from the Sibylline Oracles to portions of the Dead Sea Scrolls and *The Shepherd of Hermas.*[15]

Biblical scholars have difficulty defining the genre of apocalyptic, perhaps because (like satire) it is less a "genre" than a mode or kind of writing. The apocalyptic mode has its closest literary affinities to Hebrew prophecy, and indeed the book of Revelation often refers to itself as a prophecy. In both prophecy and apocalyptic, the writer is concerned to find a divine explanation for the plight of God's people. Both forms urge God's people to greater faithfulness. Several estimates of the *Dunciad's* biblical qualities have spoken of the "prophetic" component of its imagery and narrative, reflecting the proximity of the two modes of

---

been frequently studied for their significance to Pope — for instance, "nature" (209), "art" (200), "pride" (238), "sense" (195), "friend" (408), and "whole" (202). Emmett G. Bedford and Robert J. Dilligan, *A Concordance to the Poems of Alexander Pope,* 2 vols. (Detroit: Gale Research, 1974).

14. Leon Morris, *Apocalyptic* (Grand Rapids, Mich.: Wm. B. Eerdmans, 1972), 38.

15. The name IV Esdras (IV Ezra) comes from the Vulgate's title of this book, which is preserved in the Catholic Douai Bible of 1609-10, where it appears after the end of the Old Testament books. The book is named II Esdras in most of the Protestant English Bibles — Geneva (1560), Authorized (1611), Revised Standard (1957) — where it appears in the Apocrypha. This risks confusion with Nehemiah, which is known earlier as II Esdras as well. See Bruce M. Metzger, introduction to "The Fourth Book of Ezra," in *The Old Testament Pseudepigrapha,* ed. James H. Charlesworth (Garden City, N.Y.: Doubleday, 1983), 1:516-17. IV Esdras comes into my account of *The Dunciad* through one of its eighteenth-century readers, William Whiston, who was an object of Pope's satire (see Pope, *TE,* 6:25).

writing. Reuben Brower, for instance, refers to the "prophetic quality" compounded of "Virgilian, Miltonic, and Biblical elements" that raises *The Dunciad* above mock-epic.[16] Thomas Jemielity has written more generally of the resemblance of the personae of prophet and satirist: both of them simultaneously occupy and spurn cultural institutions; both of them protest that they come to their vocation unwillingly and lament their failure; both of them believe the contemporary moral struggle will determine the culture of the future.[17]

The differences between prophecy and apocalyptic are substantial as well. Unlike most prophecy, apocalyptic flourished when Israel (or the church) was surrounded by a foreign, hostile culture — Babylon in the case of Daniel, Rome in the case of Revelation. Part of the *Dunciad*'s strength comes from Pope's placement of his poem in a similar cultural context: the true wits are surrounded by a culture controlled by dunces. Unlike the prophet, the apocalyptist has lost all hope that God will intervene in human history to restore his people. Instead, God's intervention will put an end to history. Similarly, *The Dunciad* creates a fictional world where struggle against the empire of Dulness is futile. But unlike much apocalyptic — and especially the book of Revelation — Pope's poem does not imagine an ultimate intervention that will end the reign of Dulness. It imagines the successful restoration of her empire, and the hope of the true wits who read the poem lies in their being ironically "outside the text," intellectually and culturally, even as they read of their defeat "inside the text." *The Dunciad*, then, does not remain within the genre of apocalyptic. The ultimate victory of the forces of darkness makes it a mock-apocalypse, or even an anti-apocalypse. On the other hand, the term "anti-apocalypse" may suggest that apocalyptic is a discrete, easily classifiable genre. It is not. It "often verges off into other literary styles and conceptual modes," such as prophecy, lament, benediction, and epistle in the book of Revelation.[18]

16. Reuben Brower, *Alexander Pope: The Poetry of Allusion* (Oxford: Clarendon, 1959); see also Robert Griffin, "Pope, the Prophets, and *The Dunciad*," *Studies in English Literature* 23, no.3 (1983): 435-46.

17. See Jemielity, *Satire and the Hebrew Prophets*, 119-95.

18. Robert H. Mounce, *The Book of Revelation* (Grand Rapids, Mich.: Wm. B. Eerdmans, 1977), 18.

In this respect too, *The Dunciad* shows its similarities to apocalyptic, for the poem at many points is close to mock-epic, while at others it more closely resembles a dream vision, a theatrical farce, a "sessions of the poets" poem, and a progress poem.

Rather than attempt to fix apocalyptic as a genre, therefore, biblical scholars have tried to describe this mode by listing its general characteristics. Here too, the parallels to *The Dunciad* are striking. First, as we have seen, apocalyptic generally sets the faithful people in a hostile culture. Second, biblical apocalyptic seems contemporary to every age. Each generation has a fascination with attempts to interpret the number 666, to identify the Antichrist, or to find parallels to the persecuted church of Revelation 12–13. In Pope's day, both Sir Isaac Newton and his successor as Lucasian Professor of Mathematics, the eccentric William Whiston, devoted much intellectual energy to contemporary interpretations of biblical prophecy. Warburton himself interpreted the Reformation as having fulfilled the prophesied appearance of the "day-star" of 2 Peter 1:19.[19] The marginal note to Revelation 12:6 in the Rheims New Testament (1582), where the glorious woman is forced to flee into the wilderness, directs the reader to the contemporary persecutions of the Catholic Church in England. The measure of Pope's success in tapping this ever-contemporary source of apocalyptic fascination is found in Atkins's concern about the applicability of *The Dunciad* to deconstruction, and in Maynard Mack's application of the poem's satire to television evangelists, corporate patronage of the arts, and such artistic endeavors as covering islands in Saran Wrap.[20]

A third characteristic of apocalyptic literature is that every value held by the writer is cast into doubt, and the prognosis for renewing his or her world is generally pessimistic. The psychic and cultural structures are collapsing, writes Amos Wilder,

> with the consequent nakedness to Being or immediacy to the dynamics of existence. Hence the rhetorics of this "panic" exposure in

19. William Warburton, "Discourse 28," in *The Works of the Right Reverend William Warburton, D. D.*, ed. Richard Hurd, new ed., 12 vols. (London, 1811).

20. Mack, *Alexander Pope,* 791, 788, 796.

which all is at stake, involving antinomies of life and death, light and darkness, knowledge and nescience, order and chaos.[21]

The Dunciad both approximates this description and distances itself from it. The poem uses the structures of cosmic apocalypse figurally, as a means of describing cultural collapse. The "antinomies" listed by Wilder, especially those of darkness, nescience, and chaos, give weight to the impending cultural collapse, particularly in the early lines of each book and in the conclusion of the entire work. For example:

In eldest time, e'er mortals writ or read,
E'er Pallas issu'd from the Thund'rer's head,
Dulness o'er all possess'd her ancient right,
Daughter of Chaos and eternal Night:
Fate in their dotage this fair Ideot gave,
Gross as her sire, and as her mother grave,
Laborious, heavy, busy, bold, and blind,
She rul'd, in native Anarchy, the mind.

(1:9-16)

Yet, yet a moment, one dim Ray of Light
Indulge, dread Chaos, and eternal Night!
Of darkness visible so much be lent,
As half to shew, half veil the deep Intent.

(4:1-4)

She comes! she comes! the sable Throne behold
Of *Night* Primæval, and of *Chaos* old! . . .
Lo! thy dread Empire, CHAOS! is restor'd;
Light dies before thy uncreating word:
Thy hand, great Anarch! lets the curtain fall;
And Universal Darkness buries All.

(4:629-30, 653-56)

21. Amos N. Wilder, "The Rhetoric of Ancient and Modern Apocalyptic," *Interpretation* 25, no. 4 (1971): 440.

In the very passages where dunce and Dulness cause cosmic collapse, however, the reader is aware that the apocalyptic structures are figures — not "straight" apocalyptic elements. The apocalyptic elements lend significance to Pope's satire, but they are not simply translated into the poem, any more than the epic elements are. Pope did not see visions as St. John did. By giving apocalyptic gravity to such lightweights as Colley Cibber and Elkanah Settle, Pope simultaneously establishes the seriousness of the threat they pose to culture and deflates their importance by placing them in an ironic poem. Some recent critics, unable to see how the poem can simultaneously be fully comic and fully serious, have sought to diminish its theological significance.[22] Pope's poet-hero emerges from the allusions to Satan, writes Dustin Griffin, not as a dangerous agent of evil, but as a desperate, incompetent hack. The allusions do not induce a sense of alarm, but of amused superiority.[23] I will argue that the allusions to apocalyptic induce both alarm and amusement: they alarm by the proximity of real evil posed by cultural collapse, and they amuse by the distance between the dunces of Pope's poem and the forces of evil in biblical apocalyptic. Still, my final conclusions will be serious ones: that biblical apocalyptic and its figural use in *The Dunciad* should lead one to question the poststructuralist conclusion that such terms as "good" and "wisdom" have their opposites — evil and duncery — inscribed within them. There is a half-truth in the poststructuralist belief that no system of differences (such as those between wisdom and duncery) is stable. But biblical apocalyptic and *The Dunciad* take this instability even more seriously than poststructuralism, and give their sympathetic readers an understanding of that instability that is still contemporary.

In addition to its setting in a hostile culture, its pessimism, and its permanent contemporaneity, Pope's *Dunciad* shares a fourth characteristic with apocalyptic and visionary literature in general: it half reveals and half conceals its meaning through obscure references, bizarre sym-

22. See Leopold Damrosch, *The Imaginative World of Alexander Pope* (Berkeley: University of California Press, 1987), 263-66; Donald T. Siebert, "Cibber and Satan: *The Dunciad* and Civilization," *Eighteenth-Century Studies* 10 (1976-77): 203-21.

23. Dustin Griffin, *Regaining Paradise: Milton and the Eighteenth Century* (Cambridge: Cambridge University Press, 1986), 175-77.

bolism, and a free hand with narrative.[24] The difficulty of following *The Dunciad's* narrative is eased somewhat by Scriblerus's note (1729) that the "main action of the Poem [is] the Restoration of the Empire of Dulness in Britain," although even that leaves much unexplained. The bizarre symbolism of the poem, such as the whales who "sport in woods," makes sense within the apocalyptic new heaven and earth ushered in by Dulness (3:246). And the obscure references to scores of contemporary dunces run parallel to the obscurity that now shrouds the gematria of Revelation and the identities of the horns and heads of its beasts.

Pope indicates the importance of this characteristic in a couplet he added to the final book of the poem:

> Of darkness visible so much be lent,
> As half to shew, half veil the deep Intent.
>
> (4:3-4)

To explain this line, Pope and Warburton add the following comment (attributed to the philologist Richard Bentley in the fictional critical apparatus to the work): "the Author in this work had indeed a *deep Intent;* there were in it Mysteries or ἀπόρρητα which he durst not fully reveal. . . ." The Greek word ἀπόρρητα is ambivalent in a highly ironic manner, like the word "profound" or *altitudo* in *Peri Bathous.* With reference to sacred things it can mean "ineffable." But it can also mean "abominable."[25] In *The Dunciad* it means both. What is ineffable to the dunces who inhabit the cosmos of the poem is revealed as abominable to the witty reader outside. By half revealing and half concealing his meaning, Pope achieves a fully serious and fully ironic effect.

24. See David Aune, "The Apocalypse of John and the Problem of Genre," *Semeia* 36 (1986): 82-83.

25. H. G. Liddell and Robert Scott, *A Greek-English Lexicon,* rev. Henry Stuart Jones, 9th ed. (Oxford: Clarendon, 1940).

War in Heaven and the Fulfillment of History in *Dunciad* III

Some of the clearest markers of *The Dunciad*'s allusion to apocalyptic occur in the "War in Heaven" of book 3. In the long run, however, they are among the least significant for my purposes. The main allusive purpose of book 3 is to anticipate the restoration of Dulness in Britain by alluding to the sixth book of the *Aeneid,* where the future glories of Rome are revealed during Aeneas's trip to the underworld. In the three-book *Dunciad* (1728), the War in Heaven was part of the last 230 lines of the poem, leading to the restoration of chaos, the fleeing of the arts and sciences, and the speaking of the "uncreating word." In that early version, then, the allusions to the apocalyptic War in Heaven were closely related to the final triumph of Dulness. In the four-book 1743 version, however, the War in Heaven remained in book 3, separated from the triumph of Dulness by several hundred lines of book 4. As a result of this distance, the 1743 version of book 3 seems to evoke less of the apocalyptic conflict.

In book 3, Cibber is led to the underworld by a sibyl, where he listens to a prophecy from "Father Settle." This parallels Aeneas's conduct to the underworld by the Cumaean Sibyl, where his father Anchises prophesies the future history of Rome. At a pivotal point, Cibber is allowed to see the "charms" of his new world, when Dulness will have eliminated both "nature" and "art" from human culture — and especially from dramatic writing. What follows is a satirical vision of popular stage tricks, particularly those of the contemporary London theatrical manager John Rich.

> [Cibber] look'd, and saw a sable Sorc'rer rise,
> Swift to whose hand a winged volume flies:
> All sudden, Gorgons hiss, and Dragons glare,
> And ten-horn'd fiends and Giants rush to war.
> Hell rises, Heav'n descends, and dance on Earth:
> Gods, imps, and monsters, music, rage, and mirth,
> A fire, a jigg, a battle, and a ball,
> 'Till one wide conflagration swallows all.
> Thence a new world to nature's laws unknown,
> Breaks out refulgent, with a heav'n its own:

Another Cynthia her new journey runs,
And other planets circle other suns.
The forests dance, the rivers upward rise,
Whales sport in woods, and dolphins in the skies;
And last, to give the whole creation grace,
Lo! one vast Egg produces human race. . . .

(3:233-48)

This passage contains several allusions. Pope's note to line 246, for instance, calls attention to Horace's "Art of Poetry," where the bad innovative poet puts his dolphins in trees and boars in rivers. But the passage evokes more than the gimmicks of bad poets and stage managers. The opening lines evoke the final battle between heaven and hell, between the angels and the "ten-horned" beast and dragon, who are defeated in Revelation 19 and ultimately swallowed by the lake of fire (19:20; 20:2, 10, 14-15). Both here and in the biblical apocalypse, a new heaven and new earth are immediately revealed (Rev. 21:1), where God's blessings on creation are finally fulfilled (for instance, in the figure of the tree of life of Rev. 22:2). Pope's lines here do not have the ominous quality of his other allusions to apocalyptic, perhaps because of the clear, contemporary references to theatrical spectacles like Lewis Theobald's *Rape of Proserpine.*[26] But their allusive direction is nonetheless unmistakable. The victory of Dulness over nature and art will result in a new "nature" that Pope imagines as oviparous in origin, grotesque in operation.

A few lines later, a second passage begins by raising John Rich, manager of the theater in Lincoln's Inn, to the level of an "immortal," describing him by means of an allusion to Jahweh in his prophetic, martial character:

> The Lord . . . will not at all acquit the wicked; the Lord hath his way in the whirlwind and in the storm, and the clouds are the dust of his feet. (Nah. 3:3, AV; cf. Job 38:1; 40:6)

26. In that play, the heavens open, disclosing Jupiter, and then the earth opens so that Pluto and Proserpine may rise as from hell. The production of the human race from an egg occurred in the same play. (See Pope, *TE,* 5:177.)

The passage reads:

> "Immortal Rich! how calm he sits at ease
> 'Mid snows of paper, and fierce hail of pease
> And proud his Mistress' orders to perform,
> Rides in the whirlwind, and directs the storm.
> "But lo! to dark encounter in mid air
> New wizards rise; I see my Cibber there!
> Booth in his cloudy tabernacle shrin'd,
> On grinning dragons thou shalt mount the wind.
> Dire is the conflict, dismal is the din,
> Here shouts all Drury, there all Lincoln's-inn. . . ."
>
> (3:261-70)

The conflict between Rich's theater and Drury Lane (managed by Cibber and Barton Booth) recalls the War in Heaven of Revelation 12:7 by way of *Paradise Lost:*

> dire was the noise
> Of conflict; over head the dismal hiss
> Of fiery Darts in flaming volleys flew. . . .[27]

The passage in Revelation may be the immediate as well as the ultimate source of Pope's "dragons": "And there was made a great battel in heaven, Michael and his Angels fought with the dragon, and the dragon fought and his Angels. . . . And that great dragon was cast forth, the old serpent . . ." (Rev. 12:7, 9). Pope may also have been thinking of the "serpent" a few lines later, when Settle prays that Cibber be spared the disgrace of having to "wag a serpent-tail" in the farces and pantomimes of "Smithfield fair" (3:288).

Despite all of these allusions, however, the apocalypse prophesied in the third book doesn't succeed in threatening all of culture as the rest of the poem does. Its effects begin — and seem to end — in the theater. To be sure, the theater is a figure for the entire world, as Aubrey Williams argues,[28] but its moral failings are, for most of book 3, left

27. John Milton, *Paradise Lost,* 6:211-13.
28. Williams, *Pope's "Dunciad,"* 87-103.

at Drury Lane. It is when they emerge into the larger world, as they do at the end of book 3 and into book 4, that their threat increases. In book 4, the complete victory of Dulness is signaled by a blast from "Fame's posterior Trumpet," which summons "all the Nations . . . to the Throne" (4:71-72). This is a parodic allusion to the summoning of the nations at the throne of the Lamb and the trumpet blast that signals Christ's universal reign (Rev. 7:9; 11:15). At that point in *The Dunciad,* culture is being completely ruined and its parody of the apocalypse grows darker.

The Deep and Darkness

Among the images with apocalyptic resonance, those associated with the deep or profound are among the most significant. The importance of this image pre-dates *The Dunciad.* It appears in *Peri Bathous,* or *The Art of Sinking in Poetry,* just two months before the publication of the 1728 *Dunciad.* A collaborative effort involving Pope, Swift, and Dr. Arbuthnot, *Peri Bathous* was printed in the Swift-Pope *Miscellanies,* and continued the quarrel between the ancients and moderns. Purporting to be a treatise by Martinus Scriblerus on how modern poetry achieved its "profundity" (the obverse of ancient "sublimity"), the work catalogues the superficiality, "antinatural way[s] of thinking," and false pride of modern authors and critics.[29] Beginning with a visit from Swift in mid-March of 1726, Swift and Pope collected past works and wrote new ones for the four volumes of *Miscellanies.* Swift also persuaded Pope to proceed with an earlier sketch of *The Dunciad.*[30] As John Sitter has written, in *Peri Bathous* "we see [Pope] for the first time exploring the full reaches of antithetical logic," a technique that achieves its highest reaches in *The Dunciad.*[31]

29. The quoted phrase is from Alexander Pope, chapter 5 of *The Art of Sinking in Poetry [Peri Bathous],* ed. Edna Lake Steeves (New York: Columbia, King's Crown Press, 1952); hereafter abbreviated as *PB.*

30. Pope, *TE,* 5:201; Alexander Pope, *The Correspondence of Alexander Pope,* ed. George Sherburn, 5 vols. (Oxford: Clarendon, 1956), 2:522.

31. John E. Sitter, *The Poetry of Pope's "Dunciad"* (Minneapolis: University of Minnesota Press, 1971), 61.

In *Peri Bathous,* false logic is capable of inverting every aesthetic and human value. It twists ever so slightly the concepts and techniques that Pope seriously recommends and, in so doing, opens the possibility of literary collapse. For instance, the work uses analogy to "prove" that achieving the "true Profound" is a valid art:

> We come now to prove, that there is an Art of Sinking in Poetry. Is there not an Architecture of Vaults and Cellars, as well as of lofty domes and Pyramids? Is there not as much Skill and Labour in making of Dykes, as in raising of Mounts? Is there not an Art of Diving as well as of Flying? (*PB,* chap. 4)

Pope is not saying that all analogies are worthless, nor is he providing the deconstructive key for undermining all of his own analogies. But he is showing his full awareness that the practitioner of "the profound" has no trouble using analogy in a way that justifies the most foolish conclusions. The modern can use his or her intelligence to prove anything he or she wishes.

The modern profound is also capable of inverting one of Pope's guiding literary concepts — nature — by a brilliant misapplication of Horace's criterion that literature should delight and instruct:

> The taste of the Bathos is implanted by Nature itself in the Soul of Man; 'till perverted by Custom or Example he is taught, or rather compell'd, to relish the Sublime. . . . [I]f the Intent of all Poetry be to divert and instruct, certainly that Kind which diverts and instructs the greatest Number, is to be preferr'd. Let us look round among the Admirers of Poetry, we shall find those who have a Taste of the Sublime to be very few, but the Profound strikes universally, and is adapted to every Capacity. (*PB,* chap. 2)

One must admit that the kind of "nature" that is said to work harmoniously with human culture, and that Pope elsewhere seriously recommends (for example in the *Essay on Criticism* and the *Epistle to Burlington*), is more difficult to understand than Scriblerus's equation of nature and popular taste. It is easier to let demography determine artistic standards. In Pope's satire, the modern subversion of aesthetic values is accompanied by a relaxation of intellectual vigor, which leads in turn to moral failure.

Scriblerus indicates his moral obduracy most clearly by divorcing the profound from actual human purposes:

> The Sublime of Nature is the Sky, the sun, Moon, Stars, &c. The Profound of Nature is Gold, Pearls, precious Stones, and the Treasures of the Deep, which are inestimable as unknown. But all that lies between these, as Corn, Flowers, Fruits, Animals, and Things for the meer Use of Man, are of mean price, and so common as not to be greatly esteem'd by the Curious. (*PB,* chap. 4)

Pope's poetry is emphatically concerned with the "middle" things that are "for the meer use of Man." When criticism and poetry divorce themselves from their human purposes, their effect will be profound — but it will be profoundly destructive.

Peri Bathous is a satire, but like all of Pope's satire, it is also serious. He realizes that the modern intellectual is capable of inverting every value — aesthetic, intellectual, and moral — to which Pope subscribes. To say that Scriblerus is *capable* of working these inversions, however, does not mean that the difference between the sublime and bathetic is erased, or that a trace of the bathos fatally compromises the sublime. The irony works the other way around: a trace of the sublime remains in the bathetic. But it takes a writer like Pope — not the authors he satirizes — to give such life to "the profound" as it is capable of sustaining.

In the first scene of *The Dunciad,* the Goddess of Dulness "beholds the Chaos dark and deep, / Where nameless Somethings in their causes sleep . . ." (1:55-56). Her half-formed and monstrous creations in this opening scene issue from the deep and begin the apocalyptic process of returning culture and the entire earth back to its "uncreated" state at Genesis 1:2, when "darkness" was upon the "face of the deep."

In the poem's first book, where Colley Cibber is crowned poet laureate, the first view of Cibber is one of deep dejection. His profits from the third day of a stage play are small, and he sits "swearing and supperless" (1:115). Only when he reaches the abyss of despair does he light upon the idea of a sacrificial offering of his own works to propitiate the Goddess of Dulness, who then graciously takes him to her "Dome" of Dulness and prophesies the Laureateship — a prophecy which is immediately fulfilled. Cibber's encounter with the "profound" looks back to *Peri Bathous* and forward to the poem's apocalyptic undoing of creation:

> Then gnaw'd his pen, then dash'd it on the ground,
> Sinking from thought to thought, a vast profound!
> Plung'd for his sense, but found no bottom there,
> Yet wrote and flounder'd on, in mere despair.
> Round him much Embryo, much Abortion lay,
> Much future Ode, and abdicated Play;
> Nonsense precipitate, like running Lead,
> That slip'd thro' Cracks and Zig-zags of the Head;
> All that on Folly Frenzy could beget,
> Fruits of dull Heat, and Sooterkins of Wit.
> Next, o'er his Books his eyes began to roll,
> In pleasing memory of all he stole.
>
> (1:117-28)

The first lines indicate that Cibber is a master of the art of sinking as Scriblerus had explained it. His actual products and character, in the lines that follow, begin to draw out the monstrous possibilities of the imagined author in *Peri Bathous.* His mind is a parody of literary fertility. Rather than drawing his inspiration from a muse, Cibber owes his works to the debased union of frenzy and folly, which are capable only of embryo and abortion. The allusion in line 127 to Satan's despairing eyes in *Paradise Lost* associates his duncery with figures of evil.[32] The end result of Cibber's life and works, under the direction of the Goddess of Dulness, will be the restoration of chaos, of darkness, and of the deep.

The imagery of the deep is continued in the second book of *The Dunciad,* where parodic epic games occur. This book is sometimes disappointing to readers who find in it only a "systematic imitation" of epic, and conclude that the language loses its resonance.[33] While there is

32. The allusion is clearer in the 1728 version: "He roll'd his eyes that witness'd huge dismay" (1:115). The lines in *Paradise Lost* read, ". . . round he throws his baleful eyes / That witness'd huge affliction and dismay . . ." (1:56-57).

33. Brower, *Alexander Pope,* 344.

truth to this observation, the imagery of the deep in book 2 extends the poem's apocalpytic range. Picking up the "Art of diving" from *Peri Bathous,* the diving contest of book 2 exploits the possibilities of duncical encounters with the deep. The first diver is John Oldmixon, probably included for his polemical writings for the Whig party, who "shot to the black abyss" with his dive (2:288; see *TE* 5:450). At the bottom of Fleet Ditch are Matthew Concanen and Sir Richard Blackmore, the first identified as "a native of the deep" and the second as the most persevering of divers (2:299-304). But most significant of all is the unidentified "form" who rises "in majesty of Mud" and declares "the wonders of the deep" (2:326-30). In the 1728 version of the poem, this figure is identified as Jonathan Smedly, an antagonist of Swift and Pope, but in the final version his identity is left mysteriously vague. Pope's note to 2:329 calls attention to the likeness between this figure of "more than mortal" look and the sybil who leads Aeneas to the underworld, an allusion more fully developed in book 3 of the *Dunciad.* The "form" then "sings" of his visions in the bowers of the deep, concluding that all who drink of the fluid either grow intoxicated or are lulled to sleep. So impressed are the clerical poets and critics with these visions that one gives him the "cassock, surcingle, and vest" — the clothing symbolic of their ecclesiastical offices. These clergy are "Prompt or to guard or stab, to saint or damn, / Heav'n's Swiss, who fight for any God, or Man" (2:357-58). While the episode as a whole is not one of the central ones in the poem, it does help to establish the moral geography of Dulness. The duncical priests are mercenary Swiss guards who have abandoned their loyalty to the true God. The dunces generally are natives of the deep, and their inspiration comes from the abyss.

In the Bible, images of the deep are generally associated with mud and slime, darkness, silence, the sea, and the very limits of creation. The "miry depths" of Psalm 69, for instance, are a place of both physical darkness and moral confusion. In the depths, the authentic word from God cannot be heard, any more than authentic culture can be produced in the depths of book 2 of the *Dunciad.* The biblical deep is the habitation of sea monsters, Rahab and the Leviathan. Its power is sometimes associated with the evils of Egyptian captivity, sometimes with the pre-creation chaos that ended with the creating word of God (Isa. 27:1; 51:9-10; Job 9:13; 26:12; 38:16-19; Ps. 33:6-7; 77:16-20).

In biblical apocalyptic, the deep and the sea are the point of origin of evil, blasphemous beasts. The four beasts of Daniel 7 come up from the sea. After the two faithful witnesses of Revelation 11 finish their testimony, "the beast which ascended from the depth, shal make warre against them, and shal overcome them, and kil them" (Rev. 11:7). The beast that comes from the sea, described in Revelation 13:1-8, is usually identified with the Antichrist. He receives his authority from the dragon of Revelation 13:4, and is in turn worshiped by "al the earth." In Revelation 17:8, the angel warns John that the beast he saw "shal come up out of the bottomeles depth, and goe into destruction," inspiring "marvel" among those "whose names are not written in the booke of life." Of this verse, the biblical critic Robert Mounce writes, "Down through history [the beast] repeatedly 'comes up from the abyss,' to harass and, if it were possible, to destroy the people of God."[34]

The group of images that includes the abyss, the sea, chaos, and the deep has broad associations with evil in world mythology. But like apocalyptic, Pope's *Dunciad* associates these images more precisely with the perversion of human culture. From the deep emerges a figure whose goal is to seduce the world to false loyalties and wrong values. If possible, the deep and its inhabitants will try to seduce the faithful as well. Out of the deep, in Revelation, the beast brings an inversion of the whole structure of the true faith. Pope's dunces bring forth from the deep a mode of criticism and poetry that seeks to invert true wit. The deep, in conclusion, is part of Pope's allusive structure to apocalyptic, through the poem's figural undoing of creation and its restoration of "Night Primæval, and of Chaos old."

Darkness is a notable characteristic of the deep, both in apocalyptic and in *The Dunciad.* The descent of darkness in the final lines of the poem inverts the light of messianic birth as Pope had described it in his "Messiah" (1711; see lines 21-22). References to supernatural darkness in the Bible generally allude to the plague of darkness sent upon the Egyptians prior to the exodus of the Israelites (Exod. 10:21-23). In Revelation, for which the exodus provides one of the most important allusive backgrounds, darkness is sent as a plague upon "the seate of the beast: and his kingdom was made darke, and they together

34. Mounce, *The Book of Revelation,* 312.

did eate their tonges for paine: & they blasphemed the God of heaven because of their paines and woundes, & did not penance from their workes" (Rev. 16:10-11).[35] Commenting on the last lines of *The Dunciad,* where universal darkness "buries all," Robert Griffin writes, "[d]arkness is caused by the dunces and darkness is sent to them as a scourge."[36]

In the Catholic Scriptures, the terrors of supernatural darkness are most fully investigated in the seventeenth chapter of the Book of Wisdom.[37] In this chapter, the plague of Egyptian darkness is interpreted morally, typologically, and eschatologically by the Douai editors. The chapter begins thus:

> 1 For thy judgements o Lord are great, & thy wordes inexplicable, for this cause the souls lacking discipline have erred. 2 For whiles the wicked are perswaded that they can rule over the holie nation: fettered with the bands of darknes, and long night, shut up under roofes, they have lyen fugitives from the everlasting providence.

The Douai's marginal note to 17:2 reads the plague morally and typologically, relating darkness to the gentiles' lack of illumination prior to Christ: "Literally the Ægyptians had darknes three dayes together. . . . Morally they & other gentiles were in darknes without faith in God, til Christs Resurrection the third day." During this darkness the Egyptians — and by extension all who stand apart from people of God — are terrified by monsters, and frightened by noise. In short, they expe-

35. In addition, the darkening of the sun is associated with the fourth trumpet blast in Rev. 8:12 and with the beast's ascent from the abyss in Rev. 9:2.

36. Griffin, "Pope, the Prophets, and *The Dunciad,*" 446.

37. In Pope's day, the Book of Wisdom was considered one of the five books of Solomon in the canonical Catholic Scriptures. (Protestants put it in the Apocrypha.) In the "Argument of the Book of Wisdom," the Douai editors note the long tradition of the public reading of this book in church. Among the contents of the Book of Wisdom, according to the "Argument," are "frequent Prophecies of Christ's Coming, Passion, Ressurrection and other Christian Mysteries." This reading of Wisdom is noteworthy, especially in light of Pope's familiarity with the Douai Bible, because it provides an example of how a Catholic could legitimately interpret biblical tropes as prophecies. Of course, Pope may also have been familiar with the editors' marginal comments at Wisdom 17, to which I refer below.

rience many of the same things that Pope's dunces do (cf. *Dunciad* 3:231-72; 2:235-46). More tellingly, darkness is imagined as a kind of invisible prison or chain, similar to some of the dominant imagery of *The Dunciad:* The Egyptians are "fettered with the bands of darknes" in 17:3, and verses 15 and 17 read: "Moreover if any of them had fallen downe, he was kept shut up in prison without yron. . . . For with one chayne of darkenes they were al tyed together." In *The Dunciad,* Dulness and her agents enchain both true wit and their own duncical blood relations. "Rebel Wit" is bound in double chains by Busby's educational schemes, and Bentley's philological "Cement, ever sure to bind / [Will] bring to one dead level ev'ry mind" (4:158, 267-68).

Most significant, however, is Pope's imagery of chains for explaining intellectual darkness. At the beginning of book 4, the poet prays to Chaos and Night for "darkness visible" to reveal the intended reign of Dulness (4:1-4). His prayer is heard, and Dulness, "the Seed of Chaos, and of Night" (4:13), is revealed on her dark throne:

> Beneath her foot-stool, Science groans in Chains,
> And Wit dreads Exile, Penalties and Pains.
> There foam'd rebellious Logic, gagg'd and bound,
> There, stript, fair Rhet'ric languish'd on the ground . . .
> But held in ten-fold bonds the Muses lie,
> Watch'd both by Envy's and by Flatt'ry's eye. (4:21-25, 35-36)

As John Sitter has written, the chaining of the arts and sciences is a "profound inversion of the usual role of fetters" in seventeenth-century iconography, where the passions are typically enchained beneath the footstool of Reason.[38] In the book of Wisdom, as in *The Dunciad,* the chain of darkness is a comment on the folly of the benighted: it is a "contumelious rebuke of the glorie of their wisdom" (Wisdom 17:7). In both works, the chains of darkness are the outward sign of inner folly and moral blindness.

The Dunciad's chains of darkness have an apocalyptic resonance as well, from Revelation 20:1-3. In this passage, the beast is chained and cast into the dark, "bottomles depth." The difference in all of these

38. Sitter, *The Poetry of Pope's "Dunciad,"* 43-44; see also Pat Rogers, *Grub Street: Studies in a Subculture* (London: Methuen, 1972), 291-307.

allusions, however, is that the biblical victims of darkness deserve their fate, while the victims in *The Dunciad* are Wit and Science. The allusions simultaneously distance and approximate their biblical source. *The Dunciad* is both apocalyptic and anti-apocalpytic.

The dark conclusions of Wisdom 17 and *The Dunciad* are also parallel, particularly if one reads the final lines of the poem as the dunces' self-inflicted judgment. Despite their dark defeat "inside" the poem, the Wits who can read the poem ironically continue to live in the light. In contrast to the darkness upon Egypt, Wisdom 17 concludes,

> 19 For al the world was illuminated with a cleare light, & none was hindered in their workes. 20 But over them onlie was layd an heavie night, the image of darkenes, which was to come upon them. They therefore were unto themselves more heavie then the darkness.

The Douai Bible interprets the first verse eschatologically: "This signified the conversion of al nations to Christ." More interesting, though, is the language of the final verse. Darkness is laid over and comes upon its victims (Vulgate: *superventura* and *superposit*). The language here is quite close to the final words of *The Dunciad*, especially in the 1728 version, where "universal Darkness covers all" (3:356).

My conclusion about the imagery of darkness is more tentative than other apocalyptic images in *The Dunciad.* While the abyss and profound (like the sable throne, the ten-horned fiends, etc.) seem specifically related to apocalyptic, none of the references to darkness seem to allude unambiguously to Wisdom 17 or Revelation. On the other hand, we know that Wisdom and Revelation were part of the Catholic Church's public readings, and one of Pope's rare biblical quotations in his *Correspondence* comes from Wisdom.[39] While the provenance of Pope's imagery is less clear than his use of other apocalyptic figures, however, its function is similar: the imagery of darkness contributes to the moral seriousness of the poem through its biblical echoes. Ending with the triumph of darkness is another

39. Pope, *Correspondence,* 1:148. In a marginal note at the very beginning of Revelation, the Rheims New Testament says that the Apocalypse is read at matins, between the third and fourth Sundays after Easter.

way the poem pursues its task of inverting apocalyptic. *The Dunciad* is not "straight" apocalyptic; it is satire that uses apocalyptic methods figurally, among its other ironic resources. By using such resources, *The Dunciad* signals that its comic irony has an extremely serious purpose.

The Antichrist of Wit, the Great Mother, and the Whore of Babylon

After the proclamation of Cibber as King of the Dunces at the end of book 1, the second book of the *Dunciad* begins with a view of Cibber on his throne, parodying a similar view of Satan in *Paradise Lost:*

> High on a gorgeous seat, that far out-shone
> Henley's gilt tub, or Fleckno's Irish throne,
> Or that where on her Curls the Public pours,
> All-bounteous, fragrant Grains and Golden show'rs,
> Great Cibber sate: (2:1-5)

Pope called attention to this "Parody of Milton" in his notes to the poem, even supplying the relevant lines from *Paradise Lost:* "High on a throne of royal state, that far / Outshone the wealth of Ormus and of Ind, / [. . .] Satan exalted sate."[40] As the poem continues, however, the allusion to Cibber-as-Satan is transformed by a comparison between Cibber and a bad Italian poet much favored by Pope Leo X, Camillo Querno, who is named "the Antichrist of Wit":

> Not with more glee, by hands Pontific crown'd,
> With scarlet hats wide-waving circled round,
> Rome in her Capitol saw Querno sit,
> Thron'd on seven hills, the Antichrist of wit. (2:13-16)

These lines compared Querno to Lewis Theobald in the 1728 version of the poem. After the death of the poet laureate, Laurence Eusden (27 September 1730), Pope wrote a satirical essay suggesting that several

40. Milton, *Paradise Lost,* 2:1-5.

candidates, including Cibber, might hope to equal the glories of Querno's poetic reign under Leo. Pope's essay was published on November 19, and Colley Cibber was named laureate on December 3. When the entire poem was revised in 1743, Pope only needed to change the name in this passage. Indeed, it applied more appropriately to Cibber than to Theobald, since he was poet laureate and (like Querno) far more enmeshed in contemporary politics than Theobald. In his satirical essay, Pope calls Querno "the original and father of all Laureates" (*TE* 5:413). The idea of such a dunce occupying Rome itself brought together possibilities rich in irony. In Revelation 17 the whore of Babylon, clothed in purple and scarlet, sits upon the "seven hills" of Rome, where many Renaissance commentators thought the Antichrist would have his scat.[41] The cultural deception wrought by Querno/Cibber, together with the rich significance of "Rome," made the figure of the Antichrist perfect for *The Dunciad.* Identified with the beast from the sea by most commentators, the figure of the Antichrist in St. John's Apocalypse is usually identified with the Roman empire, especially in its character of demanding the worship of its secular authority. This authority, in turn, is represented by a human being, the emperor, who is given his authority by Satan or the dragon (Rev. 13:4; cf. Rev. 12:9). The dragon is a parody of God the Father in the book of Revelation, and the Antichrist is a parody of the Son.

As the emperor is also a "god" in Revelation, so the empress of Dulness is also a goddess in *The Dunciad.* Similarly, as the Goddess of Dulness is a parody of the Father, so Cibber is a parody of the Son. In each of her children, the Goddess "marks her Image full exprest, / But chief in BAY's [Cibber's] monster-breeding breast" (1:107-8). These lines allude to Milton's treatment of the Son, and through Milton, to St. Paul's teaching that Christ is the "image of the invisible God" in whom "dwelleth all the fullness of the Godhead."[42] As in Revelation,

41. The notes of the Rheims New Testament to Revelation 17 are concerned to refute the equation, common in sixteenth-century Protestantism (though originating earlier), of the papacy with the Antichrist, and the Catholic Church with the Whore of Babylon. They therefore stress the spiritual (rather than geographical) nature of "Rome" in this chapter. Nevertheless, its note to 17:1 acknowledges the possibility that the Antichrist will "have his seate" in Rome.

42. Col. 1:15; 2:9, AV; see Williams, *Pope's "Dunciad,"* 147n.1.

the "Antichrist" of *The Dunciad* is but the chief expression of many faithless offspring of the false god or goddess. All who follow Cibber become "sons" of the Goddess of Dulness, just as those who accept the claims of the beast in Revelation become part of the "Whore of Babylon" (Rev. 13:8; 17:1-18). The parody of true wit in *The Dunciad* greatly increases its pressure by evoking so rigorously the parody of true faith in Revelation.

Pope emphasizes Cibber's role as the son of the Goddess in every book of the poem except the third, where the highly structured, parodic trip to the underworld (alluding to *Aeneid* 6) requires Elkanah Settle to fill the paternal role of Anchises to Cibber's Aeneas. And even in the third book, Cibber is linked to the Messiah by metonymy as "th'Anointed head" (3:2). As the poem developed between 1728 and 1742, some of Pope's major additions include various extensions of the parodic image of the godhead and its adoptive "Son" (or Sons). After Dulness mounts her throne, we read, "Soft on her lap her Laureat Son reclines" (4:20). Later in book 4, the university graduate who is about to begin his grand tour is introduced to the Goddess thus: "Receive, great Empress! thy accomplish'd Son." In 4:500, Thomas Gordon ("Silenus") makes various boasts to the Goddess about "every finish'd Son" of hers. Cibber is nevertheless the chief of all her sons. As she prepares to bestow her final blessing upon her children (4:579), she sends "to ev'ry child" an aspect of his image (for the purpose of extinguishing shame): "Cibberian forehead, or Cimmerian gloom" (4:532). Cibber is the model son, and like the followers of the beast, his mark is expressed on the forehead.

In his influential chapter entitled "The Anti-Christ of Wit," Aubrey Williams notes the "designed absurdity in comparing Colley Cibber . . . with a far more awesome anti-Christ." Despite the absurdity, he writes, "there filters through the comic glaze the suggestion that even the shallowest urn may hold a formidable amount of unholy power."[43] Williams then proceeds to illustrate the impressive web of allusion that Pope reweaves from Milton, particularly in his evocation of the fallen angels and chaos.

The admitted "absurdity" of the comparison of Cibber to the

43. Williams, *Pope's "Dunciad,"* 132-33.

Antichrist is the basis for some recent critics to diminish the influence of "the School of Deep Intent" that has accepted Williams's reading: "To take anything seriously," writes Donald Siebert,

> is to invest it with power, and power gives a thing the quality of implicit respectability. . . . I do not think Pope ever intended to give Dulness that advantage, the advantage of any real power, which of course is a quality the School of Deep Intent is obsessed with.[44]

Siebert then goes on to discuss the ultimately ludicrous character of evil in *Paradise Lost.*

Such criticisms miss the mark. Evil is not less evil in *Paradise Lost* for being ludicrous. Pope knew that Milton's Satan and his fallen angels had constructed a "Paradise of Fools."[45] Of the other three poets, besides Milton, who "mark out the general course of our poetry," according to Pope, he could have learned the idiocy of evil from Spenser, the stupidity of evil from Chaucer, and the folly of evil from Dryden.[46] As early as the twelfth century, writes Jeffrey Burton Russell, Satan, "the mighty enemy of God," began to be a figure for parody, satire, and even broad humor on the medieval stage.[47] The audience was not invited to empathize with the demons, but to laugh *at* them. They were portrayed with contempt and disgust. On the lowest level, slapstick, the devils ran about the stage, screaming, leaping, farting, and making obscene gestures. On a higher level, that of satire, the devils' blessings became curses, their songs cacophony, and hell was seen as "the place where all values are inverted."[48] *The Dunciad,* like medieval drama and much of the treatment of evil in Chaucer, Spenser, Milton, and Dryden, sees evil as the demonic inversion of God's blessings. At the same time that this perversion is taken seriously, however, the Christian tradition since Augustine has also believed that the demons are ultimately

44. Siebert, "Cibber and Satan," 209.

45. Milton, *Paradise Lost,* 3:418-97.

46. See Joseph Spence, *Observations, Anecdotes, and Characters of Books and Men,* ed. James M. Osborn (Oxford: Clarendon, 1966), §410.

47. Jeffrey Burton Russell, *Lucifer: The Devil in the Middle Ages* (Ithaca: Cornell University Press, 1984), 259.

48. Russell, *Lucifer,* 260.

dunces.[49] The note to 3:333, which the 1729 Variorum *Dunciad* had applied to the last twenty-two lines of the entire poem, nicely balances the folly and seriousness of evil:

> It may perhaps seem incredible, that so great a Revolution in Learning as is here prophesied, should be brought about by such weak Instruments as have been [hitherto] described in our poem: But do not thou, gentle reader, rest too secure in thy contempt of these Instruments. Remember what the Dutch stories somewhere relate, that a great part of their Provinces was once overflow'd, by a small opening made in one of their dykes by a single Water-Rat.

Pope is using the apocalyptic image of the Antichrist figurally and ironically. *The Dunciad* is not a straight apocalyptic, where humanity is strictly divided between the righteous who follow the Lamb of God and the unrighteous who follow the Antichrist. As in all allusions, the pleasure of this image comes from both the distance and the proximity of the figure to its earlier source. The dunces represent a *cultural* threat, not a cosmic one. The influence of Cibber and the dunces will pass and Pope knows it. He is confident that the writers of true wit will be known to posterity, while the dunces' identity will be lost. In his note to 2:116 (in the 1729 Variorum), Pope writes of Congreve, Addison, and Prior: "These Authors being such whose names will reach posterity, we shall not give any account of them, but proceed to those of whom it is necessary." We know in hindsight that Pope was right. But these names reached posterity while the others were forgotten, in part, *because* Pope and the wits opposed them.

The first person of the godhead in *The Dunciad* has apocalyptic connections as well, although her "essence" seems more philosophical than apocalyptic. The Goddess of Dulness is modeled, as Aubrey Williams says, "on the Christian Supreme Being" rather than upon an anthropomorphic false deity.

> [Pope] has made her an imitation of pure being, a condition the human imagination comprehends vaguely at best. And as the human

49. Jeffrey Burton Russell, *Satan: The Early Christian Tradition* (Ithaca: Cornell University Press, 1981), 213.

> effort to realize the nature of pure being usually settles on qualities of mind, so does it, ironically, in the case of Dulness. It is her divine "mind," a pure unthinking substance, rather than any physical shape, which oozes in grey immanence throughout the poem's world. This accounts for the vagueness of her being. . . . She rules "in native Anarchy, the mind," she is called the "mindful Queen," a "Divinity without a Νοῦς," a "God without a Thought."[50]

Whatever her philosophical status, however, the character and actions of Dulness are quite anthropomorphic and reminiscent of the Whore of Babylon: she is an old harlot; and as the "principal Agent of [the] Poem," in Warburton's phrase she accomplishes "the Restoration of the Empire of Dulness" as surely as "Babylon" will extend her "kingdom over the kinges of the earth" (Rev. 17:18).

In Revelation 17, the Whore of Bablyon, clothed in purple and scarlet, symbolizes primarily the spiritual prostitution within the church, picking up the rich Hebrew imagery of the infidelities of Jahweh's once-faithful Jerusalem. Pope uses the image of the harlot to satirize contemporary figures at the end of the *Epilogue to the Satires, Dialogue I* (1738). There, the personification of Vice is degraded to a Whore. A figure with a "scarlet head," she institutes her own gospel and laws, and draws the entire world in "golden chains" (see lines 141-70).

In *The Dunciad,* the Goddess approves of the "Harlot form" of opera and scorns the "prostrate Muses," (4:45, 45n, 51). She recommends the practice of selling the works of dunces under the names of wits, as an old madam sells "each batter'd jade" under the name of the current toasts of the town (2:132-40). One might accurately name this practice "literary harlotry." Although the Goddess once had "pertness" enough, she is now "grave" and "laborious," and her possible sexual allure is suggested only at the beginning of books 3 and 4:

> But in her Temple's last recess inclos'd,
> On dulness' lap th'Anointed head reposed. (3:1-2)

In the "Argument" to this book, Pope writes that this is a "position of marvelous virtue," which causes "all the Visions of wild enthusiasts,

50. Williams, *Pope's "Dunciad,"* 144-45.

projectors, . . . and poets" (*TE* 5:319). In book 4, Cibber reclines "Soft on her lap" as she sits on the throne (4:20). The fact that he is actually asleep on her lap rather than engaging in any sexual practices only heightens the irony.

Unnatural procreation characterizes Dulness and her empire beginning with her birth, which is said to have occurred before "Pallas issu'd from the Thund'rer's head" (1:10).[51] The poem promises a vision of her "hatch[ing] a new Saturnian age of Lead" (1:28). Where the God of the Bible creates by his word, her "wild creation" is sexual in nature. The products of this debased fertility are "spawn," "maggots half-form'd in rhyme," and "momentary monsters" (1:55-84).

Cibber's literary products are similarly grotesque: "All that on Folly Frenzy could beget, / Fruits of dull Heat, and Sooterkins of Wit" (1:125-26). A sooterkin was a small animal, the size of a mouse, conceived parthenogenically by Dutch women by placing a stove under their petticoats (1:126n). As Pope was at work on *The Dunciad,* England had just finished buzzing with the report (November 1726) that a woman in Surrey, Mary Toft, had given birth to a litter of rabbits. One of the pamphlets circulating that year about Mrs. Toft was entitled "The Sooterkin Dissected," and the eccentric William Whiston later lectured on how her progeny were a direct fulfillment of a verse in the apocalyptic book of 4 Esdras: "menstrous women shall bring forth monsters" (5:8, RSV).[52] One of the physicians who examined her and wrote a pamphlet on the subject, James Douglas, F.R.S., was later included in *The Dunciad,* perhaps because of his role in this ridiculous affair (see *TE* 5:438). The poem suggests a resemblance between the works of contemporary dunces and the bizarre births that they credited. As Pope wrote of *The Dunciad,* "the Poem was not made for these Authors, but these Authors for the Poem" (*TE* 5:205).

In addition to her association with harlotry and monstrous births, the Goddess of Dulness is closely linked with the apocalyptic Whore

51. See Sitter, *The Poetry of Pope's "Dunciad,"* 11-16, for a thorough treatment of the "prodigious promiscuity" of the poem.

52. Pope was aware of the "rabbit woman," but his remarks on the subject are light-hearted. See *Correspondence,* 2:418, Spence, *Observations, Anecdotes,* §341, and Pope, *TE,* 6:259-64.

of Babylon by one of her names: the "mighty mother" or the "great mother." Where the earlier version of *The Dunciad* begins "Books and the man I sing," the later version begins, "The Mighty Mother, and her Son. . . ." Warburton's note to this line (added in 1751) cautions the reader "that the Mother, and not the Son, is the principal Agent of this Poem" (1:1n). The note to the earlier *Dunciad* (1729, 1:33) identifies Juno as the great mother and directs the curious reader to the opening of the *Aeneid.* But the Latin phrase given by Pope, *magna mater,* does not occur there. The *magna mater* is more appropriately identified as the Berecynthian mother of the *Aeneid* 6:784, or Cybele (cf. *Dunciad* 3:131-32). Pope and Warburton call attention again to her identity as the great mother in their note to 4:606, where she signifies the completion of the action of the poem (the restoration of her empire) by emitting a yawn.

Cybele, the "great mother of the gods," was a deity of Asia Minor whose cult was brought to Rome in the third century B.C. Her cult was attended by self-castrated eunuchs. One would expect Pope to pick up on this latter detail, especially if, as the deconstructive reading of Douglas Atkins maintains, Dulness is "[a] (castrated and castrating) *woman,* opposing the male *Logos* and menacing the regnant logo- and phallogocentrism. . . ."[53] But Atkins's views come from the ideological requirements of deconstruction combined with feminism, not from *The Dunciad,* whose only *castrati* are the keepers of Venetian brothels on the Grand Tour (4:310).

Pope's "great mother" is associated with grotesque procreation, not with sterility or castration. St. John was very aware of the fertility cult of Cybele, whose worship was linked to that of the goddess Roma. The churches in the province of Asia (to which Revelation is addressed) were relatively close to her Phrygian home.[54] Three of those Asian cities are known to have had temples to the goddess Roma.[55] Earlier in Revelation, the glorious woman who gives birth to a son appears to be a Christian rewriting of various myths of the generation of the gods

53. Atkins, *Quests of Difference,* 155, emphasis and parentheses in original.

54. J. P. M. Sweet, *Revelation* (Philadelphia: Westminster, 1979), 194.

55. G. B. Caird, *The Revelation of St. John the Divine* (New York: Harper & Row, 1966), 211-12.

from a single mother, with Mother Zion bringing forth the true Messiah (Rev. 12:1-6).[56] But the demonic parody of the glorious woman, the Whore of Babylon in Revelation 17:5, alludes to the pagan cult. The Vulgate provides the exact phrase "magna mater":

> et in fronte eius nomen scriptum mysterium
> Babylon magna mater fornicationum et abominationum terrae
>
> (And in her forehead a name written, *"Mysterie:"*
> Babylon the great, mother of the fornications and the
> abominations of the earth.)

G. B. Caird writes that John's purpose is to expose the "magna mater" as the great whore. He draws on "the strong repugnance expressed in the Old Testament against fornication, literal or metaphorical," both from prophets and from Proverbs, where folly keeps a "bawdy-house."[57] Like the biblical "magna mater," Pope's is a mother of abominations and ultimately a mother of folly. Neither figure is sterile, as Atkins's deconstructive reading suggests; neither turns the landscape into a wasteland. The one in Revelation attempts to seduce the church into apostasy; the one in *The Dunciad* populates culture with pedants and virtuosos — all of them ineducable, all of them degree-holders. Both figures bring forth a bizarre progeny.

In addition, both women are associated with "mysteries" that contrast with the true revelations of their respective texts. The Rheims New Testament identifies the whore's "mysterie" with the "secrete and close working of abominations, the mysterie of iniquitie" of 2 Thessalonians 2:7. Warburton's note to 4:517 offers a long description of how the great Mother initiates her aspirants into "the participation of the Mysteries" through the proffering of a cup of Nepenthe.[58]

56. G. R. Beasley-Murray, *The Book of Revelation* (London: Oliphants, 1974), 191-97.

57. Caird, *The Revelation of St. John the Divine,* 212; Prov. 9.

58. I do not believe this cup alludes to the "cup of abominations" in Revelation 17:4. The cup is offered by a wizard, not the Goddess. In addition, Pope indicates both by the text (of 4:517-19) and by the note to 4:518 that its significance, like that of the cup of Nepenthe (*Odyssey* 4:220-21), is to induce forgetfulness. For a different view, see Griffin, "Pope, the Prophets, and *The Dunciad,*" 444.

Shortly after the cup is drained, the Goddess's "sable Throne" appears, signifying her complete victory over true wit (4:629). This scene alludes to the white throne of Revelation 20:11, whose appearance signifies Christ's complete victory over Babylon, Satan, and death itself. In *The Dunciad,* the arts and sciences, which are our cultural means of revealing the mysteries of the heavens and earth, then expire or flee (4:631-52). In Revelation, the earth and heavens flee from the white throne before the revelation of the new heaven and new Jerusalem.[59] True religion and true wit have their mysteries, which, like every other aspect of the truth, are parodied by the "mysteries" of apostasy and duncery.

* * * * *

The great mother, like the Antichrist of wit and the imagery of darkness and the deep, contributes to an allusive structure linking *The Dunciad* and biblical apocalypse. But the allusions are highly ironic, establishing the poem's distance from as well as proximity to the biblical text, just as its even more evident allusions to the *Aeneid* show the poem less as an epic or even mock-epic than an "anti-epic." It differs from *The Rape of the Lock* in that, within its own system of language, it defeats the very genres to which it alludes.

To read Pope without irony, as proposing the division of mankind along cultural lines, would make *The Dunciad* ridiculous and even blasphemous. It would suggest that the reader's chief purpose should be victory in the culture war. It would make the poem fall into the second temptation of Christ, especially as rendered in *Paradise Regained,* where the devil offers Christ cultural authority if only he will abandon the one true God.[60] This temptation, "rejected by Jesus at the outset

59. *The Dunciad* 4:647 reads "See Mystery to Mathematics fly," which Warburton's note (added in 1743) explains as a satire on the "sort of men . . . [who have] attempted to shew that the mysteries of Religion may be mathematically demonstrated; as the authors of Philosophic or Astronomic Principles, natural and reveal'd." Warburton and Pope may have had in mind the rationalist philosopher-theologians mentioned by the Twickenham editor, but they were particularly thinking of a work by the Cambridge mathematician and clergyman William Whiston, *The Astronomical Principles of Religion, Natural and Reveal'd* (1725).

60. John Milton, *Paradise Regained,* 4:25-393; cf. Luke 4:1-13.

of his public ministry," writes Robert Mounce, "reappears at the end of history in its most persuasive form" through the Antichrist's seduction of all whose names are not written in the book of life.[61] Human culture becomes a figure for the entire cosmos in *The Dunciad*, where apocalyptic wars and judgment are followed by the cosmic rule of Dulness. But one must remember that the image of culture-as-cosmos is a figure for the cosmos of the *dunces*. The dunces are the ones who "Make God Man's Image, Man the final Cause . . ." (4:478). Theirs is the kingdom where culture is all in all. Pope's irony suggests a distinction between culture and the divine maker of the cosmos, whose blessings include those of culture. To obscure this distinction is to invite the demonic inversion of culture that one finds in the apocalypse of Revelation and in the parodic apocalypse of *The Dunciad*. Yet many of the parodic gestures of *The Dunciad* are performed without irony by the most recent "modern" challenge to the "ancients": deconstruction. These readers assume that the correct cultural critique will reveal the true meaning of "the Logos." Culture will then enter a new epoch, and will finally be free of the Logos.

There are two quite different, mistaken ways of reading the dunces in Pope's poem. In one, the divisions between dunce and wit are thought to be so obvious that there is no serious contest between them. In the other, which is the deconstructive approach of G. Douglas Atkins, Pope himself feels the resistless sway of Dulness to such a degree that *The Dunciad* unconsciously defeats its own design and deconstructs the very values it seems to promote.[62]

The first mistake may be avoided by remembering that apocalyptic makes things obvious to its readers that are not obvious in any other way. The writer of Revelation did not expect his readers to have his degree of perception any more than Pope did. Pope is aware of the thin line that divides wit and duncery. When Dulness creates a poet in book 2, the text reads:

> Never was dash'd out, at one lucky hit,
> A fool, so just a copy of a wit;

61. Mounce, *The Book of Revelation*, 255; see Rev. 13:4-8.
62. Atkins, *Quests of Difference*, 161-62.

So like, that critics said, and courtiers swore,
A Wit it was, and call'd the phantom More. (2:47-50)

Foolishness can copy wit — although it doesn't really produce wit in the end. In the wonderfully ironic world of *The Dunciad,* though, one sees that only a true wit can copy foolishness. Apocalyptic writing clarifies the distinctions between good and evil, and wisdom and folly, but one source of its appeal is that the distinctions are not initially clear to its readers. The seven churches of Revelation 1–3 and the readers of *The Dunciad* are both audiences that need clarity. Appearances, Pope knows, are deceiving: "Ah think not, Mistress! more true Dulness lies / In Folly's Cap, than Wisdom's grave disguise" (4:239-40). He knows too that no rules may be codified to separate mechanically the exhibitions of duncery from those of true wit. For instance, *Peri Bathous* satirizes the same trope — turning water into flame — that Pope uses in the *Dunciad's* pissing contest: "Thro' half the heav'ns he pours th'exalted urn; / His rapid waters in their passage burn" (2:183-84; see *PB,* chap. 7). He knows that all of his dearest concepts can be deconstructed: nature can be inverted by a dunce to prove that the bathetic is more natural than the sublime. The sabbath can become a figure for stupidity and nescience — where "Christians, Jews, one heavy sabbath keep, / And all the western world believe and sleep" (3:99-100) — rather than the aesthetically demanding exercise of praise that Milton envisioned.[63] In every true work of prophecy or apocalyptic, there is a real possibility of kinship with evil.

The alternative, deconstructive approach is really just a variation of the first sort of misreading. It begins by assuming that "characteristic of Pope, in fact is a quest of clear, distinct lines and absolute differences." He is "caught in the trap of binary oppositions."[64] But this approach can never really confront the complexities of Pope's actual poetry (however well it conforms to deconstructive theory). It must see the inversions cited above as evidence that "like other texts, Pope's deconstruct themselves."[65] It cannot consider the possibility that, by embracing

63. Milton, *Paradise Lost,* 7:591ff.
64. Atkins, *Quests of Difference,* 13, 164.
65. Atkins, *Quests of Difference,* 12.

these oppositions in an ironic mode, Pope's poem makes the reader continually ask the most important questions about where to find wisdom and true art.[66]

In common with other ideological criticism, deconstruction discovers that Pope is implicated in certain mistakes (here "binary oppositions") that function rather like original sin for the ideology in question. The next steps are common to other ideological criticism as well: the text becomes a confirmation of deconstruction; the text then loses its capacity to raise questions about human nature and society outside of the categories of deconstruction itself. Perhaps most tellingly, the text no longer retains the capacity to make the deconstructive critic *self*-critical: the text can no longer raise questions about oneself and one's system. In what sense, then, is the deconstructive critic capable of truly learning anything new from a literary text?

The Goddess of Dulness Reads Derrida

C. S. Lewis somewhere remarks that literary criticism rarely prepared him to read literature. The process rather worked the other way around: imaginative literature prepared him to read criticism. *The Dunciad* has

66. Interestingly, Warburton's kinship with the very rationalists who are targeted in the note to 4:647 ("See Mystery to Mathematics fly!") is apparent in a later sermon. Warburton's 1743 note condemns writers like William Whiston (who attempted to infer the truth of the biblical account of the deluge by deducing the previous orbits of the comet of 1680/1). Yet Warburton later writes that the worldwide distribution of fossils provides "an incontestable proof of the truth of the Mosaic relation" of the flood (Sermon 13 in Warburton, *Works,* 9:259). Warburton's conclusion in his sermon is that "there are some Sciences little conversant in that kind of proof by which the truths of Religion are supported," among which he specifically includes Mathematics. On the other hand, the study of natural philosophy, "profane history," and the customs of ancient times have contributed new supports for the truth of Christianity (9:264, 259). This distinction seems strained to me. But the sermon is particularly useful because it attempts to rebut the charge that "the revival of learning" since the Renaissance has hurt Christianity. *The Dunciad,* in turn, may be read in part as a rebuttal of the Enlightenment attack upon ancient learning, as I shall argue later. Pope's poem succeeds where Warburton's sermon fails, I think, because its irony acknowledges a "kinship" with its opponents.

a similar relationship to deconstruction: its inversion of human values and welcoming of a new age offer a powerfully ironic comment on a literary theory that claims to overthrow an entire logocentric "epoch" and initiate a new one. Like deconstruction in the enthusiastic description of Christopher Norris, Dulness is "the active antithesis of everything that criticism ought to be if one accepts its traditional values and concepts."[67] But Pope's Goddess goes even deeper, ironically questioning whether "active" antitheses should be privileged over "passive" ones.

Jacques Derrida's *Of Grammatology* begins with a critique of "logocentrism: the metaphysics of phonetic writing."[68] Logocentrism is "the illusion that the meaning of a word has its *origin* in the structure of reality itself and hence makes the *truth* about that structure seem directly *present* to the mind."[69] Deconstruction begins with the insight of Ferdinand de Saussure that linguistic meaning rather arises from the specific ways a word contrasts with other possible words. Consider the speech of the philologist Aristarchus:

> 'Tis true, on Words is still our whole debate,
> Disputes of *Me* or *Te*, of *aut* or *at*,
> To sound or sink in *cano* O or A,
> Or give up Cicero to C or K.[70]

On the lowest level, "sound" means something different from "sink" from the contrast in their spelling. But on a more significant level, we understand the meaning of "sound" from its contrast to related words that are part of a general category of noises (singing, warbling, etc.); and we understand "sink" from its contrast to related actions like plunging, diving, groping, and so on. The source of meaning for each

67. Christopher Norris, *Deconstruction: Theory and Practice* (London: Methuen, 1982), xii.

68. Jacques Derrida, *Of Grammatology*, trans. Gayatri Chakravorty Spivak (Baltimore: Johns Hopkins University Press, 1976), 3.

69. John Ellis, *Against Deconstruction* (Princeton: Princeton University Press, 1989), 36-37. Some of the following discussion is indebted to pp. 37-48.

70. Pope, *The Dunciad*, 4:219-22. These lines satirize the disproportionately ponderous disputes among classicists over a word (*me* or *te*?) in a Horatian ode; the proper metrical quality of *cano* (does the *o* or *a* receive the stress?); and the proper pronunciation of the orator's name (Cicero or Kikero?).

of these two categories of actions is the system of differences that comprises them, a system that has no existence outside of language. "Saussure's point," writes John Ellis,

> was that languages are a repository of very specific decisions to divide up the endless continuum of experience into arbitrarily defined and demarcated, i.e., differentiated, units and to make a finite system out of what was infinite.[71]

But deconstruction here goes beyond Saussure, exploiting the two meanings of the French verb *différer,* to differ and to defer. Meaning doesn't simply come from the differences between concepts, according to Derrida; it is endlessly deferred. In *Positions* Derrida says the silent "a" of *différance* (a combination of the French for "deferral" and "difference") produces "conceptual effects and verbal or nominal concretions" that are simultaneously imprinted and fractured by the "strange 'logic'" of "a."[72] The meaning of concepts is never *established* by a system of contrasts, according to deconstruction. It is deferred. The relationship between the concepts, moreover, is not one of contrast, in Derrida's typical formulations, but one of limitless play, so that meaning becomes radically indeterminate, never fully "present." There is no place outside the text where its meaning comes to rest, as Derrida states.[73] The "deconstruction of presence" is Derrida's announced "final intention" in *Of Grammatology,* and he anticipates the limitlessness of play to follow from its accomplishment.[74] Both Derrida's antagonists and defenders agree that linguistic meaning derives from contrasts, and that literary language is full of "play," although not necessarily in the way he describes it.

In the general system of *The Dunciad's* language, for instance, Pope yokes two categories — sounding and sinking in the example I've given — that are different from each other in ordinary usage. In *The*

71. Ellis, *Against Deconstruction,* 54.

72. Jacques Derrida, *Positions,* trans. Allen Bass (Chicago: University of Chicago Press, 1982), 40. See also Jacques Derrida, *Margins of Philosophy,* trans. Allen Bass (Chicago: University of Chicago Press, 1982), 3-27.

73. Derrida, *Of Grammatology,* 158.

74. Derrida, *Of Grammatology,* 70.

Dunciad, however, the particular shade of meanings of the first category (the singing, sounding, and warbling of duncical poets) derives from their similarities to and contrasts with the second category (the sinking, plunging, and diving of duncical critics), and from their contrasts with the activities of witty poets and critics. My conclusion is that Pope playfully yokes these two divergent activities (sounding/sinking) and thereby produces new insight into the difference between true art and duncery.

Deconstructive readers often write as if they are the first to have thought very much about the odd or playful yokings within literary texts. They do not recognize that Pope (for instance) is very much aware of this yoking, and that he depends upon the reader's recognition of it for the reader to gain any meaning from the poem. Moreover, the deconstructionist would take Pope's ironic yoking a crucial step further: he or she would assert that the poem's meanings are *endlessly* deferred, and therefore indeterminate, because of *limitless* play between the various categories and their respective terms.

Further, this radical indeterminacy of meaning adheres to every opposition within the poem: Muse/Dulness; wit/dunce; good/evil. Pope's acceptance of dualistic oppositions, privileging the first term over the second, allegedly catches him "in the trap of binary oppositions," according to Atkins's deconstructionist reading. In so doing, Atkins continues,

> Pope denies himself what he seeks. Inverting, Pope understands Dulness and the dunces as merely destructive, indeed as (maternal) absence and non-being, and so he opposes to them (paternal) presence and Being. Another procedure, eschewing oppositionalism and inversion, would lead to a sense of relatedness to those from whom Pope wants to difference himself absolutely.[75]

Actually, *The Dunciad* locates "paternal presence" in another dunce, "Father" Elkanah Settle (3:43-338), not in a supposed "Being" that would render Pope secure. In fact, the poem longs for the "maternal absence" of the "prostrate Nine" Muses (4:51). Once again, Atkins's

75. Atkins, *Quests of Difference,* 164-65.

ideological commitments (here, to feminism as well as deconstruction) cause him to misread the poem: he must find that Pope adheres to "binary oppositions" that function as privileged hierarchies and ultimately deconstruct themselves. It makes for consistent deconstructive interpretation, but misrepresents the structures of the poem.

The kinship (as well as difference) between true wit and duncery is not a new point. Atkins's new procedure is to deconstruct the wit/duncery opposition, which (like all of the oppositions overturned by deconstructionists) is supposedly unstable because the inferior, second term (duncery) is actually inscribed within the first term (wit). Next he argues that the entire system of meanings in *The Dunciad* is destabilized by Pope's failure to recognize his connection with the dunces: "like [Dulness], he defeats his own design" by refusing to accept his relationship with the dunces, whom he nevertheless resembles in spite of himself.[76] Within the language system of *The Dunciad* (like every other piece of literature), the deconstructionist argues that one can never arrive at a place where the author's meaning is said to be fully "present." One can never establish a stable difference between wit and duncery.

The assumption that "present" meanings are superior to "absent" ones is among the many supposed hierarchical polarities of Western metaphysics whose "overturning and displacing" is one of Derrida's major goals.[77] For him, the "privileging" of speech over writing in the Western tradition (because a speaker who is "present" may always be called upon to explain his or her "true meaning") becomes the paradigmatic logocentric act, something on the order of original sin. By regarding writing as a mere "supplement" to speech, the Western tradition has overlooked the strange logic of supplementarity. "The supplement is an inessential extra," explains Jonathan Culler, "added to something complete in itself, but the supplement is added in order to complete, to compensate for a lack in what was supposed to be complete in itself."[78] The privileged term, then, is thus seen to be incomplete

76. Atkins, *Quests of Difference*, 157-58, 162, 165.

77. Derrida, *Margins of Philosophy*, 329.

78. Jonathan Culler, *On Deconstruction: Theory and Criticism after Structuralism* (Ithaca: Cornell University Press, 1982), 103.

apart from its "supplement," and their relationship can no longer be seen as existing in a stable hierarchy. Speech/writing, presence/absence, coitus/auto-affection — all of the "supplements" on the right hand destabilize the hierarchy of which they are a part, displacing and endlessly redefining their relationship with the left-hand terms.[79]

In "White Mythology," Derrida writes an obituary for Western metaphysics, calling it "the white mythology which reassembles and reflects the culture of the West: the white man takes his own mythology, Indo-European mythology, his own *logos,* . . . for the universal form of that he must still wish to call Reason."[80] In particular, by subjecting the concept of metaphor to the " 'logic of the *abyme*' " (infinite reflection/abyss/deep), Derrida strives to achieve the " 'figurative ruination' of logic" and the death of philosophy. It is a kind of *Peri Bathous* without the irony. We see Derrida, like Pope's Scriblerus, " 'plunging into the abyss' of a particular metaphor" (especially that of the sun) and concluding that metaphor "always carries death within itself."[81]

Deconstructionists dwell at length on the ruinous possibilities within language, and surmise that previous literature sought protection from these possibilities under the shelter of the "transcendental signified." But this is not so. At the end of chapter 7 of *Peri Bathous* Pope is aware, preternaturally aware, of what the imagination can bring forth from the depths. Of Broome's couplet, "Thus Phœbus thro' the Zodiack takes his way, / And amid Monsters rises into Day," Scriblerus writes,

> What a Peculiarity is here of Invention? The Author's Pencil, like the Wand of Circe, turns all into Monsters at a Stroke. A great Genius takes things in the Lump, without stopping at minute Considerations: In vain might the Ram, the Bull, the Goat, the Lion, the Crab, the Scorpion, the Fishes, all stand in his way, as mere natural Animals: much more might it be pleaded that a pair of Scales, an old Man, and two innocent Children, were no Monsters: There were only the Centaur and the Maid that could be esteem'd out of Nature. But what of that? with a Boldness peculiar to these daring Genius's, what he found not Monsters, he made so.

79. See Derrida, *Of Grammatology,* 152-57, 244-45.
80. Derrida, *Margins of Philosophy,* 213.
81. Derrida, *Margins of Philosophy,* 262n., 271.

Like the deconstructionists, Scriblerus seeks to undo the relationship between concepts such as natural/monstrous which previous authors had used to distinguish sublime from bathetic poetry. By following the strange logic of the "happy and anti-natural way of thinking," a trace of which may be found in all genius and wit, Scriblerus destabilizes the critical tradition and shows that the epics of Sir Richard Blackmore, rather than those of Homer, Virgil, and Milton, embody the true principles of heroic poetry.[82]

The irony of *Peri Bathous* suggests that Pope does not see sublimity/bathos as a binary opposition, where the "presence" in sublimity contrasts absolutely with the "absence" of bathos. Bathos is an inversion of sublimity, not its opposite; in *The Dunciad*, duncery is an inversion of wit, not its opposite. Deconstruction gets it half right: the terms it examines are related, though "hierarchy" is an ideological simplification and distortion of those relationships.[83] And even in those cases where the relationship is a hostile one, such as wit/duncery, where the right-hand term inverts the left-hand term, the situation is the opposite of what deconstruction describes. In actuality, the "trace" of wit "supplements" duncery and gives it such existence as it has; the trace of the sublime provides such power as bathos has; the trace of "original brightness" gives the symbol of evil such energy as he has.[84] Pope was part of the tradition which saw evil as an inversion of good. But the deconstructive idea that good is ultimately meaningless without evil, to take the most intriguing of these pairs, was rejected by that tradition, though not without centuries of conflict and doubt, beginning with Lactantius, through Augustine's debates with the Manicheans, and continuing in Luther's theology.[85]

Regarding the hierarchy that most annoys Derrida, speech/writing, *Of Grammatology* blames the logos (as understood in Christian terms) for its establishment:

82. For an extended discussion, see Sitter, *The Poetry of Pope's "Dunciad,"* 55-65.

83. I tried to show the distortions of a similar hierarchical understanding of Milton's male/female relationships in chapter 3. Other relationships that are important to Pope and are similarly distorted by this procedure include nature/art, nature/culture, author/critic.

84. The last example is drawn from Milton's description of Satan in *Paradise Lost,* 1:592.

85. Russell, *Satan,* 149-218.

> The epoch of the logos thus debases writing considered as mediation of mediation and as a fall into the exteriority of meaning. . . . [Reading and writing] are preceded by a truth, or a meaning already constituted by and within the element of the logos. Even when the thing, the "referent," is not immediately related to the logos of a creator God where it began by being the spoken/thought sense, the signified has at any rate an immediate relationship with the logos in general (finite or infinite), and a mediated one with the signifier, that is to say with the exteriority of writing.[86]

As his critique continues, Derrida attempts to show how the logos is implicated in the supplementary, "right-hand" terms (in the following case, in "auto-affection") that the hierarchies of its epoch attempt to subordinate.

> God's infinite understanding is the other name for the logos as self-presence. The logos can be infinite and self-present, it can be *produced as auto-affection,* only through the *voice. . . .*[87]

In times other than ours, it would strike many observers as bizarre that the "epoch" associated with the theological traditions of Judaism and Christianity would be censured for their debasement of writing. One of their most striking features is their reliance upon the Scriptures, the written word. As I showed in the second chapter, "the canon" is one of the master tropes for certain literary critics who wish to censure the Judeo-Christian tradition or Western literature on precisely *opposite* grounds: for using certain writings to exclude noncanonical texts, preliterate cultures, and alternative "voices."[88] It is noteworthy that Jonathan Culler has criticized the tradition on both grounds: for valuing written texts too much and for valuing writing too little. These criti-

86. Derrida, *Of Grammatology,* 12-15.

87. Derrida, *Of Grammatology,* 98, emphasis in original. Derrida is here referring specifically to "God" as understood in the "epoch" from Descartes to Hegel, and particularly as understood by Rousseau. However, he links Rousseau's understanding with the views of Plato and Aristotle and nowhere suggests that a biblical view of the logos is discontinuous with the one he here criticizes.

88. See, for instance, Jonathan Culler's essay on William Empson, "A Critic against the Christians," *TLS,* 23 November 1984, 1327-28.

cisms are ultimately self-contradictory. Like other problems of ideology, however, self-contradiction does not trouble someone who is committed to an ideological program.

A biblical poetics is virtually the reverse of what one would expect from Derrida's critique of the logos. To be sure, creation is said to begin with a spoken word: "And God said, 'Let there be light,'" but surely no one believes that the Jewish and Christian traditions teach that divine sound waves are responsible for creation. As we have seen in the chapter on Milton, the "logocentric" tradition that Derrida attacks does not teach that Scripture shows us God in himself, but rather that Scripture accommodates its language to fallen human understandings to represent God as he is *toward us.*

Derrida's hierarchies of speech/writing cannot even begin to explain the richness, tensions, and paradoxes of "the word" in the Hebrew and Christian Scriptures. To begin with, the biblical word is not merely something written. In the Apocalypse, John does not write anything at all until he "sees" the word in his visions (Rev. 1:2). In the Gospel of John, the ability to "see" the word aright is a powerful trope. This figure runs from the first true recognition by John the Baptist ("Behold the Lamb of God," John 1:29) through the climactic series of recognitions at the raising of Lazarus (John 11), until Christ's final questions to Peter at the end of the book. In addition to being spoken, read, and seen, language is "tasted" in various ways throughout Scripture, and even touched as the Psalmist clings to it (Ps. 119:31). In short, the oppositions of speech/writing in the Bible, the ur-text of the "logocentric" tradition, are woefully inadequate for understanding that text.

The treatment and use of language in Scripture has far too great a variety to be captured by Derrida's categories. Its origin, in the blessing at creation, is in pleasure rather than in the implicitly hostile oppositions of deconstruction. Nor is the meaning of the first human words, before the fall, "already constituted by and within" the logos, as Derrida would imply: Adam has the autonomy to name the animals as seems reasonable to him, and God waits "to see what he would call them" (Gen 1:19). The only unfallen speech of Adam — the poetic recognition of woman ("this is now bone of my bones . . .") — does not identify "absence" in the female and thus see her as a "supplement" to the male. In fact,

Calvin and Milton give precisely the opposite reading: it suggests a deficiency in the solitary creature, Adam. The language of Derrida may be built on a hierarchical system of presence/absence, but the biblical system of differences, under its original blessing at creation, is not slave to a merely binary mode of opposition. Biblical language reaches toward fullness and complementarity, toward fertility and pleasure. The language of deconstruction, by contrast, for all its alleged "play," strikes many as tedious and dry. To paraphrase C. S. Lewis, set before almost anyone the book of Genesis and the book *Of Grammatology,* and I think I know which will tire him the faster.

Derrida criticizes the "epoch of the logos" as a "mediation of a mediation." It puts writing at two removes by viewing writing as the mediation of speech/thought, which in turn is a mediation of the logos. His solution is to proclaim an end to the rule of theology over writing, and "announce that the science of writing — *grammatology* — shows signs of liberation all over the world, as a result of decisive efforts" — namely, his own work.[89] Some critics of Derrida, like John Ellis, cannot understand why deconstructionists use the rhetoric of liberation to describe their project. Pope would. Pope's dunces are drawn to such language at the end of *The Dunciad,* where, by dint of its deep logic, the new dispensation kills off the old gods and inaugurates a new age:

> We nobly take the high Priori Road,
> And reason downward, till we doubt of God:
> Make Nature still incroach upon his plan;
> And shove him off as far as e'er we can:
> Thrust some Mechanic Cause into his place;
> Or bind in Matter, or diffuse in Space.
> Or, at one bound o'er-leaping all his laws,
> Make God Man's Image, Man the final Cause. . . . (4.471-78)

The deconstructionist largely accepts this. His or her conclusions about Pope and other texts flow *a priori* from deconstructive theory: "like other texts, Pope's deconstruct themselves" as Atkins states. Next, the removal of God is accompanied by the attribution of a new "cause," namely *différance,* which in Atkins's usage functions as theological

89. Derrida, *Of Grammatology,* 4.

"grace." Finally, instead of reading God's laws to learn about ourselves, Atkins reads "language [for what it] has to 'say' about God" in the new deconstructive dispensation.[90]

A biblical poetics takes a different view of the final historical role of the logos. "The word" at the end of history is the apocalyptic word. Apocalyptic is distinguished among biblical modes in the priority it gives writing over speech. Three times in Revelation, Christ declares, "I am the Alpha and Omega, the beginning and the end," possibly alluding to Old Testament acrostics (such as Ps. 119), and certainly suggesting that he "exceeds . . . the whole traditional edifice of Western attitudes to thought and language," to borrow a phrase from Christopher Norris.[91] Only, instead of dismantling language, he will reconstruct a purified language (see Zeph. 3:9). St. John would agree with Derrida's statement that, in a sense, Christ "is the text, and there is nothing outside of the text." But this is not because of "the strange logic of Alpha and Omega," but rather because St. John believes Christ rose from the dead. He will undo the first speech-act of creation, not by uncreating light, or by plunging all into the abyss, but by fulfilling it: he will "be" the light of the new Jerusalem (Rev. 21:23). The abyss will be answered by a "sea of glass," but rather than being the site where metaphor dies, as in Derrida, it will be a place of harmony and song (Rev. 15:3). Instead of the weariness that characterizes the poststructuralist's negotiations with his or her own cultural tradition, the blessing that was given at creation and extended to human culture will be renewed upon a new heaven and new earth (Rev. 21:1-7). Instead of endlessly retracing the inner collapse of a culture in which one no longer finds pleasure or delight, the Apocalypse imagines a new world, symbolized by the rebuilding of cities and temples, and the replanting of trees. The Apocalypse, in short, goes beyond deconstruction and imagines the reconstruction of the blessing upon creation and human culture.

* * * * *

At this point I should note some of the similarities between deconstruction and other ideologies that dominate literary study. I will begin

90. Atkins, *Quests of Difference,* 12, 15.

91. Norris, *Deconstruction,* 29.

with general similarities and then reverse the process to show the more local ways in which Pope's satire anticipates deconstruction.

Rather than producing new knowledge, deconstruction, like ideological criticism in general, is a theory of development — or in this case, a theory of collapse. The deconstructionist knows in advance that the text will undermine itself and, more interestingly, forward the cause of undermining the Western, logocentric tradition, where cultural oppression has its locus. While some Marxists and feminists have criticized deconstruction for its apparent conclusion that no description of reality (including Marxism and feminism) is ultimately superior to any other, many within the deconstructive fold have sought to mitigate that charge — by distinguishing Derrida's version of deconstruction from that of Paul de Man, or by finding a rapprochement between the two.[92] Derrida himself undertakes a long explanation on whether the dialectics of Marxism-Leninism "[escape] from the dominance of metaphysics."[93] And a recent practitioner, Jeffrey Nealon, seems pleased with the varieties of deconstruction that are consistent with feminist, postcolonial, and Marxist ideologies.[94]

Derrida's polemical rhetoric against the Western tradition has much in common with other ideologies, particularly in its assumption that there is an oppressive structure that must be overcome. "[W]e must traverse a phase of *overturning*," he writes. "To do justice to this necessity is to recognize that in classical philosophical opposition we are not dealing with the peaceful coexistence of a *vis-à-vis,* but rather with a violent hierarchy."[95] The "Western tradition" or the "epoch of the logos" functions as the oppressive structure that deconstruction seeks to undermine, particularly its "hierarchy and . . . order of subordination."[96] In addition to presence/absence and speech/writing, these hierarchies include soul/body, writer/critic, divine/human, male/female, and culture/nature, which David Richter calls "the dia-

92. Jeffrey Nealon distinguishes Derrida's deconstruction from that of Paul de Man in "The Discipline of Deconstruction," *PMLA* 107, no. 5 (1992): 1266-79. Michael Ryan finds rapprochement between the two in *Marxism and Deconstruction: A Critical Articulation* (Baltimore: Johns Hopkins University Press, 1982).

93. Derrida, *Positions,* 62-67.

94. Nealon, "The Discipline of Deconstruction," 1268.

95. Derrida, *Positions,* 41.

96. Derrida, *Margins of Philosophy,* 329.

lectical polarities that have formed the basis of Western culture."[97] Richter's astonishing oversimplifications are typical of ideologies which, as Hannah Arendt explains, can account for everything by deducing it as the logical consequence from a single premise.[98]

Like other ideologues, deconstructionists locate their solidarity not upon an idea of common humanity, but rather upon agreement with its "claims to possess either the key to history, or the . . . intimate knowledge of the hidden universal laws which are supposed to rule nature and man."[99] In this case the key is the shared vocabulary of *différance,* "supplement," "play," and so on, and their shared technique of showing how the logocentrism of Western literature makes possible the destabilization of its texts.

Like other ideologues, the deconstructionists resemble the three "masters of suspicion" described by Paul Ricoeur: they "clear the horizon for a more authentic word, for a new reign of Truth, not only by a means of a 'destructive' critique, but by the invention of an art of *interpreting.*"[100] Even more obviously than the other ideologies, the achievement of the correct critique is the condition for deconstructive liberation: the critique itself is the "decisive action" of cultural liberation. There is no need for a customary form of politics or cultural change.

It goes without saying that deconstructionists, like other ideologues, are never wrong. None of my arguments about Pope or apocalyptic will carry weight with them. Deconstructionists typically accuse their critics of incompetence, of overlooking some essential point, of misreading, or of "turning against [Derrida's] texts criticisms one forgets one has found in them first . . ."[101]

97. David H. Richter, *The Critical Tradition* (New York: St. Martin's, 1989), 946.

98. Hannah Arendt, *The Origins of Totalitarianism* (New York: Harcourt, Brace, Jovanovich, 1973), 468.

99. Arendt, *The Origins of Totalitarianism,* 159-61.

100. Paul Ricoeur, *Freud and Philosophy,* trans. Denis Savage (New Haven: Yale University Press, 1970), 33.

101. Derrida, *Positions,* 52; see Ellis, *Against Deconstruction,* 13-15. The one exception to this may be the case of Paul de Man, whose collaboration with the Nazis is now so offensive that the commonsense reactions — disgust and outrage — seem to have prevailed over the prodigious efforts to reinterpret it. This scandal may have

Pope's satire anticipates deconstruction in many ways. In particular, he sees how a war over words may be linked to party spirit and a critique of religion. He consciously adopts the imagery of "centering" to describe the party program of his dunces, which provides an ironic contrast to the impulse towards "decentering" in deconstruction. And he anticipates the exaltation of the critic over the author, which is common in poststructural thought.

Some of Pope's sharpest satire in *The Dunciad* concerns the unquestioning expectation of solidarity among dunces who "war with Words alone." His first gesture is to link the verbal pedantry of the dunces to a kind of ideological conformity that the deconstructionist would do well to consider:

> "Oh (cry'd the Goddess) for some pedant Reign!
> Some gentle JAMES, to bless the land again;
> To stick the Doctor's Chair into the Throne,
> Give law to Words, or war with Words alone,
> Senates and Courts with Greek and Latin rule,
> And turn the Council to a Grammar School!
> For sure, if Dulness sees a grateful Day,
> 'Tis in the shade of Arbitrary Sway.
> O! if my sons may learn one earthly thing,
> Teach but that one, sufficient for a King;
> That which my Priests, and mine alone, maintain,
> Which as it dies, or lives, we fall, or reign:
> May you, may Cam, and Isis preach it long!
> 'The RIGHT DIVINE of Kings to govern wrong.' " (4:175-88)

It is astonishing that in his comment on line 178, the deconstructionist Atkins shies away from the very relationship he wants to force upon Pope — the relationship with the dunces:

> duncery relates to deconstruction as a caricature of it, not a faithful representation (deconstruction is not, for example, in any simple sense a war with words alone). In opposing and inverting, Pope

---

damaged deconstruction irreparably. Nealon attempts to save the appearances, however, by driving a wedge between de Man and Derrida.

> ensures that he not be able to recognize that the "other" is a part of him as he is a part of the "other." The implications of such a relationship of "self" and "other" are far-reaching. . . .[102]

Since deconstruction denies that *any* language works by "faithful representation," Atkins can hardly fault Pope for failing to achieve the impossible. Moreover, Pope knows that his dunces are not carrying on "war with words alone." Duncery begins with deep discussions of the *O* and *A*, but it involves the inversion of *all* value. The fact that duncery is a caricature of deconstruction should be a source of endless play of meaning, inviting Atkins to show his own relationship with duncery. But for all his talk of play, the deconstructionist cannot take a joke: Pope's irony is too serious. He is suggesting that those who take upon *themselves* the task of arbitrarily giving law to words will be arbitrary rulers. The fact that college students now speak of concealing their true beliefs from ideologically committed professors comes as no surprise to someone who reads *The Dunciad* with sympathy.

The Dunciad later yokes the dunces' hostility to religion with their slavery to words and thence to "party" spirit in a speech by "Silenus" (Thomas Gordon):

> Then thus. "From Priest-craft happily set free,
> Lo! ev'ry finish'd Son returns to thee:
> First slave to Words, then vassal to a Name,
> Then dupe to Party; child and man the same. . . ." (4:499-502)

Released from their subservience to the clergy, the free-thinking Sons of Dulness fall into a slavery similar to that of ideological conformity. The phrase "child and man the same" indicates that there is no place of growth: having received the key to all knowledge (through their Party), the "Son" knows as much as he ever will. Whereas wisdom, in Pope and in the Bible, is associated with growth and blessing as a

102. Atkins, *Quests of Difference,* 167. Of course it is difficult to think of many poets who placed a higher value upon their relationships with "others" — Pope called them "friends" — than Alexander Pope. Atkins ignores these relationships in his chapter on *The Dunciad.*

consequence of creation, duncery is associated with stagnation and conformity, resulting in "uncreation."

A similar conformity is evident in passages like the one in which Atkins hopes that his book is "faithful to basic principles and strategies of deconstruction."[103] Conformity is a subject of Frederick Crews's criticism of one of the leading American deconstructionists: "Nietzsche, Marx, Freud, Durkheim, Saussure, Derrida, Althusser, Barthes, and Foucault appear in [Jonathan] Culler's pages, not as proponents of ideas that bear testing, but as tutelary figures deserving of automatic honor."[104] Likewise, Jeffrey Nealon's article on the decline of deconstruction seeks a solution from Derrida, wondering why he hasn't criticized the theorists who (according to Nealon) are responsible for the theory's decline and, paraleptically, "not" calling upon him to "issue a sort of deconstructive papal bull on a doctrinal matter."[105] Perhaps even more troubling, the mimic war against "logocentrism" demands loyalty to this party: either you are with them, or you are complicit in the major structure of oppression that has deformed the history of the world.

Apart from the satirical connection between the war of words and ideological conformity, Pope's *Dunciad* anticipates deconstruction in two other areas: the treatment of "the center" and the relationship between author and critic. Destabilizing a text by showing that its apparent meaning becomes radically decentered is a favorite deconstructive gesture. The notes accompanying *The Dunciad,* Atkins argues, show that

> *The Dunciad* qua poem is not, then, a whole — only holey. The notes *supplement,* trying to plug some of these holes. As they supplement the flawed "text," the notes break down any "rigid" separation between "text" and notes. What is ostensibly a satirical technique turns out to be more: Pope's own text displays the same de-centering for which he satirizes the dunces. . . . [The notes] open up the text, destabilizing it and exposing it as something other than — because more than — a fixed and complete object, a well-wrought urn.[106]

103. Atkins, *Quests of Difference,* 4.

104. Frederick Crews, *Skeptical Engagements* (New York: Oxford, 1986), 127.

105. Nealon, "The Discipline of Deconstruction," 1276.

106. Atkins, *Quests of Difference,* 157-58.

It seems almost too obvious to say this, but Pope intended for *The Dunciad* to seek instability. The satirical notes don't simply "turn out" to be more than notes. As the poem grew, with its Advertisements, Testimonies, Appendices, Prefaces, Lists of Errata, Indexes, and Critical Remarks (by Aristarchus, Scriblerus, Dennis, et al.), surely it is apparent that Pope (and later, Warburton) intended the project to satirize book making, critical commentary, editing practices, puffery, and many other practices of contemporary letters. *The Dunciad,* in an important sense, isn't even "Pope's own text," but that of the dunces.

Pope is not the one who seeks the stability of a center in *The Dunciad.* The dunces do. "Centering" is a characteristically duncical act in the poem: "All nonsense thus, of old or modern date, / Shall in thee centre, from thee circulate," prophesies Settle to Cibber (3:60). In book 4, after the summoning of all the nations to the Throne of Dulness, "The gath'ring number . . . / Roll in her Vortex, and her pow'r confess" (4:81, 84). As Sitter writes, this vortex "grows naturally out of similar metaphors in Book III of circular energy — both whirling and rolling. All of these images imply not only confusion but confusion with a purpose, motion with a goal or center."[107] The dunces "coher[e] around" the Goddess, who is called "their Centre" at 4:77-78. The circle is an image of stupidity in *The Dunciad,* closely related to effluvium and to the nod ("nutation") of sleep:

> As what a Dutchman plumps into the lakes,
> One circle first, and then a second makes;
> What Dulness dropt among her sons imprest
> Like motion from one circle to the rest;
> So from the mid-most the nutation spread
> Round and more round, o'er all the sea of heads. (2:405-10)

Even the image of the dome, the circular symbol of artistic wholeness, boldness, and regularity in the *Essay on Criticism,* is degraded into the dome of Dulness by this poem (*Dunciad,* 1:265).

The Dunciad's eccentricity is part of Pope's conscious design. It "constitutes the text," as de Man says of deconstruction. Pope's full and

107. Sitter, *The Poetry of Pope's "Dunciad,"* 46.

ironic knowledge of his poem's instability suggests that the ultimate revelation for current readers is the light *The Dunciad* casts upon deconstruction, rather than vice versa.

The Dunciad's ironic endorsement of eccentricity is one of many examples of how this old poem anticipates and moves beyond current critical theory. It forces one to question the critic's claim to superiority over the author, common both to current literary theory and to Pope's poem. These claims are most explicit in the work of Paul de Man and Geoffrey Hartman. In *Criticism in the Wilderness,* Hartman offers Derrida's *Glas* to illustrate his view that "literary commentary is literature." Criticism can become "conscious of itself as a form of 'serious play' similar to art" and attack the isolation of the critic from the source of creative power.[108] De Man, more cannily, simply declares victory over literature: the difference between literature and criticism is delusive, he writes, but the literary critic can nevertheless enlist under Nietzsche's philosophical banner in his struggle with the poets.[109] The notion that the critic surpasses the poet was suggested by William Wotton, one of the main characters in Swift's *Tale of a Tub.* Modern criticism, he wrote in 1694, will "often raise a judicious Critic as much above the Author upon whom he tries his skill as he that discerns another Man's Thoughts, is therein greater than he that thinks."[110]

Pope satirizes this modern disposition toward the ancients. He anticipates de Man's language of "struggle" by exploiting the double meaning of "standard-Authors": they are both standard literary authorities and military "standards" (banners) to be captured:

> When Dulness, smiling — "Thus revive the Wits!
> But murder first, and mince them all to bits;
> As erst Medea (cruel, so to save!)
> A new Edition of old Æson gave,
> Let standard-Authors, thus, like trophies born,

108. Geoffrey H. Hartman, *Criticism in the Wilderness* (New Haven: Yale University Press, 1980), 202-3, 238-39.

109. Paul de Man, *Allegories of Reading: Figural Language in Rousseau, Nietzsche, Rilke, and Proust* (New Haven: Yale University Press, 1979), 17, 19.

110. Quoted in Mack, *Alexander Pope,* 483.

> Appear more glorious as more hack'd and torn,
> And you, my Critics! in the chequer'd shade,
> Admire new light thro' holes yourselves have made. (4:119-26)

The first gesture of the dunces, as editors and printers in lines 119-24, is the simultaneous revival and deconstruction of wit. Their second step, as critics, is to admire older writers for the degree to which they allow the critic to find pleasure in his own "light." The lines remind us as well of the pleasant "Checker'd shade" of "L'Allegro," even as they recall a duncical critic like Bentley, who considered himself capable of emending Milton. Criticism by the dunces no longer merely "supplements" older poetry. As the reference to Medea shows, the dunces believe that ancient poetry is lifeless without modern criticism. Like the deconstructionists, Pope's dunces demonstrate that criticism is really prior to poetry.

At this point, Pope returns us to the issues with which my book begins: the relationship between ancients and moderns, and all of the questions regarding learning and life that are raised by Swift's *Tale of a Tub.* Like Swift, Pope's text raises questions about his own poetry and his own life. Pope had his shortcomings — large editorial mistakes in the edition of Shakespeare, mistaken inclusions (rare) of valuable authors like Defoe among the dunces, and lapses in charity. But one of Pope's achievements, like those of Johnson and Burke and unlike the ideological critic of any stripe, is that he can be held to his own standards. Self-criticism, which used to be counted among the goals of literary study, is a natural outcome of an education in Swift and Pope, Milton, Johnson, and Burke. A master of Eton College put it this way: In school,

> you are not engaged so much in acquiring knowledge as in making mental efforts under criticism. . . . But you go to a great school not so much for knowledge as for arts and habits; for the habit of attention, for the art of expression, for the art of assuming at a moment's notice, a new intellectual position, for the art of entering quickly into another person's thoughts, for the habit of submitting to censure and refutation, for the art of indicating assent or dissent in graduated terms, for the habit of regarding minute points of

> accuracy, for the art of working out what is possible in a given time, for taste, discrimination, for mental courage and mental soberness. And above all you go to a great school for self-knowledge.[111]

However much the criticisms of "logocentrism" may follow *a priori* from the assumptions of deconstruction and present themselves as new discoveries, a study of *The Dunciad* and the relevant, apocalyptic part of a biblical poetics shows that little in deconstruction is really new. But I hope my study has gone further than this. I hope it has shown that an engagement with the actual literary tradition of which we are a part, from the Bible through the eighteenth century, provides more pleasure and more intellectual challenge than the ideological critiques of that tradition.

* * * * *

It may be that deconstruction will sink under its own weighty prose. Some conclude that they should therefore ignore it and go on with their own, more positive encounters with literature. Dr. Arbuthnot had similar advice for Pope, when he urged him "study more to reform than chastise."[112] Pope rightly took this as advice to make his satire more general and stop descending to the level of his antagonists, but he responded that "[t]o reform and not to chastise, I am afraid is impossible. . . . To attack Vices in the abstract, without touching Persons, may be safe fighting indeed, but it is fighting with Shadows."[113] Nor can misbegotten criticism simply be disdained. In the opening lines of *An Essay on Criticism,* Pope indicates that bad literary criticism is a more dangerous offense than bad poetry, for while bad poetry merely bores us, bad criticism "mis-lead[s] our Sense."

Even if deconstruction continues to decline in popularity, many of its effects will remain — the culture of suspicion toward literature in general and toward critics outside of the ideological avant-garde; the

111. Quoted in Michael Oakeshott, *Rationalism in Politics and Other Essays,* new ed., ed. Timothy Fuller (Indianapolis: Liberty Press, 1991), 491n.

112. Pope, *Correspondence,* 3:417.

113. Pope, *Correspondence,* 3:419.

language of "privileging" and "valorizing," with their implied distrust of previous estimates of literary value; a technique of implying that the aesthetic, intellectual, and moral values in the literary tradition are radically unstable, held in place only by a violent hierarchy.

Everyone knows that deconstruction will not really end the "epoch of the logos" and bring in a new one. Everyone knows that *The Dunciad* is not a "real" apocalypse. Both systems make use of apocalyptic rhetoric, the one seriously, the other ironically, to describe a contemporary cultural crisis. *The Dunciad* recognizes its distance from true apocalyptic as it simultaneously approximates it. As an ironic work, *The Dunciad* is ultimately a more serious work than deconstructive criticism. Its allusive irony, in turn, can lead us back to more instructive and delightful encounters with the texts from which it springs, to *Paradise Lost,* the *Aeneid,* and the Bible.

Conclusion

IDEOLOGICAL APPROACHES to literature are deeply mistaken because they are half-true. The half of the truth they perceive is that our reading should somehow relate to our other profound concerns — gender and race relations, the philosophy of language, the need to question traditional learning, and so on. But they fail to perceive many other, equally important truths. They fail to acknowledge the rationality of traditional ways of learning, except for the purpose of regarding those ways with suspicion. They fail to see that cultural achievements cannot be subsumed within a project of liberation except at the cost of the very intellectual freedom that makes learning possible. They cannot acknowledge that many people of good will find parts of the multiculturalist and feminist agendas questionable. An ideologue rarely questions his tendency to regard work outside his ideological camp as corrupt at worst, uninteresting at best. As the ideological project proceeds, intellectual error creeps into literary interpretation until, in an Orwellian fashion, those who attempt to discriminate between better and worse readings risk being identified with the forces of oppression. The more timid will withdraw into self-censorship; the less restrained may lash out in anger.

Most scholars I know, whether liberal or conservative, share an interest in good relations between the sexes and races. Like the five literary figures examined in this book, they acknowledge the political, social, and moral roles of literature. Like Pope, they recognize the ambiguous relationships between language and reality. But they oppose ideological trends, in part, because the current ideological critiques often worsen human relationships, and because deconstruction and the new historicism are obstructing our access to the very questions we need to ask in order to improve those relationships. In my studies of Milton and Burke I have tried to provide examples of the kinds of questions that could be raised about gender and race if our conversations about books and poems can be reconstructed without having to pass ideological tests.

The furor over "political correctness" has brought home to secular higher education something that Christians in higher education have known for a long time: even if you believe you know a large part of the truth, a crucial difference remains between educating students and indoctrinating them; a difference remains between pursuing your disciplinary knowledge on the basis of that truth and simply using your discipline as an instrument for propagandizing or proselytizing. As soon as that difference evaporates, students begin to feel like catechumens in a church they never joined. Outside the classroom, what purports to bc "the new scholarship" is actually felt to be so only by one's ideological soulmates. Rather than true intellectual advance, one begins to engage in "group thinking," to use David Bromwich's phrase, in which individual scholars hedge their best thoughts out of anxiety over what the larger group outside will think.[1]

One can see group thinking in the nervous *autos da fe* situated at the outset of many literary essays. To take just one example from the previous chapter, G. Douglas Atkins begins his book by hoping that it proves "faithful to basic principles and strategies of deconstruction."[2] This would be parallel to a Christian scholar nervously declaring his or her doctrinal purity in order to give value to his or her work as a whole. In neither case does literary study have any significant autonomy. Since one's belief system explains everything, fidelity to that system is the most important consideration. Of secondary importance is the

1. David Bromwich, *Politics by Other Means: Higher Education and Group Thinking* (New Haven: Yale University Press, 1992), 181.

2. G. Douglas Atkins, *Quests of Difference* (Lexington: University of Kentucky Press, 1986), 4.

production of excellent work from within a discipline that has its own, relatively autonomous traditions of understanding.

This is not to say that the nervous declarations of faith are unjustified. The history of academic freedom at Christian colleges and universities — which would include virtually all older Western universities, if one begins at the beginning — is a troubled one. Likewise, the current academic climate causes many a young professor to keep quiet about his or her true thoughts until tenure is won. Just to give a couple of indicators of this climate, in 1991 the Modern Language Association established a project on "antifeminist harassment" whose mandate was so broad that virtually any criticism of feminist thought could be construed as harassment.[3] The prominent multiculturalist James Banks criticizes alternative models of multiculturalism (proposed by Diane Ravitch and Chester Finn) for promoting a faulty "Western-centric, male-dominated paradigm."[4] The implication is that if you want to avoid siding with the forces of oppression, you cannot disagree with Banks's version of multiculturalism or the MLA's version of feminism.

When humanists confront ideological misreading, they often avoid talking about fundamental issues altogether. Instead, they "concentrate on the texts." When pushed, however, distinguished humanists like David Bromwich and Donald Greene will write autobiographically — as ideologues themselves often do — speaking of the role literature had in their personal development or larger understanding of the world.[5] I do not believe their personal testimony will shake a committed ideologue. The ideologue can always point to some version of "false consciousness" that kept Bromwich and Greene from interpreting their experience correctly.

My proposal of a biblical poetics will meet with no more approval

3. *MLA Newsletter,* Spring 1991, 21.

4. James A. Banks, "A Curriculum for Empowerment, Action, and Change," in *Empowerment through Multicultural Education,* ed. Christine E. Sleeter (Albany: State University of New York Press, 1991), 130.

5. Bromwich, *Politics by Other Means,* 170-71. Greene's essay, "Literature or Metaliterature? Thoughts on Traditional Literary Study," along with an engaging, semi-autobiographical piece by Morris Brownell, may be found in *Theory and Tradition in Eighteenth-Century Studies,* ed. Richard B. Schwartz (Carbondale, Ill.: Southern Illinois University Press, 1990).

from the ideologues than the testimonies of Bromwich and Greene. I have greater hopes, however, for thc more general reader. Just as I can accept the validity of Bromwich's and Greene's literary interpretations without accepting every aspect of their view of the world, they could accept my readings without accepting every aspect of my basic beliefs.

I believe that all nonideological humanists who are concerned about the erosion of intellectual freedom by secular ideologies would do well to consider the place of religion in a truly pluralistic, humane, liberal education. As postmodernism deteriorates further into ideological conformity on the one hand and endless deconstructive play on the other, some alternative methods of reading will be needed.

A biblical poetics can provide an alternative way of relating literature to one's deepest beliefs without forcing literature into dogmatic categories. It need not (and should not, in my view) regard every good essay and pedagogical gesture as playing a role in the drama of delivering us from evil, as ideological criticism does. A successful biblical poetics does not promise a "Christian civilization" in the way that a successful ideological critique, to use Gramsci's terms, looks forward to a new hegemony. Indeed, for a biblical poetics to be used in those ways — as the mirror image of ideological criticism — would be a disaster in my view, for it would turn the biblical word into a partisan for one's particular cultural interests.

* * * * *

I began this book by laying out three questions for each of my chapters: What can we learn from biblical ways with language? How does this language provide a basis for literary study? and How does this poetics differ from recent ideological approaches? Of these three questions, only the third is necessarily related to today's critical controversies. Despite its current significance, in the long run I believe this is the least important of the three questions. A biblical poetics may be concerned (as I have been) with current modes of interpretation, but its larger significance extends far beyond our current troubles.

The field of a biblical poetics is quite diffuse, embracing at least three broad areas: the interpretation of secular texts, the poetics of biblical authors themselves, and the influence of the Bible in shaping the writings of secular authors. Thomas Jemielity's intertextual treatment of biblical prophecy and satire, *Satire and the Hebrew Prophets,* may serve as an example of the first type of criticism. He locates similarities between the satiric and prophetic modes in their common assumptions that the outcome of the contemporary moral battle will determine the course of the future, and that the collapse of the social world is due to a massive failure of moral firmness.

As an example of the second type of criticism, Robert Alter and many others have focused their attention on the biblical writings themselves, producing something like a poetics of scriptural narrative, verse, imagery, and other biblical tropes and genres. Clearly there is a good deal of overlap between biblical poetics and biblical hermeneutics here. The hermeneutical assumptions of Alter are very different from those of postmodern critics. The postmoderns focus on the hermeneutical method as our only access to the text. Where they emphasize the power of the interpreter, Alter emphasizes the power of the text. Alter's emphasis has profound implications for reading. It assumes that the biblical tradition is truly "other" than oneself. It assumes that the biblical tradition — like the secular literary tradition — has something to teach.

Literary historians like Barbara Lewalski and Ernst Curtius have addressed the third area, the Bible's shaping power over authors, from Philo onward through the Middle Ages and Renaissance.

My book has largely been an attempt to discover the significance of a biblical poetics for interpreting secular texts. Each chapter has looked at an issue in biblical language, broadly speaking, and attempted to locate a parallel issue in the literary texts. I began with Swift not only because he treats so effectively the quarrel between ancients and moderns, but because the parallel biblical issue, "fulfillment," could serve as a model for the book as a whole. The meaning of gender in *Paradise Lost* moves closer to fulfillment, I would maintain, by an understanding of blessing; diversity in Burke by an understanding of sympathy; and cultural collapse in Pope by an understanding of his allusions to apocalyptic. My book attempts to fulfill what is lacking in earlier readings, not to displace them with a new system.

The theoretical questions raised by a biblical poetics are probably most intense during times of great spiritual upheaval, such as our own day, the early Enlightenment, the Reformation, and the early Christian era. In such times, the consensus over what constitutes good writing, and good culture generally, is very much in doubt. Is writing to be valued when it conforms to an ideological dogma, whether biblical or secular? when it imitates certain tropes? During such moments, there arise many competing explanations of the proper relations between literary delight and instruction. More fundamentally, there arise many competing explanations of what constitutes the good life.

It is no accident that Christian writers are acutely aware of the fallenness of language, even as they attempt to write about spiritual truths. Milton, speaking more broadly about the pursuit of Christian knowledge, writes in the *Areopagitica* that this side of Eden, we know good "by" evil. That is, we come to see the good by its contrast with evil, truth by contrast with falsehood, virtue by contrast with vice. As the heresy of Arianism helped Christians develop the theology of the Trinity, the current ideological approaches to literature could enable readers once again to reestablish the integrity of literary study. The moderns helped Swift to identify the qualities of "ancientness" that he truly valued; the dunces helped Pope to identify the qualities of art that he wished to preserve.

I have tried to suggest that one reason for the current shortcomings of ideological criticism, clever and appealing as much of it is to current sensibilities, is a failure to engage the kinds of questions raised by a biblical poetics. The Christian critic Michael Edwards makes a similar point in his critique of deconstruction. Having first assumed that the biblical concept of the Logos is that of a tranquil guarantor of the sign, deconstruction concludes in a "Derridean complacency in signlessness, in an inferno of endless signifying where nothing is signified."[6] The true complacency is in current ideology, not in the poetics of the logos. The deconstructionist accuses previous criticism of "logocentrism" — the belief that language naturally and directly expresses an independently existing real order of things. But whatever their accuracy regarding previous criticism, these conclusions fail to notice the fallenness of language as recognized by the biblical word. The logos does not remain in Eden as a tranquil guarantor of meaning. It is involved in the

6. Michael Edwards, *Towards a Christian Poetics* (Grand Rapids, Mich.: Wm. B. Eerdmans, 1984), 232.

mysteries of the incarnation and crucifixion, which were made necessary by the fall. It became flesh and was even accounted sinful for a space of three days. It did not reign in a sphere of Platonic idealism or Cartesian clarity, or even God-like majesty. The logos "emptied himself," as Paul writes, and endured a cursed death so that the original blessing upon creation could be fulfilled. The biblical word, then, is more aware of the fallenness of language than those who present themselves as today's deepest skeptics.

* * * * *

What I have been doing in this book is a form of traditional literary study that looks to biblical and literary sources to answer the very questions posed by postmodernism. The approaches of the traditionalist and the postmodern, as Alasdair MacIntyre explains, are "rival versions" of inquiry.[7] Where the traditionalist finds his or her identity in the communities of which he or she is a part, and in the texts that are its central documents, the postmodern "genealogist," as MacIntyre calls him, constructs a subversive narrative of the past to expose the latent will-to-power in all traditional texts and communities. Where the traditionalist's reasoning is inseparable from the history, circumstances, and traditions of his or her communities, the genealogist finds in those same histories abundant illustrations of the underlying pursuit of power that actuates human relationships. Where the traditionalist sees a quest for unity, the genealogist sees an unacknowledged quest for dominance.

What unites me with traditional literary scholars and separates me from the postmoderns is a common agreement on the high value of the literary tradition. Its texts are essential to my identity. My first impulse is not to interrogate those texts or to question their privileged status, as the postmodern vocabulary puts it. In my view, the insights of the past question the privileged status of current literary theory. Its texts interrogate me — and each other, and sometimes themselves.

7. Alasdair MacIntyre makes the distinctions between the postmodern "genealogist" and the traditionalist in *Three Rival Versions of Moral Enquiry* (Notre Dame: University of Notre Dame Press, 1990).

In modern times, most of us belong to several communities — academic, religious, national, local, ethnic, and so on. Many of us acknowledge several traditions. Clearly, my deepest loyalties are to the biblical tradition. Partly as a response to the postmodern charge that traditional scholarship has obscured its own assumptions, I have tried to show how the biblical and literary traditions may be used openly, for the pursuit of new knowledge and insight. I see no reason why traditional scholars cannot, in good faith, enjoy the literary tradition again. After one has become wise as a serpent in one's dealings with postmodernism, it is time to pick up a book, innocent as a dove. Good books do an even better job than our current literary quarrels of raising troubling questions.

Index

Allegoresis, in Bible, 120n.1; distinguished from hermeneutics of Milton, Reformers, 154-58; in Middle Ages, 120; as technique of ideological analysis, 76, 82, 120n.1, 121, 123, 124-25, 135-36, 158-59
Alter, Robert, 237, 293
Ancients versus Moderns, 21-70, 266; ancients and traditional approaches to learning, 29, 31, 54, 58; ancients' use of language, 29-30; and classic literature, 27-28; gentleman as ancients' ideal, 45; and modern ideologies, 1, 5-6, 12-13, 19, 27, 79; moderns' assumption of superiority to past, 34-36, 45, 47, 48, 49, 79, 286; Swift's characterization of, 5-6, 21-24
Arendt, Hannah, 280
Arnold, Matthew, 1-3
Asante, Molefi Kete, 28, 29
Atkins, G. Douglas, 235, 240, 263, 264, 266, 267, 271-72, 281-82, 283, 290

Bacon, Sir Francis, 32, 47
Banks, James, 185, 193, 194, 199, 221, 291
Basil, Saint, 144
Battle of the Books. *See* Ancients versus Moderns
Bentley, Richard, 26, 27, 30, 31, 32, 38, 236, 243, 254, 286
Bible: Acts, account of Pentecost, 186, 223, 226-31; Genesis and naming, 159-62, 225; Genesis, blessing, and culture, 136-46, 224, 225; Genesis, Tower of Babel story, 186, 223-26, 229-31; hermeneutics, 120, 120n.1, 133, 154-58, 169, 293; Matthew as fulfillment of Old Testament, 60-66; Revelation and apocalyptic literature, 232-33, 234, 238-43, 245-47, 252-55, 257-58, 263-66, 278; Titus, use of pagan culture, 143-44. *See also* Wisdom, Book of
Biblical poetics, 13-18, 119-20, 144, 276, 291-96; apocalyptic as model, 237, 240-43, 245-47, 257-58, 265-67; autonomy of culture in, 17-18, 59, 67, 127, 129, 161, 176, 179, 222, 229, 230, 290-91; blessing and culture, 18, 121, 127, 129, 137, 142-45, 153, 176, 225, 252, 259, 266; compatible with traditional literary study, 208, 222, 229-

31, 287, 292, 295; dissimilarities between sacred and secular literature, 115-17, 127n.20, 222; diversity of cultures, 222-31; New Testament fulfillment of Old Testament as model for literary interpretation, 60-70; similarities to and differences from ideological approach, 17-18, 58-59, 66, 67-69, 120, 122, 127, 294; and "the word" of God, 63, 121-22, 127, 235, 251, 275, 276, 278, 294. *See also* Blessing, Deconstruction
Blackmore, Richard, 104-5, 251
Blessing: Calvin's view of, 134, 136-37, 142-43, 266; different from salvation, 127, 137-39, 142, 143, 147, 229; and diversity, 222-31; language of, 129, 142, 144-45, 149, 159, 179, 276, 278; marriage, 136, 139, 140-41, 166-68; proper realm for culture, 18, 127, 129, 138-45, 237; wisdom, 146-47, 149, 266, 282. *See also* Biblical poetics, *Paradise Lost*
Boswell, James, 101, 103. Works: *Life of Samuel Johnson,* 91, 100-101
Boughton, Lynne Courter, 77n.9
Bromwich, David, 13, 17, 290, 291, 292
Brueggemann, Walter, 225, 227
Bruns, Gerald, 75-76, 78, 82
Burke, Edmund, 8, 180-231; allusion in, 217-20; conventions of language, eloquence, 212-14; critique of systemic oppression, 208-9, 221; knowledge of India, 215; sympathetic understanding of others, 182, 185-86, 208, 210-17, 221, 222; sympathy and moral, natural law, 212, 219-20. *See also* East India Company. Works: *Correspondence,* 211, 218, 219, 222; *Philosophical Enquiry,* 211, 212, 213, 215; *Speech on Fox's India Bill,* 214-17, 218; Speeches on Impeachment of Warren Hastings, 218-20

Caird, G. B., 264
Calvin, John, 82n.22, 136, 225; biblical hermeneutics, 133, 155-58; blessing, culture, 121, 123, 134, 141-44, 178; common grace, 14n.24, 136; gender, 133-34; Swift's satire of Calvinism, 32-33, 44, 59
Cambridge University: associated with modern learning, 44
Canon, 71-118; as applied to Bible, 75-88; as applied to literary texts, 72-74, 76, 89-90; authoritative collection versus authoritative books, 72, 77-80, 85, 100, 113, 115; criteria for biblical canon, 78, 84, 96, 111-12; Johnson's definition, 90; new canon-makers, 71-72, 85, 89, 100, 109-10, 115; origin of term in literary discussion, 72, 114-15; parallel between biblical canon and secular literature, 111-17. *See also* Johnson, Samuel
Christopher, Georgia, 127, 153, 154
Cibber, Colley, 244, 246, 249-51, 257, 262; as Antichrist, parody of Christ, 236, 256-59; as King of Dunces, 233, 256
Clarke, Samuel: influence on Johnson, 74, 92-93, 96, 100; writings on New Testament canonization, 90, 93-96
Classic: as an ideal, 23. *See also* Tradition
Crane, Mary, 120
Culler, Jonathan, 272, 273, 283
Culture Wars. *See* Ancients versus Moderns, Tradition
Curtius, Ernst, 293

Damrosch, Leopold, 106
Deconstruction, 235, 236, 269-88;

deferred meaning, 270-71; idea of the trace, 249, 274; as ideology, 266, 268, 271-72, 274, 277, 278-87; instability of systems of difference, 242, 248, 267, 269, 272-73, 279-80; logocentrism, 269, 272, 276, 279-80, 287; logos, 263, 274-77, 278, 279, 294. *See also* Biblical poetics
de Man, Paul, 284-85
Derrida, Jacques, 269-70, 272-80, 285, 294. *See also* Deconstruction, *Dunciad*
Dodd, C. H., 61, 61n.49
Dunciad, The, 232-88; allusive strategies, 233-35, 236, 244, 255, 265, 266, 288; apocalyptic qualities, 234-35, 238-47, 250-56, 257-68; and deconstruction, 242, 243, 266-78, 279, 281-89; evil in, 251-53, 258-60, 261, 271; genre considerations, 233-34, 239-40, 242; goddess of Dulness, 257-58, 260-65; inversion of values, 267-68, 271, 273-74, 282, 284; as mock-epic, 233, 234, 250, 265. *See also* Deconstruction; Pope, Alexander

Eagleton, Terry, 2-3, 9, 29
East India Company, 180, 209, 214. *See also* Burke, Edmund
Edwards, Michael: biblical poetics, 15-16, 117, 223, 294
Ellis, John, 270, 277

Feminism, 119-78; critique of Milton, 129-36, 158, 165-66, 177; and deconstruction, 263, 271-72, 279; as ideology, 10-11, 79, 128, 291; and multiculturalism, 191, 193; Swift's Laputa as image of control, 66-67. *See also* Ideology
Fitzgerald, Robert P., 45-46
Froula, Christine, 86, 113, 121, 123, 133, 158, 169

Gadamer, Hans-Georg, 4, 13. *See also* Tradition
Gates, Henry Louis, 2, 6, 9-10, 11n.20, 27, 34
Geneva Bible, 133, 137, 141, 164, 165, 171
Gentleman, 23, 45. *See also* Tradition
Gilbert, Sandra, 131, 177
Graff, Gerald, 27, 34
Gramsci, Antonio: concept of hegemony, 181, 184-85, 195, 196-200, 203-7
Grant, Carl, 193, 194, 199
Gray, James, 93
Gray, Thomas, 107
Green, Garrett, 170n.96
Greene, Donald, 36-37, 291, 292
Griffin, Robert, 253

Hagstrum, Jean, 105
Hammond, Henry, 60, 62n.52
Hastings, Warren, 209, 214. *See also* Burke, Edmund; East India Company
Homer, 93; educator of Hellas, 71

Ideology: autonomy, dissent impossible, 11, 18-19, 29, 34, 120, 122, 128, 131, 162, 185, 192-93, 196, 229-30, 279, 282, 290-91; denunciation of opponents, 9-10, 19, 29, 123, 185, 280; different from acknowledging historical context, 182-83, 203, 207, 212, 220; different from "point of view," 7-8; method and outcome the same, 10, 59, 69, 184-85, 277; past portrayed in negative light, 29, 35-36, 68, 122-24, 131, 148, 182, 192, 200, 272, 279; social liberation as goal, 8-9, 68, 128, 143, 193, 199, 229, 277, 280; system of power as the cause of evil, oppression, 3-4, 8-9, 28, 31, 72-74, 75-76, 79, 81-82, 85, 87, 108-9, 126, 160, 178, 181, 190, 193, 197, 205-6, 279; as technique of literary criticism, 3-4, 13, 31, 36, 123-24, 201-2, 280; test for, 17; unresponsive to argument, historical data, 9, 10, 38, 67, 81, 87, 96, 125-26, 132, 135, 177, 190, 195, 198, 200-201, 205-6, 276, 280; validity of, 3, 8, 289; as way of gaining power, 34-35, 72, 123, 128, 177, 191, 197-202, 272. *See also* Allegoresis, Ancients versus Moderns, Biblical poetics, Deconstruction, Feminism, Multiculturalism, Tradition

India. *See* Burke, Edmund; East India Company

Irenaeus, 82-83, 94

Jemielity, Thomas, 15-16, 57, 239, 293

Jerome, Saint, 78, 82n.22, 119, 133, 144

Johnson, Samuel, 71-118; common reader, 89, 105, 106-8, 109, 111; distinction between sacred and secular literature, 73, 76, 89, 90; empirical rather than systematic criticism, 107-8, 110; familiarity with biblical canonization process, 83, 90, 92, 94; literary pleasure, 74, 76, 89, 90, 100-105, 108, 111, 113; religious happiness, 89, 97-100; task of the critic, 89, 107, 109, 111-13. Works: *Diaries, Prayers,* 98, 115-16; *Dictionary,* 90, 93, 101, 110; *Idler,* 109; *Lives of the English Poets,* 72, 102-3, 108-9, 111-14, 116; *Preface to Shakespeare,* 102, 103-4, 105-8; *Rambler,* 99; *Sermons,* 93, 97-98; *Vanity of Human Wishes,* 98; *Vision of Theodore,* 98. *See also* Canon

Jones, William, 204

Justin Martyr, 83, 84, 86

Kaplan, Carey, 71, 73n.2, 79, 109

Kass, Leon, 79-80

Kernan, Alvin, 100, 108-10

Kolodny, Annette, 2, 3, 6, 10-11, 35, 59

Language: of blessing, 129, 142, 144-45, 149, 159, 179, 276, 278; conventions of, 213; satire of scientific, 53; in Swift's writings, 29-30, 52; as used in ideological theories, 29-30, 124-25, 288, 295. *See also* Biblical poetics, Blessing, Deconstruction

Leonard, John, 172, 173

Levine, Joseph, 22-27

Lewalski, Barbara, 153-54, 293

Lewis, C. S., 18, 116-17, 135-36, 268

MacCallum, H. R., 154-55, 170n.96

McColley, Diane, 126, 127, 130, 132, 166, 177

Mack, Maynard, 235-36, 240

Marsh, Narcissus, 55

Marxism. *See* Gramsci, Antonio

Metzger, Bruce, 76-78, 83-86, 96

Milton, John, 58, 102, 105, 207-8, 276, 286; biblical hermeneutics, 133, 154-57, 169; and Christian's relation to culture, 121-22, 151, 153-54; considered oppressive to women, 36, 126, 129-36; considered sympathetic to women, 125; knowledge, 147-49, 151, 162-63, 171; marriage, 141, 170; and pagan culture, 147-49, 150-51. Works: *Areopagitica,* 121, 144, 147, 294; *Christian Doctrine,* 169; *Comus,* 125, 167-68; Divorce Tracts, 141, 170; *Of Education,* 147; *Paradise Regained,* 144, 150, 265; *Samson Agonistes,* 149. *See also Paradise Lost*

Minogue, Kenneth, 8, 58, 196

Mohler, Nora, 51, 53

Mounce, Robert, 252, 266

Multiculturalism: Afrocentrism, 189-90, 194-95; diversity, lack of diversity, 192-94, 196, 199-200, 225-26, 227-31; ideological versus pluralistic multiculturalism, 181-85, 190-92, 291; race-based values, 184, 191, 195. *See also* Burke, Edmund; Ideology; Psalmanazar, George

New Historicism, 2, 67, 69, 76, 290
Nicolson, Marjorie, 51, 53
Norris, Christopher, 269
Nyquist, Mary, 123, 124, 134-35, 158, 165

Oakeshott, Michael, 29n.14, 69
Oates, Titus, 188, 189
Ohmann, Richard, 197-98
Orientalism, 202-8, 220, 231
Origen, 82n.22, 83, 85, 94, 155
Oxford University, 187; Christ Church, 27, 31

Pagels, Elaine, 77, 78-79, 82-83
Paradise Lost, 123-79, 234, 250; Adam, 162-65, 171; culture and blessing, 151-53, 166-67, 174, 176, 178; Eve, 125, 126, 129-30, 159, 165-66, 171, 173-76; fall of Adam and Eve, 149, 167; marriage of Adam and Eve, 130-33, 162-63, 166-68, 170, 171-76; naming in, 159, 162-66, 171, 173; Satan, 130-31, 176, 177, 250, 256, 259. *See also* Milton, John
Pechter, Edward, 123-24, 133
Perrault, Charles, 51n.35
Poetics. *See* Biblical Poetics
Pope, Alexander, 55, 112, 114, 232-88, 247, 294; and Martinus Scriblerus, 233-34, 243, 247, 248, 273-74. Works: *Correspondence,* 255, 287; *Essay on Criticism,* 284, 287; *Peri Bathous,* 243, 247-51, 267, 273. *See also* Deconstruction; *Dunciad*
Postcolonial studies. *See* Multiculturalism
Psalmanazar, George, 185, 186-96

Radzinowicz, Mary Ann, 127
Ramsey, George W., 160-61
Ravitch, Diane, 28, 29, 182, 183, 200, 291
Rawson, Claude, 42
Ricoeur, Paul, 280
Rose, Ellen Cronan, 71, 73n.2, 79, 109
Rousseau, Jean-Jacques, 213
Royal Society, 43-44, 49, 53, 56, 187, 202
Russell, Jeffrey Burton, 259

Said, Edward, 203-5, 207
Scholes, Robert, 74n.3
Schwartz, Richard B., 91
Shakespeare, William, 102, 103-4, 106, 192, 207-8, 286
Shullenberger, William, 129-30, 177
Siebert, Donald, 259
Sitter, John, 247, 254
Sleeter, Christine, 191, 193, 194, 199
Smith, Barbara Herrnstein, 72, 81, 104-5
Stout, Gardner D., 37n.23, 39
Swaim, Kathleen, 173n.98
Swift, Jonathan, 1, 21-58, 62, 66-70, 92, 294; on religious enthusiasm, 32-33; skepticism of schemes and systems, 33-34, 52; treatment of language, 29-30. Works: *Battle of the Books,* 28-32, 39, 47, 48n.32; *Gulliver's Travels,* 22, 25, 38-58, 66-67; "Letter to a Young Gentleman," 23-24; *A Tale of a Tub,* 5-6, 17, 22, 32-39, 44, 51-52, 53, 54, 57, 285. *See also* Ancients versus Moderns

Temple, Sir William, 22, 25, 27, 46, 47, 60
Tertullian, 83, 84, 86, 94, 119, 148
Theobald, Lewis, 233, 245, 256, 257
Toland, John, 92-95
Tracy, Clarence, 111
Tradition, 4, 13, 37, 182, 208, 287, 295; and culture wars, 1, 4, 59,

184-85, 192-93, 265, 273; learning from past, 48-49, 107, 123, 293; as opposed to ideology, 57, 128, 129-31, 184, 191-92, 195, 197, 201, 205, 235, 295; traditional literary study, 4-6, 12-13, 58, 124-26, 128, 177, 197-98, 208, 210-12, 217-18, 286, 289, 292; self-criticism, 37, 39, 54, 73, 194, 198, 203, 209, 221, 230, 286; and Swift's "ancients," 5-6, 29, 31, 48, 54, 58. *See also* Ancients versus Moderns
Trible, Phyllis, 134, 159-60
Trinity College (Dublin), 54, 55
Tuve, Rosemond, 157-58

Viswanathan, Gauri, 181-82, 184-85, 205-8

Warburton, William, 233, 240, 243, 264, 268n.66
Webber, Joan, 168, 177
Westermann, Claus, 137-38, 139, 140, 146-47, 161-62
Whiston, William, 240, 262, 268n.66
Wilder, Amos, 240-41
Williams, Aubrey, 235, 246, 258
Wisdom, Book of: imagery of darkness and Pope's *Dunciad,* 253-55
Wotton, William, 25-26, 27, 285